365 *plus one*
Vegetarian Puddings, Cakes & Biscuits

GW00547107

365 plus one Vegetarian Puddings, Cakes & Biscuits

Delicious wholesome sweet treats for every day of the year

Janet Hunt

Thorsons

An Imprint of HarperCollins*Publishers*

Thorsons
An Imprint of HarperCollins*Publishers*
77–85 Fulham Palace Road,
Hammersmith, London W6 8JB.
1160 Battery Street,
San Francisco, California 94111-1213

Published by Thorsons 1994
1 3 5 7 9 10 8 6 4 2

A catalogue record for this book
is available from the British Library

ISBN 0 7225 2865 5

Typeset by Harper Phototypesetters Limited,
Northampton, England
Printed in Great Britain by
The Bath Press, Bath, Avon

Contents

Introduction   6

1. Individual Cakes   9
2. Large Cakes and Gateaux   19
3. Biscuits   30
4. Chilled Desserts   38
5. Pancakes   47
6. Souffles, Mousses, Whips and Creams   54
7. Wholesome Nibbles   62
8. Suet and other Winter Puddings   67
9. Cheesecakes   77
10. Fruit Based Desserts   85
11. Traditional Sweets   94
12. Flans and Pies   100
13. Sauces, Spreads and Jams   109
14. Sweets from other Cultures   117

Directory of Recipes   125
- *Vegan Recipes*   125
- *Children's Parties*   127
- *Dinner Party Desserts*   127
- *Sweets on the Move*   127
- *Sweet Gifts*   128

General Index   131

Introduction

Throughout history, sweets and sweet foods have been associated with reward, with pleasure and with love. In some parts of the world they are offered as gifts to appease the gods; in others they are an integral part of wedding and birthday celebrations. In Mexico, on the Day of the Dead, sugar skulls are sold on the streets. In Britain, too, most of our traditional festivities include sweet foods – mince pies at Christmas, chocolate eggs at Easter, pancakes on Shrove Tuesday.

It seems we have an insatiable appetite for sweet things, and until recently, there has been nothing wrong with that. Even sweets, ice creams, cakes and so on can be made of good and wholesome ingredients. It is only in recent years that commercially-made versions containing more chemicals than nutrients – and far more calories than they ought! – have resulted in sweet foods being labelled sinful, wicked, harmful and even dangerous. And with their high white sugar content it's a reputation that is justified. This innocent looking, yet highly addictive ingredient is now recognized as being implicated in a variety of health problems including diabetes, allergies, tooth decay, thrombosis, ulcers, and some cancers. And it makes you fat. When you consider that the British consume more sweets, per head, than anyone else in the world, and that the majority of these are commercially made, it's not surprising that our doctors are so busy.

Yet sweet foods undoubtedly have a place in our lives. Without them life would indeed be bland, for children and adults alike. If you eat a lot, it might be advisable to cut your consumption, keeping them as occasional treats rather than everyday eats. Making more of your own means you'll know exactly what is in them – and can adjust the ingredients to suit yourself. You might even be able to persuade other members of the family to join you in the kitchen, turning what could be a chore into a get-together. This book will give you plenty of ideas, from simple to sumptuous.

But why *vegetarian* sweets? After all, no-one eats meat or fish for pudding, do they?

While that's certainly true of most people, commercially made sweets and sweet foods are fraught with hidden dangers for anyone who aims to avoid eating animal products. Look along the shelves at your local supermarket: the most obvious examples are suet puddings (suet being an animal fat), and jellies made from gelatine (produced by boiling animal bones and hooves). But there are plenty more you may well be unaware of. Some commercially produced yogurts are thickened with gelatine, as are some ice creams, sweets, margarines – even apple pies! Colourings can be animal derived; cochineal is the best known, made from the crushed bodies of insects. Albumin, emulsifiers, glycerine, lecithin, stearic acid, edible fats and oils – names you'll find on countless sweet products – could all be taken from either animal or vegetable sources, a detail that is rarely specified. The famous 'E numbers', which aimed to make matters clearer, have confused rather than helped. For example, E120, 542, 631, 635, 901, 904 and 920 are all animal derived ingredients, though without a reference book you'd be unlikely to know that.

Although savoury foods are increasingly often labelled as suitable for vegetarians, this doesn't yet seem to apply to sweet products. It's therefore important that when you *do* buy commercially produced products you check the ingredients list carefully, maybe even writing to manufacturers for clarification when in doubt.

There is another reason for a book of vegetarian sweets. Many people who give up flesh foods do so because they care about being healthy. They want to reduce their consumption of saturated fats, to avoid artificial additives and to eat nutritious food in as natural a condition as possible. Sadly – and incorrectly – there has long been a belief that eating for health automatically means giving up sweet things. But if you make your own foods you can make them as healthy as you like. Base your sweets on ingredients that contain nourishment, keep the sugar content to the minimum, try to refrain from eating everything in one go . . . and enjoy!

Some tips on ingredients

Flour

Wholemeal flour is made from wheat and contains wheatgerm and bran in their most natural forms – a real benefit for anyone interested in healthy eating. A variety of grades of flour is now available, ranging from superfine (especially good for lighter textured baked goods such as sponges) to coarse, and to flour with added grains (for making granary bread). 81% flour has already had the bran removed. Use whichever you prefer. Organic flours, made from grains grown with the minimum of artificial tampering, are obviously preferable when available.

Unless otherwise specified, whenever flour is included in recipes in this book, it means *plain* flour, and when a lifting agent is needed you will be asked to add baking powder or bicarbonate of soda. Self-raising wholemeal flour will have already had this added, so if you use this bear this in mind. You may prefer to have only plain flour in the house and to adapt this as necessary. As wholemeal flour will get stale quicker than refined flour (one of the main reasons wheatgerm is removed being to extend the shelf life of white flour), buying small quantities and using them quickly ensures that the flour is in good condition.

Thickeners

Whenever these are needed use wholemeal flour (sift out the bran first), cornflour or arrowroot. Arrowroot has a few more nutrients than cornflour, although the latter gives smoother results. All should be blended with a small amount of water to make a paste, before being added to other ingredients.

Fats

I use two margarines when cooking. One is a soft, polyunsaturated soya margarine – most supermarkets now sell a dairy-free variety under their own label which is inexpensive and ideal for both vegetarians and vegans. When block margarine is suggested I use Tomor, widely available in speciality and wholefood shops.

Although not suitable for vegans, vegetarians may like to use butter occasionally. While high in saturated fats, butter is a more natural product than margarine. Use it when its difference really will be appreciated, preferably a low-salt variety which will probably be free from artificial colouring as well.

Vegetable oils should be from one source only, not blended. Sunflower, soya and safflower are all excellent. Cold-pressed oils are preferable, although not essential.

Sweeteners

Always use raw cane sugar. While this has the same amount of calories as refined white sugar, it also contains small amounts of nutrients such as calcium, phosphorus, magnesium, sodium, potassium and iron. In general, the darker the sugar, the more nutrients it will contain and the richer will be its flavour. Try different varieties to find which you prefer. Keep amounts used to a minimum – you might find you can reduce the amount given in the recipes that follow – but do not change those given in the sweets section or they may not set properly. If you cannot find caster sugar in the shops, powder larger grained sugar in a small coffee grinder or blender – also good when icing sugar is required.

You can reduce your consumption of sugar further by using other sweeteners in your cooking. Honey is becoming increasingly popular and is available both set and runny and in a wide variety of colours and flavours. It can be used whenever a recipe asks for sugar – use three quarters of the amount suggested for sugar and adjust the liquid accordingly. However, as honey is an animal-derived ingredient, vegans may prefer to avoid it. As an alternative try some of the many excellent syrups – corn, barley malt, date, rice and so on – each of which has a distinctive flavour and is suitable, not just for vegetarians but for vegans too.

In many recipes concentrated apple juice can be used as a sweetener. Look out too for Pear and Apple Spread, one of a range of spreads which has the double attributes of both sweetening and binding ingredients. This makes them especially useful for vegans as a few spoonfuls of the spread can be added to replace both sugar and eggs. When using jams or marmalades, try to use those made with raw cane sugar.

Chocolate and carob

These appear frequently in this book, and are interchangeable, carob being more nutritious and less likely to cause allergies. If using these in bar form, look out for chocolate made with raw cane sugar. Unless specified in the recipe, use milk or plain chocolate as preferred. Cocoa is chocolate in powdered form – it has not been sweetened which means you can adjust the flavour of the finished product more accurately. Carob powder also needs to be sweetened.

Several recipes contain white chocolate – for fun. To date no white chocolates have been made with raw cane sugar. As these also contain milk they are not suitable for vegans.

Milks and creams

Any milk can be used for most of the recipes. Low fat milks to you keep the fat content low, if this is a priority. Goats' and sheep's milk can be used by those who have trouble digesting products made with cows milk.

Vegans will find soya milk can be used whenever milk is listed as an ingredient. Concentrated soya milk is a good alternative for cream, but do look out too for a specially created soya 'cream' which makes the perfect topping for all sorts of dessert dishes.

Dairy creams can be very rich sources of fat. I have not used double or clotted cream in the book for this very reason. Where cream is listed it is either single cream, or whipping (which is halfway between single and double in fat content). Better still, use fromage fraîs or crème fraîche which are both very creamy to taste, yet considerably healthier. Sour cream, which is single cream treated with a bacterial culture, is another good alternative.

Yogurt

The selection of commercially made yogurts grows daily! I would suggest making your own so that you know exactly what is in it, how fresh it is – and you need never run out. When listed in recipes, the yogurt referred to is always natural and flavour free.

Vegan yogurt can be used as an alternative to dairy yogurt.

Tofu

A bland curd made from soya beans and widely used in Chinese cookery, tofu is also surprisingly useful when making sweet foods, especially non-dairy cheesecakes. The softer variety – called silken tofu – is usually recommended for sweet recipes but I prefer the firm variety. Use whichever you prefer.

Flavourings and colourings

The recipes that follow include few of the prettily decorated and highly coloured cakes and biscuits you will find in supermarkets. If, however, you want to make your food look more decorative (especially if it is to be served at a children's party, for example), look out for vegetable dyes which will add colour without adding chemicals. There are also some excellent essences now available which are as close to natural as possible. Check your wholefood or health food store's shelves.

You should also be able to find glacé cherries (a delicious one comes preserved in corn syrup rather than white sugar), naturally dyed angelica, and so on. Look out, too, for stem ginger preserved in honey or a raw cane sugar syrup. Mixed candied peel usually contains some kind of preservative but read the labels – some, for example, are dyed whereas others are not. Buy those that have had the least done to them!

When buying dried fruits, try to find those that have not been sprayed with mineral oil (to stop them sticking), or treated with sulphur dioxide. If in doubt, wash your fruits in hot water, making sure they are dry before using.

When using coffee in recipes try to use decaffeinated – the healthier alternative.

Nuts and seeds

Buy from a wholefood or health food store where they will not have been treated with chemicals. Buy small amounts at a time and store them in airtight containers until needed. If they are to be chopped or ground for a recipe, do this just before using them.

Tahini

This is a paste made from sesame seeds which is high in protein, calcium and other nutrients. It is also delicious, and very versatile. It is available in light and dark varieties, the light having a more delicate flavour. Personally, I prefer this one when baking, but the choice is yours.

Coconut

Coconut gives ice creams, cakes and desserts a slightly exotic flavour without masking all others. The recipes that follow call for it in desiccated form (unsweetened), and as larger coconut flakes (available from wholefood and health food stores – roast them lightly for extra flavour). For coconut cream you can use powdered coconut mixed with water or milk, or block coconut. This needs to be grated – a sharp knife or cheese grater is ideal – and then mixed with water, milk or fruit juice. It gives a thicker, smoother texture than the milk.

Fruit

Try to use fresh fruit when recipes call for it. However, as supplies can be limited at certain times of the year, frozen fruit makes a good alternative. If using canned fruit, buy the kind that has been preserved in natural juice.

1
Individual Cakes

Though less impressive in appearance than larger cakes, small cakes have one big advantage – they can be cooked more quickly. (Besides, you can always add icing, or warmed jam and chopped nuts to dress them up.) Ideal for children's parties, lunch boxes and picnics, they are also perfect at tea-time or for late night nibbles. Try some of them for breakfast too – for example, muffins. Get in to the habit of making up the batter before you go to bed, then you can have fresh-from-the-oven muffins before the coffee has percolated.

Use up less-than-fresh cakes in trifles.

Carrot Muffins

55g (2 oz)	margarine, melted	¼ cup
55g (2 oz)	sugar	⅓ cup
1 medium	free-range egg, beaten	1 medium
200ml (⅓ pt)	milk	¾ cup
1 large	carrot, grated	1 large
170g (6 oz)	wholemeal (wholewheat) flour	1½ cups
1 tsp	ground mixed spice	1 tsp
½ tsp	ground ginger	½ tsp
2 tsp	baking powder	2 tsp
55g (2 oz)	sultanas (golden seedless raisins)	⅓ cup

1 Stir together the margarine and sugar, add the egg, milk and carrot.
2 Sift together the flour, spices and baking powder. Combine both mixtures and beat well to let air into the batter. It should be quite moist so if it seems too heavy, add a little more milk. Stir in the sultanas.
3 Lightly grease 10 muffin tins. Spoon some of the batter into each, leaving space at the top for the muffins to rise.

4 Bake at 200°C/400°F (Gas Mark 6) for 20 minutes, or until a sharp knife inserted into a muffin comes out clean. Cool briefly, then remove from the tins and leave on a wire rack to cool. Serve sliced and buttered.

Note: For a change, replace the sultanas with candied peel or add chopped cashews.

Blueberry Buttermilk Muffins

115g (4 oz)	margarine	½ cup
115g (4 oz)	sugar	⅔ cup
2 medium	free-range eggs, beaten	2 medium
170g (6 oz)	wholemeal (wholewheat) flour	1½ cups
2 tsp	baking powder	2 tsp
1 tsp	ground cinnamon	1 tsp
140ml (¼ pt)	buttermilk	⅔ cup
115g (4 oz)	blueberries, cleaned	4 oz

1 Beat together the margarine and sugar. When light and fluffy, add the eggs.
2 Sift together the flour, baking powder and cinnamon. Add to the first mixture, then stir in the buttermilk. Whisk to lighten the batter, adding more buttermilk if it seems too heavy. Gently stir in the blueberries.
3 Lightly grease 12 muffin tins. Pour some of the batter into each, filling them three-quarters full. Bake at 190°C/375°F (Gas Mark 5) for 30 to 40 minutes, or until well risen. Cool briefly before transferring to a wire rack. Serve warm or cold.

Note: Buttermilk helps give these American–style muffins their distinctive flavour, but you can use milk instead. British grown fresh blueberries can be found in an increasing number of shops in late summer, but if you cannot track any down, use either frozen or tinned (draining them well), or replace with other berries.

Peanut Butter Muffins

225g (8 oz)	wholemeal (wholewheat) flour	2 cups
2 tsp	baking powder	2 tsp
2 tsp	soya flour	2 tsp
30g (1 oz)	margarine	2½ tbs
115g (4 oz)	crunchy peanut butter	¾ cup
85g (3 oz)	sugar	½ cup
140ml (¼ pt)	soya (soy) milk	⅔ cup
140ml (¼ pt)	water	⅔ cup
4 tbs	banana chips, coarsely crushed	4 tbs

1 Sift together the flour, baking powder and soya flour.
2 In another bowl beat the margarine to soften, then mix with the peanut butter. Add the sugar, together with the dry ingredients.
3 Stir in the milk and water, mixing well. The batter should be thick and creamy but not too heavy – add more liquid if necessary. Add the banana chips.
4 Spoon into 12 lightly greased muffin tins, allowing room for the muffins to rise. Bake at 200°C/400°F (Gas Mark 6) for 30 minutes, or until cooked. Cool briefly then transfer to a wire rack. Serve warm, spread with your favourite jam.

Note: Vegans should check that the banana chips are sweetened with sugar and not honey. Alternatively, replace them with raisins.

Fruity Marmalade Muffins

225g (8 oz)	wholemeal (wholewheat) flour	2 cups
2 tsp	baking powder	2 tsp
1 tsp	bicarbonate of soda	1 tsp
55g (2 oz)	margarine	¼ cup
55g (2 oz)	sugar	⅓ cup
200ml (⅓ pt)	milk	¾ cup
85g (3 oz)	sultanas (golden seedless raisins)	¾ cup
3 tbs	marmalade	3 tbs

1 Sift together the flour, baking powder and bicarbonate of soda.
2 In a small saucepan, gently melt the margarine, add the sugar and then the milk. Mix quickly with the dry ingredients, sultanas and marmalade, stirring just long enough to moisten everything. (Over-mixing will make the muffins heavier.)
3 Bake at 180°C/350°F (Gas Mark 4) for 20 minutes, or until a sharp knife inserted in the centre comes out clean. Eat while fresh.

Note: For spicier muffins, use ginger preserve instead of the marmalade.

Apricot Doughnuts

340g (12 oz)	wholemeal (wholewheat) flour	3 cups
115g (4 oz)	margarine	½ cup
115g (4 oz)	sugar	⅔ cup
1 medium	free-range egg, beaten milk to mix	1 medium
12 tsp	apricot jam vegetable oil for frying	12 tsp

1 Sift the flour into a bowl, then use fingertips to rub in the fat to make a crumb-like mixture. Stir in most of the sugar, the beaten egg, and just enough milk to make a soft dough.
2 With floured hands, knead the dough gently for a few minutes, then divide into 12 equal portions and flatten each one slightly. Put a teaspoon of jam into the centre of each and roll into a ball around the jam.
3 In a deep pan, heat a generous amount of oil (enough to cover the balls) to a temperature of 180°C/350°F (Gas Mark 4). (If you don't have a thermometer, test by dropping in a cube of day-old bread which should turn golden in a minute.)
4 Fry the doughnuts a few at a time, lowering the heat and cooking them gently so that they cook through. They are ready when you can press a knife against them and no dough oozes out.
5 Drain well and serve warm or cold.

Note: Other fillings can be used in the same way, for example different jams, marmalade, lemon curd, stewed apples or other fruit purées – whatever you fancy.

Creamy Custard Puffs

225g (8 oz)	puff pastry, frozen	8 oz
1	free-range egg white - optional	1

For filling		
285ml (½ pt)	milk	1⅓ cups
1½ tbs	arrowroot	1½ tbs
55g (2 oz)	sugar	⅓ cup
1 tsp	vanilla essence	1 tsp
1 tsp	ground cinnamon flaked almonds or grated chocolate	1 tsp

1 Defrost the pastry, then roll it out to a thickness of approximately ¼ in. Use a cutter approximately 7cm (2½ in) across to make 8 circles, then use a smaller one to mark a ring in the centre of each of the dough circles. Brush with lightly beaten egg white, if liked.
2 Arrange these on a baking sheet. Bake at 220°C/425°F (Gas Mark 7) for 10 minutes, or until golden. Set aside to cool.
3 In a small saucepan, gently heat most of the milk. Mix

the remaining milk with the arrowroot to make a paste. Pour the hot milk over the paste, stir well and return to the saucepan. Bring to the boil, stirring continually, then lower the heat and cook for a few minutes until the custard thickens. Add the sugar and vanilla essence, and leave to cool.

4 Use a sharp knife to cut the centres from the puffs, then fill each one with some of the custard, piling it high. Sprinkle with cinnamon and either almonds or chocolate. Serve at once.

Note: Exactly how many of these sweet vol-au-vents you make will depend on how many you cut from the dough. Do not be tempted to roll the pastry too thin as the results will be rather flat. Use other fillings instead of custard, for example apple purée, whipped cream, low sugar jam. Vegans can use blended tofu flavoured with maple syrup or simply replace the dairy milk with soya.

Jam Crowns

225g (8 oz)	puff pastry, frozen	8 oz
6 tbs	raw cane or low sugar jam	6 tbs
55g (2 oz)	hazelnuts, coarsely chopped	½ cup

1 Defrost the pastry, then roll it out thinly. Cut into 6 squares. Fold in each of the corners to make a smaller square.
2 Spoon a tablespoon of jam into the centre of each, sprinkle with the nuts.
3 Bake at 200°C/400°F (Gas Mark 6) for 15 minutes, or until puffed up and golden. Serve warm or cold.

Note: These are perfect for unexpected guests as they can be put together in no time, yet taste really special. Use other fillings as desired - fruit purées such as blackberry and apple go wonderfully with the light flaky pastry case.

Wholemeal Hot Cross Buns

Buns

340g (12 oz)	wholemeal (wholewheat) flour	3 cups
¼ tsp	salt	¼ tsp
1 tbs	ground mixed spice	1 tbs
55g (2 oz)	block margarine	¼ cup
15g (½ oz)	easy-blend dried yeast	2 tsp
55g (2 oz)	sugar	⅓ cup
55g (2 oz)	sultanas (golden seedless raisins)	⅓ cup
55g (2 oz)	currants	⅓ cup
140ml (¼ pt)	milk	⅔ cup
1 medium	free-range egg, beaten	1 medium

Glaze

30g (1 oz)	sugar	2 tbs
1 tbs	water	1 tbs

1 Sift together the flour, salt and spice, then use fingertips to rub in the fat. Stir in the yeast, sugar, and dried fruit. Make a well in the centre.
2 Warm the milk until hand hot, pour it into the dry ingredients and add the lightly beaten egg. Use a wooden spoon to mix thoroughly to make a soft dough, adding a little more milk if necessary.
3 Turn the dough onto a well-floured board and knead for 5-10 minutes, or until it is elastic and smooth. (Re-flour your hands if the dough gets sticky as you work.) Transfer it to a large oiled bowl, cover with a tea-towel, and leave in a warm place for about 1 hour or until well risen.
4 Grease and lightly flour 2 baking sheets. Knock down the dough and knead briefly again, then divide into 12 even-sized pieces and shape into buns. Place these on the baking sheets, press down lightly. Use the back of a knife to mark a cross on each, then leave in a warm, draught free place for a further 30 minutes.
5 When well risen, mark the crosses again. Bake at 200°C/400°F (Gas Mark 6) for 15 to 20 minutes or until they sound hollow when tapped. Transfer to a wire rack.
6 To make the glaze, dissolve the sugar in the water, simmer for a minute more, then brush over the buns while they are still hot. They are best served warm.

Note: Block vegetable margarine gives these buns a better texture, although you can, if you prefer, use a soft margarine. Vegans can simply omit the egg and use soya milk and a vegan margarine. To freshen up day-old Hot Cross Buns, wrap in silver foil and put into a hot oven for a few minutes.

Honey Squares

225g (8 oz)	wholemeal (wholewheat) flour	2 cups
2 tsp	baking powder	2 tsp
1 tsp	ground mixed spice	1 tsp
115g (4 oz)	margarine	½ cup
4 tbs	thick honey	4 tbs
55g (2 oz)	raisins	⅓ cup
55g (2 oz)	blanched almonds, chopped	½ cup
2 tbs	orange peel, grated	2 tbs
2 tbs	orange juice	2 tbs
2 medium	free-range eggs, lightly beaten	2 medium

1 Sift together the flour, baking powder and spice.
2 In a saucepan, heat the margarine and honey and stir in the raisins, almonds, orange peel and juice, mixing well. Cool slightly before adding the eggs. Pour onto

the dry ingredients and mix well. The dough should be soft – add more juice or milk if it seems too firm.

3 Line and grease a medium-sized, shallow square cake tin. Pour in the mixture and smooth the top. Bake at 180°C/350°F (Gas Mark 4) for 50 minutes, or until set – check by pressing gently with your fingers. Leave to cool briefly then transfer to a wire rack. Serve cut into squares.

Note: For special occasions, spread the squares with extra honey and top with whole almonds. If you don't like honey, use marmalade instead.

Carob and Walnut Brownies

115g (4 oz)	margarine	½ cup
2 tbs	carob powder	2 tbs
2 medium	free-range eggs, lightly beaten	2 medium
170g (6 oz)	sugar	1 cup
85g (3 oz)	wholemeal (wholewheat) flour	¾ cup
1 tsp	baking powder	1 tsp
55g (2 oz)	walnuts, coarsely chopped	½ cup

1 Melt the margarine and stir in the carob powder.
2 In a separate bowl, combine the eggs and sugar, then stir in the margarine and carob.
3 Sift together the flour and baking powder. Add to the other ingredients with the walnuts.
4 Grease a medium-sized square cake tin and line with greased silver foil. Pour in the mixture and bake at 180°C/350°F (Gas Mark 4) for 35 to 45 minutes. Leave to cool slightly before transferring to a wire rack. When cold, cut into squares.

Note: Use chocolate instead of carob if preferred.

Ginger Brownies

115g (4 oz)	chocolate, broken into pieces	4 oz
115g (4 oz)	margarine	½ cup
115g (4 oz)	sugar	⅔ cup
1 tbs	milk	1 tbs
2 medium	free-range eggs, beaten	2 medium
115g (4 oz)	wholemeal (wholewheat) flour	1 cup
1 tsp	baking powder	1 tsp
1 tsp	ground ginger	1 tsp
2 tbs	preserved stem ginger, finely chopped	2 tbs
	icing sugar - optional	

1 Place the chocolate in a bowl suspended over a pan of hot water and stir gently until melted. Add the margarine and heat for a few more minutes, then stir in the sugar and milk.
2 Remove from the heat and gradually add the eggs.
3 Sift together the flour, baking powder and ground ginger. Add to the first mixture, making sure it is thoroughly mixed. Stir in the chopped stem ginger.
4 Pour into a well-greased square cake tin. Bake at 180°C/350°F (Gas Mark 4) for 45 minutes or until firm. Cool in the tin, dust with icing sugar and cut into squares.

Note: Add a little of the juice in which the ginger was preserved if you like – reduce the raw cane sugar accordingly.

White Chocolate Brownies

85g (3 oz)	margarine	⅓ cup
170g (6 oz)	white chocolate, coarsely chopped	6 oz
115g (4 oz)	sugar	⅔ cup
2 medium	free-range eggs, beaten	2 medium
85g (3 oz)	wholemeal (wholewheat) flour	¾ cup
1 tsp	baking powder	1 tsp
55g (2 oz)	hazelnuts, roasted and chopped	½ cup

1 Gently melt the margarine and a third of the white chocolate in a bowl over a saucepan of hot water. Stir so that they are thoroughly blended.
2 Add the sugar. Leave to cool briefly before stirring in the eggs, then the flour, baking powder and chopped hazelnuts.
3 Pour into a greased, shallow, medium-sized tin and smooth the top. Bake at 180°C/350°F (Gas Mark 4) for 20 to 30 minutes, or until just firm. Allow to cool.
4 Melt the remaining white chocolate. Dot spoonfuls across the top of the cooked cake and spread quickly with a knife. Leave until the top has hardened, then cut into squares.

Note: The white chocolate topping looks attractive with the wholemeal flour which gives the cake a golden colour. For a specially effective topping, melt 55g/2 oz plain chocolate and dab spoonfuls of both colours across the top, swirling with a fork to give a marbled effect.

Lemon Cream Tarts

Pastry

170g (6 oz)	wholemeal (wholewheat) flour	1½ cups
85g (3 oz)	margarine	⅓ cup
2-3 tbs	water	2-3 tbs

Filling

115g (4 oz)	tofu, drained	½ cup
4-6 tbs	vegan lemon curd (see page 114)	4-6 tbs
1 tsp	lemon juice	1 tsp
1 tbs	finely chopped lemon peel	1 tbs

1 Place the flour in a bowl, rub in the margarine with fingertips to make a crumb–like mixture, then add water to bind. Knead briefly, wrap in cling–film and chill for 30 minutes.
2 Roll out the pastry and use to line eight small tins. Press down firmly, prick the bases, and bake blind at 190°C/375°F (Gas Mark 5) for 10 minutes or until crisp and golden. Set aside to cool.
3 Blend or mash the tofu and combine with the other ingredients.
4 Carefully remove the cool tart bases from the tins and fill each one with some of the lemon cream. Serve fairly soon after preparation.

Note: When using white flour it is necessary to line tart bases with foil and then fill with beans or rice to hold them down while baking them blind. Wholemeal flour has less tendency to rise so this isn't absolutely necessary, although you can do it if you like. Ordinary lemon curd can be used by non–vegans.

Nutty Egg Custard Tarts

Pastry

170g (6 oz)	wholemeal (wholewheat) flour	1½ cups
55g (2 oz)	almonds, ground	½ cup
115g (4 oz)	block margarine, cut into pieces	½ cup

Egg custard

2 medium	free-range eggs, beaten	2 medium
1	free-range egg yolk	1
55g (2 oz)	sugar	⅓ cup
200ml (⅓ pt)	milk	¾ cup
½ tsp	vanilla essence	½ tsp
140ml (¼ pt)	single cream	⅔ cup
30g (1 oz)	flaked almonds	¼ cup

1 Stir together the flour and ground almonds, then use fingertips to rub in the margarine. Knead to make a firm dough. If time allows, wrap in cling–film and chill

for 30 minutes. Then carefully roll out, cut into circles, and use to line six small patty tins.
2 In a small saucepan, combine the eggs and egg yolk, sugar, milk, vanilla essence and cream. Heat gently until mixture begins to thicken. Cool slightly before dividing between the cases. Sprinkle each one with some nuts.
3 Bake at 200°C/400°F (Gas Mark 6) for 20 to 30 minutes, or until set. Serve warm or cold.

Note: These are not just delicious but very nutritious – ideal for ailing appetites!

Strawberry and Kiwi Tarts

Pastry as for Lemon
Cream Tarts

Filling

200ml (⅓ pt)	water	¾ cup
1 tsp	rosewater	1 tsp
1 tsp	sugar	1 tsp
1 tsp	arrowroot	1 tsp
225g (8 oz)	strawberries, washed and hulled	8 oz
4	kiwi fruits, peeled	4

1 Make the pastry, roll out, and use to line eight small tins. Bake blind.
2 Meanwhile, put most of the water into a small saucepan. In a bowl mix the rest of the water with the rosewater, sugar and arrowroot. Add this to the pan and heat gently, stirring continually, until the sauce thickens and clears.
3 Slice the fruit and arrange decoratively in the cooked tart bases. (Do not remove them from the tins at this stage.) Pour a little of the arrowroot mixture over each, spreading it evenly. Return the tarts to the oven for 2 minutes only. Allow to cool before serving.

Note: Other fruits, for example wild strawberries, can be used in the same way, either alone or in combination.

Star Mince Pies

Pastry

170g (6 oz)	wholemeal (wholewheat) flour	1½ cups
85g (3 oz)	margarine	⅓ cup
2 tbs	orange peel, finely grated	2 tbs
2-3 tbs	orange juice	2-3 tbs

Filling

approx. 340g (12 oz)	vegetarian mincemeat (see page 115)	approx. 12 oz
	drop of milk	
	caster sugar	

1 Put the flour into a bowl and use fingertips to rub in the margarine to make a crumb-like mixture. Stir in the peel and just enough juice to bind the ingredients. Knead briefly then wrap in silver foil and chill for 30 minutes.

2 When ready, roll the pastry out onto a floured board and cut two-thirds of it into rounds. Use to line small patty tins. Fill each one with some of the mincemeat. Cut the remaining pastry into stars and place these over the mincemeat. Brush with milk and sprinkle with sugar.

3 Prick the top of the pies with a fork. Bake at 200°C/400°F (Gas Mark 6) for 15 to 20 minutes, or until the pastry is cooked. Serve hot with cream, custard, or vanilla soya dessert, perhaps spiced with a spoonful of brandy. These tarts are equally good warm or cold.

Note: Do not overfill the tarts as the fillng might bubble out. You can, of course, use circles of pastry to cover the mincemeat completely. As an alternative, use either shop bought or home-made mincemeat (*see page 115*) to fill puff pastry vol-au-vents. If you don't have enough mincemeat in the cupboard, try extending it with coarsely chopped bananas.

Spiced Apple Scones

225g (8 oz)	wholemeal (wholewheat) flour	2 cups
4 tsp	baking powder	4 tsp
1 tsp	ground cinnamon	1 tsp
½ tsp	ground nutmeg	½ tsp
55g (2 oz)	block margarine, cut into pieces	¼ cup
200ml (⅓ pt)	apple purée (see page 110)	¾ cup
approx. 140ml (¼ pt)	milk	⅔ cup

1 Sift the flour into a bowl with the baking powder and spices. Rub in the margarine so that the mixture resembles fine breadcrumbs. Stir in the apple purée and add just enough milk to make a medium-firm dough.

2 Gently roll out onto a floured board to a thickness of 15mm (½ in), then use a cutter or glass to cut into rounds. Transfer to an ungreased baking sheet and bake at 230°C/450°F (Gas Mark 8) for about 10 minutes, or until firm when lightly pressed. Cool slightly on a wire rack. Scones are best eaten while still warm, sliced and buttered.

Note: For a Christmas version, replace the apple purée with mincemeat.

Date Scones

225g (8 oz)	wholemeal (wholewheat) flour	2 cups
4 tsp	baking powder	4 tsp
55g (2 oz)	block margarine, cut up	¼ cup
55g (2 oz)	sugar	⅓ cup
85g (3 oz)	dates, chopped	½ cup
200ml (⅓ pt)	milk	¾ cup

1 Sift together the flour and baking powder. Use fingertips to rub the margarine into the dry ingredients to make fine crumbs. Add most of the sugar and the dates.

2 Add milk to make a soft dough and mix well. If necessary use a little more milk. Roll out onto a floured board to a thickness of 15mm (½ in). Cut into diamonds and arrange these on an ungreased baking sheet. Brush the tops with a little extra milk and sprinkle with the remaining sugar.

3 Bake at 230°C/450°F (Gas Mark 8) for 10 minutes or until cooked. Eat when fresh.

Note: While dates are a traditional favourite with scones, other dried fruit can also be used. Whatever you choose, make sure that you chop it finely.

Maple Sesame Scones

225g (8 oz)	wholemeal (wholewheat) flour	2 cups
2 tsp	baking powder	2 tsp
30g (1 oz)	margarine	2 tbs
30g (1 oz)	sugar	2 tbs
1 tbs	sesame seeds	1 tbs
2 tbs	maple syrup	2 tbs
4 tbs	buttermilk	4 tbs
	extra sesame seeds for topping	

1 Sift together the flour and baking powder, then use fingertips to rub in the margarine to make a crumb-like mixture. Stir in the sugar and seeds, add the maple syrup and mix well. Add enough buttermilk to make a fairly thick dough.

2 Knead the dough briefly, then form into a round and press down to a thickness of about ¾ in. Scatter a few more seeds over the top. Use a knife to mark the round into sections.

3 Place on a baking sheet and bake at 220°C/425°F (Gas Mark 7) for 10 to 15 minutes, or until just firm to touch. Cool on a wire rack. Split and eat buttered.

Note: If you cannot get buttermilk, use milk, preferably sour.

Yogurt and Honey Eclairs

Choux pastry

140ml (¼ pt)	water	⅔ cup
30g (1 oz)	block margarine or butter	2½ tbs
85g (3 oz)	81% wholemeal (wholewheat) flour	¾ cup
3 small	free-range eggs, well beaten	3 small

Filling

140ml (¼ pt)	thick yogurt	⅔ cup
2 tbs	thick honey, or to taste	2 tbs
115g (4 oz)	strawberries, coarsely chopped – optional extra honey – optional	4 oz

1 Gradually combine the water and margarine or butter in a pan, cover, and cook gently until the mixture boils.
2 Remove the pan from the heat and add all the flour, then use a wooden spoon to beat the mixture well. Return it to a low heat and continue cooking, still beating, until the dough comes away cleanly from the sides. Cool briefly.
3 Gradually add the eggs, a spoonful at a time, beating well after each addition. Continue beating until the mixture is thick and smooth. Leave to cool.
4 Pipe the mixture into finger shapes onto greased and floured baking sheets, using kitchen scissors to cut into lengths of about 9cm (3½ in). Bake at 190°C/375°F (Gas Mark 5) for 15 to 20 minutes or until puffed up and golden. Test by tapping the pastry: it should sound hollow. When cool enough to handle, split lengthways (this will allow steam to escape as well as being necessary for the filling).
5 Beat together the yogurt and honey, draining off any excess liquid (the mixture should be as thick as possible). Stir in the strawberries, if using. Fill each éclair with some of the mixture. You may also spread the top with a little warmed honey. Serve at once.

Note: Choux pastry is not as difficult to make as many people think, although it does take a little practice. Using 81% flour, which has had the bran removed, helps you to achieve the traditional light and delicate results. Use this basic mixture for making profiteroles and choux buns too, filling them with crème fraîche, fruit, custard, and so on. An unusual but delicious filling is Chestnut Chocolate Sauce (*see page 93*). The famous chocolate éclairs are made as above but are filled with double cream, and topped with chocolate icing.

Apricot Danish Pastries

30g (1 oz)	sugar	3 tbs
140ml (¼ pt)	milk	⅔ cup
15g (½ oz)	fresh yeast	½ oz
115g (4 oz)	margarine *or* butter	½ cup
225g (8 oz)	81% wholemeal (wholewheat) flour	2 cups
285ml (½ pt)	apricot sauce, well drained (*see page 110*)	1⅓ cups
approx. 3 tbs	apricot jam, warmed	3 tbs
30g (1 oz)	flaked almonds	¼ cup

1 Dissolve 1 tsp of the sugar in the milk, stir in the dried yeast, and set the mixture aside until it becomes frothy.
2 Cut the margarine or butter into small pieces. Sift the flour into a bowl reserving the bran for use in another recipe. Stir in the remaining sugar followed by the yeast mixture and mix well together.
3 Knead the dough on a lightly floured surface until smooth and roll it out to an oblong measuring about 35.5 × 18cm (14in×7in). Spread the dough with the apricot sauce and then roll up like a Swiss roll. Cut into thick slices to make whirls.
4 Arrange the rolls on a greased baking sheet and leave for an hour to rise. Bake for 10 to 15 minutes at 220°C/450°F (Gas Mark 7).
5 Spread the top of the whirls with the warmed apricot jam and sprinkle with the nuts. Eat warm.

Note: You can shape this dough into windmills, triangles, or any shape and fill them with a variety of ingredients, for example, jams, dried fruits and nuts. You can top them with icing too. Frozen puff pastry could be used as an alternative.

Brandy Snaps with Crème Fraîche

55g (2 oz)	margarine	¼ cup
55g (2 oz)	sugar	⅓ cup
55g (2 oz)	syrup	¼ cup
1 tsp	lemon juice	1 tsp
55g (2 oz)	wholemeal (wholewheat) flour	½ cup
1 tsp	ground ginger	1 tsp
½ tsp	baking powder	½ tsp
200ml (⅓ pt)	crème fraîche	¾ cup

1 Melt the margarine with the sugar, syrup and lemon juice. Sift together the flour, ginger and baking powder and stir into the first mixture, making sure they are well blended.
2 Drop teaspoons of the mixture onto well-greased baking sheets, allowing room for them to spread.

3 Bake at 190°C/375°F (Gas Mark 5) for 8 to 10 minutes or until well spread out and beginning to harden at the edges.

4 Leave to cool for just 1 or 2 minutes, then roll each biscuit around the greased handle of a wooden spoon and hold for a few seconds. Slip the roll off the spoon, and continue with the remaining biscuits, working carefully but quickly. (If they begin to set on the tray, return to the oven for a minute or two more.)

5 Leave to cool on a wire rack then store in an airtight tin. When ready to serve them, simply fill each one with some of the crème fraîche and arrange decoratively on a plate.

Note: Vegans can use a thick soya custard instead of the crème fraîche, or puréed tofu, sweetened with maple syrup.

Wholemeal Rock Cakes

225g (8 oz)	wholemeal (wholewheat) flour	2 cups
2 tsp	baking powder	2 tsp
115g (4 oz)	margarine	½ cup
115g (4 oz)	caster sugar	⅔ cup
55g (2 oz)	dates, chopped	⅓ cup
55g (2 oz)	sultanas (golden seedless raisins)	⅓ cup
1 medium	free-range egg, beaten	1 medium
2-3 tbs	milk	2-3 tbs

1 Sift together the flour and baking powder then use fingertips to rub in the margarine so that the mixture resembles fine breadcrumbs. Add the sugar and dried fruit, mix well, then stir in the beaten egg and enough milk to make a fairly soft dough.

2 Drop from a spoon onto a greased baking sheet, leaving room to spread. (The heaps should be rough – hence the name!).

3 Bake at 220°C/425°F (Gas Mark 7) for 15 minutes. When firm to touch, remove from the oven and allow to cool on the sheets for 5 minutes, before transferring to a wire rack. Rock cakes are best eaten when fresh.

Note: These are nice sprinkled with extra sugar before baking for those who aren't watching their diets.

Orange and Hazelnut Slices

55g (2 oz)	fresh wholemeal (wholewheat) breadcrumbs, extra fine	1 cup
approx 6 tbs	orange juice	approx 6 tbs
2 tbs	orange peel, grated	2 tbs
115g (4 oz)	hazelnuts, ground	1 cup
1 tbs	orange flower water	1 tbs
3 medium	free-range eggs separated	3 medium
115g (4 oz)	sugar	¾ cup
	extra hazelnuts for topping - optional	

1 Mix together the breadcrumbs, orange juice and peel. In another bowl, combine the hazelnuts and orange flower water.

2 Whisk the egg yolks with the sugar until thick and creamy and then add to the nuts. Stiffly beat the egg whites and use a metal spoon to fold into the mixture. Sprinkle the base of a greased medium-sized square cake tin with the breadcrumbs, press down, top with the second mixture and smooth the top. Sprinkle with the extra hazelnuts.

3 Bake at 180°C/350°F (Gas Mark 4) for about 40 minutes, until just firm. Cool briefly before turning out of the tin and transferring to a wire rack. Leave to get completely cold and cut into slices.

Note: For a quick and unusual dessert, try serving these slices topped with whipped cream.

Spiced Banana Cakes

115g (4 oz)	margarine	½ cup
170g (6 oz)	sugar	1 cup
2 large	ripe bananas, mashed	2 large
1 tsp	bicarbonate of soda	1 tsp
2 tbs	hot milk	2 tbs
225g (8 oz)	wholemeal (wholewheat) flour	2 cups
1 tsp	baking powder	1 tsp
½ tsp	ground ginger	½ tsp
½ tsp	ground mixed spice	½ tsp
55g (2 oz)	peanuts, coarsely chopped	½ tsp
55g (2 oz)	granola, coarsely crushed - optional	2 oz

1 Cream together the margarine and sugar until thick and smooth. Add the bananas. Dissolve the bicarbonate of soda in the milk and then add this to the first mixture.

2 Sift together the flour, baking powder and spices and combine with the first mixture. Add the nuts.

3 Divide between twelve small greased cake tins, sprinkling them with granola, if using it.

4 Bake at 180°C/350°F (Gas Mark 4) for 10 to 15 minutes until a sharp knife inserted in the centre comes out clean. Cool briefly in the tin and then transfer to a wire rack.

Note: You can also top these with icing – great for kids parties.

Madeleines

115g (4 oz)	margarine	½ cup
115g (4 oz)	sugar	⅔ cup
½ tsp	vanilla essence	½ tsp
2 medium	free-range eggs, beaten	2 medium
115g (4 oz)	wholemeal (wholewheat) flour	1 cup
1 tsp	baking powder	1 tsp
approx. 6 tbs	Apple and Raspberry spread, warmed	approx. 6 tbs
85g (3 oz)	desiccated coconut	1 cup
6	glacé cheries, halved angelica	6

1 Cream together the margarine and sugar, making sure that they are well-blended. Add the essence, then gradually beat in the eggs.
2 In a separate bowl, sift the flour and mix with the baking powder. Tip in the bran that is left in the sieve, and mix the dry ingredients with the margarine and sugar.
3 Three-quarters fill twelve greased and floured dariole moulds, then bake at 170°C/325°F (Gas Mark 3) for 12 minutes or until a sharp knife inserted in the centre comes out clean. Turn them out and leave to cool. If the bases are uneven, use a sharp knife to cut them so that they make a firm standing surface.
4 Heat the spread slightly and brush the sides and tops of the cakes with an even covering, then sprinkle them with desiccated coconut. Decorate each of the tops with half a glacé cherry and angelica cut to look like tiny leaves.

Note: Although traditionally made with raspberry jam, madeleines are delicious made with this low sugar spread. If you prefer, use raw sugar, jam, marmalade or even lemon curd.

Fig Crumble Slices

Pastry

115g (4 oz)	margarine	½ cup
55g (2 oz)	caster sugar	⅓ cup
140g (5 oz)	wholemeal (wholewheat) flour	1¼ cups

Filling

140g (5 oz)	dried figs, chopped	1 cup
2 tbs	concentrated apple juice	2 tbs

Crumble topping

55g (2 oz)	wholemeal (wholewheat) flour	½ cup
1 tsp	ground cinnamon	1 tsp
30g (1 oz)	margarine	2½ tbsp
55g (2 oz)	sunflower seeds	⅓ cup

1 Beat together the margarine and sugar until light and fluffy, stir in the flour. Press across the base of a lightly greased Swiss roll tin. Bake at 180°C/350°F (Gas Mark 4) for 10 minutes or until lightly browned. Set aside.
2 In a small saucepan, combine the figs and apple juice and cook gently until soft enough to mash to a purée. Spread the mixture over the cooked base.
3 Combine the topping ingredients to make a crumble. Sprinkle this over the figs. Bake at the same temperature for 30 minutes more or until the topping is lightly browned. Leave to cook in tin before cutting into generous slices.

Note: You can also use other purées such as date and apricot, or even a well-drained apple purée in this recipe.

Date and Apple Slices

Pastry

115g (4 oz)	margarine	½ cup
225g (8 oz)	wholemeal (wholewheat) flour	2 cups
2-3 tbs	cold water	2-3 tbs

Filling

455g (1 lb)	cooking apples, peeled and chopped	1 lb
115g (4 oz)	dates, coarsely chopped	¾ cup
2 tbs	lemon juice	2 tbs
55g (2 oz)	almonds, coarsely chopped	½ cup
30g (1 oz)	coconut flakes	⅓ cup

1 To make the pastry, rub the fat into the flour to make a crumb-like mixture, then add just enough cold water to bind the ingredients to a dough. Wrap in silver foil and chill for 30 minutes.
2 Meanwhile, put the apples into a saucepan with the dates and lemon juice and cook gently for 5 to 10 minutes. As they cook, mash them with a wooden spoon to make a thick purée. If it seems too dry, add a little water.
3 Roll out the pastry and shape into an oblong. Place on a baking sheet. Spread with the purée and sprinkle with the nuts and coconut, then bake at 200°C/400°F (Gas Mark 6) for 20 minutes. Leave to cool slightly, then cut into slices and transfer to a wire rack to cool completely.

Note: Although these slices are surprisingly sweet for a sugar-free cake, you may like to add one or two spoonfuls of concentrated apple juice to the fruit as it cooks. You can, of course, add sugar or syrup if you have an especially sweet tooth.

Parsnip Cup Cakes

115g (4 oz)	margarine	½ cup
3 tbs	Pear and Apple Spread	3 tbs
2 tbs	orange juice	2 tbs
2 large	free-range eggs	2 large
115g (4 oz)	wholemeal (wholewheat) flour	1 cup
1 tsp	baking powder	1 tsp
1 tbs	orange peel, grated	1 tbs
225g (8 oz)	parsnip, peeled and finely grated	8 oz
55g (2 oz)	walnuts, chopped	½ cup

1 Blend together the margarine, spread and orange juice. Add the eggs one at a time, beating well after each addition.
2 Sift together the flour and baking powder, then add to the first mixture with the peel, parsnip and nuts. Mix well.
3 Lightly grease twelve small cake tins, spoon some of the mixture into each. Bake at 180°C/350°F (Gas Mark 4) for 20 to 30 minutes or until golden. Cool on a wire tray.

Note: This unusual combination will have your guests guessing! It is also good with raisins added.

Orange Carob Oat Munchies

225g (8 oz)	orange flavoured carob bar, broken into pieces	8 oz
55g (2 oz)	margarine	¼ cup
1 tbs	syrup	1 tbs
225g (8 oz)	granola or other oat crunch cereal	8 oz
2 tbs	orange peel, finely grated	2 tbs

1 In a bowl placed over a pan of hot water, gently melt the carob bar and margarine, stirring as you do so. Add the syrup.
2 Stir in the granola making sure that all of it is coated with some of the carob and margarine mixture. Add the orange peel.
3 Drop spoonfuls into paper cake cases. Set aside to cool.

Note: These easy cakes are ideal for children's parties. You can use other cereal flakes instead of the granola and raw cane sugar chocolate instead of the carob.

Eccles Cakes

340g (12 oz)	puff pastry, frozen	12 oz
115g (4 oz)	currants	¾ cup
300g (1 oz)	sugar	2 tbs
30g (1 oz)	margarine, melted	2 tbs
	cold water	
	extra caster sugar	

1 Defrost the pastry, roll it out on to a floured board, then cut 8 large circles.
2 Stir together the currants, sugar and melted margarine, then divide between the circles.
3 Pull the edges of the pastry towards the centre and press together firmly before flattening to make smaller circles. Transfer to a baking sheet and make four parallel cuts across the top of each. Brush with water and sprinkle with more water.
4 Bake at 220°C/425°F (Gas Mark 7) for 10 to 15 minutes, or until the pastry is cooked. Carefully transfer to a wire rack to cool.

Note: For more fancy Eccles Cakes, add some candied peel to the currants.

2
Large Cakes and Gateaux

These are mostly special occasion cakes although many of them would also make superb desserts, either just as they are, or with cream or fruit purée toppings.

Don't forget that appearance is important when serving cake to guests – and that includes the plate and even the napkins you use.

Several of these cakes are simpler fare – hearty loaves that can be sliced and then buttered or spread with something sweet. Two slices sandwiched together make good lunch box fillers.

Carob Sponge with Hazelnut Filling

Sponge

115g (4 oz)	margarine	½ cup
115g (4 oz)	sugar	⅔ cup
2 medium	free-range eggs, beaten	2 medium
115g (4 oz)	wholemeal (wholewheat) flour	1 cup
55g (2 oz)	carob powder	½ cup
1 tsp	baking powder	1 tsp
55g (2 oz)	hazelnuts, ground	½ cup
140ml (¼ pt)	milk	⅔ cup

Filling

55g (2 oz)	margarine or butter	¼ cup
55g (2 oz)	sugar	⅓ cup
55g (2 oz)	hazelnuts, coarsely chopped	½ cup

1 Cream together the margarine and sugar until light and fluffy, then stir in the eggs and mix well.
2 Sift together the flour, carob powder and baking powder and add to the first mixture with the ground

hazelnuts. Stir in the milk, beat the mixture to lighten and pour into a lightly greased medium-sized round tin.
3 Bake at 190°C/375°F (Gas Mark 5) for 20 to 30 minutes. The cake is cooked when you can press it gently with your fingertips and leave no mark. Cool slightly then transfer to a wire rack and leave to get cold.
4 Cream together the remaining margarine or butter and sugar, then add the nuts. Slice the cake in half diagonally, spread with the filling and replace the top. Serve cut into slices.

Note: Use chocolate instead of carob powder if preferred. Although margarine works in the filling, butter tastes better! Alternatively, try other fillings – a banana cream goes especially well.

Cherry and Brazil Nut Sponge

115g (4 oz)	margarine	½ cup
115g (4 oz)	sugar	⅔ cup
2 medium	free-range eggs, beaten	2 medium
115g (4 oz)	glacé cherries, halved	4 oz
1 tbs	lemon peel, grated	1 tbs
115g (4 oz)	wholemeal (wholewheat) flour	1 cup
1 tsp	baking powder	1 tsp
approx. 4 tbs	milk	approx. 4 tbs
55g (2 oz)	Brazil nuts, coarsely chopped	½ cup
2 tbs	extra sugar - optional	2 tbs

1 Cream together the margarine and sugar until light and fluffy, then gradually add the eggs, beating well after each addition. Stir in the cherries and peel.

2 In a separate bowl, sift together the flour and baking powder, then add the first mixture to this with just enough milk to give a soft dropping consistency. Beat well.

3 Turn into a greased, small square tin, smooth the top and sprinkle with the nuts and the sugar, if using it. Bake at 190°C/375°F (Gas Mark 5) for 20 to 30 minutes. The cake is cooked when you can press it with your fingertips and leave no mark. Cool in the tin for a few minutes, then carefully transfer to a wire rack and leave to get cold.

Note: For an even lighter sponge, use 81% wholemeal flour in this recipe.

Lemon Crumble Cake

Cake

225g (8 oz)	wholemeal (wholewheat) flour	2 cups
2 tsp	baking powder	2 tsp
140g (5 oz)	margarine	⅔ cup
115g (4 oz)	sugar	⅔ cup
3 tbs	candied lemon peel, finely chopped	3 tbs
3 tbs	lemon juice	3 tbs
2 medium	free-range eggs, beaten	2 medium

Topping

30g (1 oz)	margarine	2½ tbs
55g (2 oz)	wholemeal (wholewheat) flour	½ cup
55g (2 oz)	sugar	⅓ cup
30g (1 oz)	flaked almonds, crumbled	¼ cup

1 Sift the flour and baking powder into a bowl, then use fingertips to rub in the margarine to make a crumb-like mixture.

2 Stir in the sugar, chopped peel, lemon juice, and finally the beaten eggs, mixing well. The mixture should be moist and heavy - add a drop more lemon juice if necessary.

3 Turn into a greased and floured, medium-sized round cake tin and smooth the top.

4 To make the crumble topping, rub the margarine into the flour and stir in the sugar and chopped nuts. Sprinkle over the cake and press down lightly.

5 Bake at 180°C/350°F (Gas Mark 4) for 45 minutes, or until it feels firm when gently pressed. Allow to cool briefly before removing from the tin and placing on a wire rack to cool completely.

Note: As the crumble topping is easy to dislodge, this cake is best cooked in a loose-bottomed tin.

Gingerbread

2 tbs	molasses	2 tbs
2 tbs	syrup	2 tbs
115g (4 oz)	block margarine	½ cup
55g (2 oz)	sugar	⅓ cup
225g (8 oz)	wholemeal (wholewheat) flour	2 cups
1 tbs	ground mixed spice	1 tsp
1 tsp	ground ginger	1 tsp
¼ tsp	bicarbonate of soda	¼ tsp
140ml (¼ pt)	milk	⅔ cup
85g (3 oz)	sultanas (golden seedless raisins)	½ cup
85g (3 oz)	candied peel	½ cup

1 In a small saucepan, combine and gently heat the molasses, syrup, margarine and sugar. Stir well.

2 Sift together the flour, spices and bicarbonate of soda. Add to this the first mixture and the milk and blend well. Stir in the fruit.

3 Grease a medium-sized square tin, line with silver foil and pour in the prepared mixture. Bake at 170°C/325°F (Gas Mark 3) for 50 minutes to 1 hour or until a sharp knife inserted in the centre comes out clean. Leave to cool briefly before carefully removing from the tin and placing on a wire rack to cool completely. Serve cut into squares.

Note: This is one of the few cakes that really does benefit from being kept for several dayss. Wrap it well and store in an airtight tin.

Malt Loaf

455g (1 lb)	mixed dried fruit (raisins, sultanas, currants, apples etc.)	3 cups
200ml (⅓ pt)	cold tea (black)	¾ cup
170g (8 oz)	sugar	1 cup
225g (8 oz)	wholemeal (wholewheat) flour	2 cups
2 tsp	baking powder	2 tsp
1 large	free-range egg, lightly beaten	1 large

1 Wash and dry the fruit, then add to the cold tea and leave to soak overnight. In the morning stir in the sugar, then the flour and baking powder, mixing well.

2 Add just enough of the beaten egg to give the mixture a fairly stiff consistency. Spoon it into a lightly-greased large loaf tin and smooth the top.

3 Bake at 180°C/350°F (Gas Mark 4) for about 1½ hours, or until cooked. Test by inserting a sharp knife in the centre, which will come out clean when the cake is ready. Cool on a wire rack. Serve sliced, lightly spread with butter, margarine or jam.

Note: It is the tea which gives this old favourite its malty taste.

Grapefruit Cake

115g (4 oz)	margarine	½ cup
115g (4 oz)	sugar	⅔ cup
225g (8 oz)	wholemeal (wholewheat) flour	2 cups
2 tsp	baking powder	2 tsp
1 tsp	ground mixed spice	1 tsp
115g (4 oz)	sultanas (golden seedless raisins)	⅔ cup
2 tbs	grapefruit peel, finely chopped	2 tbs
140ml (¼ pt)	grapefruit juice	⅔ cup

1 Beat together the margarine and sugar until thick and creamy.
2 In a separate bowl, sift together the flour, baking powder and spice, then stir in the sultanas and peel.
3 In a saucepan, gently bring the grapefruit juice to the boil, then pour it onto the flour mixture and blend thoroughly. Stir in the margarine and sugar.
4 Spoon into a small, greased loaf tin and smooth the top. Bake at 150°C/300°F (Gas Mark 2) for one hour, or until a sharp knife inserted in the centre comes out clean. Leave to cool briefly, then remove from the tin carefully and transfer to a wire rack.

Note: To give the cake a firmer texture add an egg.

Chocolate and Almond Roulade

Roulade

3 medium	free-range eggs, beaten	3 medium
3 tbs	honey	3 tbs
2 tbs	hot water	2 tbs
55g (2 oz)	ground almonds	½ cup
55g (2 oz)	wholemeal (wholewheat) flour	½ cup
1 tbs	cocoa	1 tbs

Filling

| 115g (4 oz) | ricotta cheese | ½ cup |

1 Whisk together the eggs and honey until well mixed. Add the water and beat again.
2 Use a metal spoon to fold the nuts into the mixture, then add the flour, stirring gently but making sure all the ingredients are well mixed.
3 Line a Swiss roll tin with greased foil. Pour in the mixture and bake at 180°C/350°F (Gas Mark 4) for 12 to 15 minutes, or until the cake is just firm to touch. Turn out, using the foil to help you lift it. Trim with a knife then roll up into a Swiss roll shape and leave on a wire rack to cool.

4 When ready to serve the roulade, unroll it and spread with the ricotta cheese. Roll it up again and serve cut into generous slices.

Note: This Swiss roll can be served at teatime or as a dessert, topped with fresh fruit salad or stewed red berries. Ricotta cheese is creamy, has a subtle taste and is low in fat. If you prefer use crème fraîche and yogurt.

Pear and Ginger Loaf

170g (6 oz)	wholemeal (wholewheat) flour	1½ cups
1 tsp	bicarbonate of soda	1 tsp
2 tsp	ground ginger	2 tsp
55g (2 oz)	margarine	¼ cup
3 tbs	syrup	3 tbs
30g (1 oz)	stem ginger, chopped	1 oz
115g (4 oz)	dried pears, chopped	1 cup
approx. 140ml (¼ pt)	milk	⅔ cup

1 Sift together the flour, baking powder, bicarbonate of soda and ground ginger.
2 Use fingertips to rub in the margarine to make a crumb-like mixture. Add the syrup, stem ginger and pears, and enough milk to make a soft dough.
3 Transfer the mixture to a greased, small loaf tin. Bake at 180°C/350°F (Gas Mark 4) for 50 minutes to 1 hour, or until a sharp knife inserted in the centre comes out clean. Cool the cake briefly in the tin, then turn out and stand on a wire rack until cold. Serve thinly sliced.

Note: Vegetarians can add an egg to give the cake a firmer texture. Any syrup can be used for this cake, but the syrup in which the ginger was preserved will greatly enhance the flavour.

Buttermilk Cake

Cake

285g (10 oz)	wholemeal (wholewheat) flour	2½ cups
1½ tsp	bicarbonate of soda	1½ tsp
1 tsp	baking powder	1 tsp
1 tsp	ground cinnamon	1 tsp
½ tsp	ground nutmeg	½ tsp
½ tsp	ground cloves	½ tsp
115g (4 oz)	margarine, melted	½ cup
340ml ⅔ pint	buttermilk	1½ cups
2 medium	free-range eggs, beaten	2 medium

Topping

55g (2 oz)	sugar	⅓ cup
2 tsp	ground cinnamon	2 tsp
55g (2 oz)	raisins	⅓ cup
30g (1 oz)	walnuts, chopped	¼ cup

1 Sift together the flour, baking powder and spices. Add the margarine and mix well, then add the buttermilk and finally the eggs.
2 Pour into a greased, medium–sized square cake tin. Mix together the ingredients for the topping and sprinkle over the first mixture, pressing down lightly. Bake at 180°C/350°F (Gas Mark 4) for 40 minutes. Cool briefly before removing from the tin. Serve cut into squares.

Note: Buttermilk is a by-product of the butter-making process and is both low in fat and high in protein. It has a unique, slightly acid flavour. If you cannot find it, use yogurt instead.

Apricot Frangipane

Cake

170g (5 oz)	wholemeal (wholewheat) flour	1½ cups
55g (2 oz)	sugar	⅓ cup
2 small	free-range eggs yolks	2 small
85g (3 oz)	margarine, melted	⅓ cup

Filling

115g (4 oz)	whole dried apricots, soaked	1 cup
3 tbs	apricot jam	3 tbs
85g (3 oz)	margarine	½ cup
85g (3 oz)	sugar	½ cup
2 small	free-range eggs, beaten	2 small
1 tbs	lemon juice	1 tbs
1 tbs	lemon peel, finely grated	1 tbs
¼ tsp	almond essence	¼ tsp
115g (4 oz)	almonds, ground	1 cup
55g (2 oz)	wholemeal (wholewheat) flour	½ cup

1 Stir together the flour, sugar, egg yolks and margarine. When well mixed, turn onto a floured board and knead to make a soft dough. Wrap in foil and chill briefly.
2 Roll out and use to line a shallow, oblong medium-sized tin. Bake blind at 190°C/375°F (Gas Mark 5) for 10 minutes. Drain the apricots well. Spread the cooked base with apricot jam and dot with the whole apricots.
3 Cream together the margarine and sugar and gradually add the eggs. Stir in the juice and peel. Add the almond essence and the almonds, mixing well. Fold in the flour.
4 Pour this mixture over the apricots and return the cake to the oven. Cook at the same temperature for 20 minutes, then lower the heat to 180°C/350°F (Gas

Mark 4) and bake for 20 minutes more. Cool before removing from the tin. Cut into slices to serve.

Note: This unusual version of frangipane can be varied by using other fruit instead of the apricots, for example, fresh plums or greengages in summer.

Tahini Cake

340g (12 oz)	wholemeal (wholewheat) flour	3 cups
3 tsp	baking powder	3 tsp
1 tsp	bicarbonate of soda	1 tsp
170g (6 oz)	sugar	1 cup
55g (2 oz)	walnuts, chopped	½ cup
55g (2 oz)	raisins	⅓ cup
55g (2 oz)	candied peel	2 oz
115g (4 oz)	tahini	⅓ cup
200ml (⅓ pt)	orange juice	¾ cup
200ml (⅓ pt)	water	¾ cup

1 Sift together the flour, baking powder and bicarbonate of soda. Stir in the sugar, nuts, raisins and peel.
2 In a separate bowl, whisk together the tahini, orange juice and most of the water. Add the flour mixture and stir well to make a thick smooth batter – add more water as necessary.
3 Line a large square cake tin with greased foil. Pour in the mixture and smooth the top. Bake at 180°C/350°F (Gas Mark 4) for 45 minutes to 1 hour. The cake is cooked when a sharp knife inserted in the centre comes out clean. Cool briefly, transfer to a wire rack to cool completely, and serve cut into squares.

Note: Tahini is a nutritious paste made from sesame seeds. It is available in dark and light versions. The lighter one, which has a more delicate flavour, is best for this recipe.

Christmas Fruit Cake

225g (8 oz)	margarine	1 cup
570ml (1 pt)	water	2½ cups
225g (8 oz)	sugar	1⅓ cups
450g (1 lb)	mixed dried fruit	3 cups
1 tsp	ground cinnamon	1 tsp
1 tsp	ground ginger	1 tsp
1 tsp	ground allspice	1 tsp
½ tsp	ground nutmeg	½ tsp
2 tsp	vanilla essence	2 tsp
2 tbs	syrup	2 tbs
2 tsp	bicarbonate of soda	2 tsp
1 tbs	lemon juice	1 tbs
2 tbs	lemon peel, grated	2 tbs
395g (14 oz)	wholemeal (wholewheat) flour	3½ cups

55g (2 oz)	*soya flour*	*½ cup*
55g (2 oz)	*hazelnuts, coarsely chopped*	*½ cup*
55g (2 oz)	*walnuts, coarsely chopped*	*½ cup*
1 tbs	*brandy - optional*	*1 tbs*

1 Put the margarine, water, sugar, fruit and spices in a large saucepan and boil for 10 minutes. Set aside to cool. Add all the remaining ingredients, making sure the mixture is thoroughly blended.
2 Lightly grease a large cake tin and pour in the mixture. Bake at 150°C/300°F (Gas Mark 3) for 2 hours. Alternatively, divide the mixture between two small tins and reduce the cooking time by about 30 minutes. When cold, store in an airtight container.

Note: To make this even more special, brush the top with warmed apricot jam then decorate with whole brazil and pecan nuts, glacé cherries, candied pineapple, angelica - or whatever comes to mind.

Mincemeat Cake with Marzipan Cream Filling

Cake

115g (4 oz)	*margarine*	*½ cup*
115g (4 oz)	*sugar*	*⅔ cup*
2 large	*free-range eggs, beaten*	*2 large*
170g (6 oz)	*wholemeal (wholewheat) flour*	*1½ cups*
2 tsp	*baking powder*	*2 tsp*
340g (12 oz)	*vegetarian mincemeat (see page 115)*	*12 oz*

Filling

115g (4 oz)	*marzipan (see Marzipan Mice page 95)*	4 oz
2 tbs	crème fraîche	2 tbs

1 Cream together the margarine and sugar. When light and fluffy add the eggs.
2 Sift together the flour and baking powder, then combine with the first mixture. Add the mincemeat, making sure it is evenly distributed.
3 Transfer the mixture to a medium-sized greased round cake tin and smooth the top. Bake at 180°C/350°F (Gas Mark 4) for 1 hour, or until a knife inserted in the centre comes out clean. Cool on a wire rack.
4 To make the filling, grate or chop the marzipan, then mash together with the cream. Halve the cake diagonally and spread with the cream. Serve cut in wedges.

Note: This is an unusual alternative to Christmas Fruit Cake.

Honey Dundee Cake

170g (6 oz)	*margarine*	*⅔ cup*
115g (4 oz)	*sugar*	*⅔ cup*
3 medium	*free-range eggs, beaten*	*3 medium*
4 tbs	*honey*	*4 tbs*
225g (8 oz)	*wholemeal (wholewheat) flour*	*2 cups*
1½ tsp	*baking powder*	*1½ tsp*
1 tsp	*ground mixed spice*	*1 tsp*
2-4 tbs	*milk*	*2-4 tbs*
55g (2 oz)	*blanched almonds, chopped*	*½ cup*
55g (2 oz)	*glacé cherries*	*½ cup*
55g (2 oz)	*candied peel*	*½ cup*
340g (12 oz)	*mixed dried fruit*	*2 cups*
30g (1 oz)	*blanched almonds, split*	*¼ cup*
	egg white	

1 Cream together the margarine and sugar until smooth and light. Add the eggs and honey.
2 Sift together the flour, baking powder and spice, and add to the first mixture with just enough milk to give the mixture a soft dropping consistency. Fold in the chopped almonds, cherries, peel and fruit, mixing gently but thoroughly.
3 Grease and flour a medium-sized round cake tin. Pour in the mixture and decorate with the split almonds, brushed with a little egg white. Bake at 170°C/325°F (Gas Mark 3) for 1½ hours, then reduce the heat to 140°C/275°F (Gas Mark 1) for another ½ hour, or until a sharp knife inserted in the centre comes out clean. Cool briefly in the tin, then turn onto a wire rack and leave to cool completely. Store wrapped in silver foil in an airtight tin.

Note: This is a heavy, rich cake, so will go a long way. Although glacé cherries cannot be called a healthfood, they are traditional. To help prevent them sinking, lightly flour them.

No-bake Fruit Cake

225g (8 oz)	*dates*	*1½ cups*
225g (8 oz)	*dried apricots*	*1½ cups*
115g (4 oz)	*raisins*	*⅔ cup*
115g (4 oz)	*currants*	*⅔ cup*
115g (4 oz)	*pecans or* walnuts	1 cup
55g (2 oz)	almonds	½ cup
115g (4 oz)	sunflower seeds	1 cup
115g (4 oz)	coconut flakes	1⅓ cups
1 medium	orange, washed, seeds removed	1 medium
2 tsp	cinnamon	2 tsp
2 tbs	lemon juice	2 tbs
4 tbs	corn syrup	4 tbs
30g (1 oz)	sesame seeds, roasted	¼ cup

1 Use a food processor to grind the dried fruit and nuts. Cut the orange into segments (do not remove the peel) and add to the other ingredients.
2 Add the cinnamon, lemon juice and syrup.
3 Grease a medium-sized cake tin and spoon in the mixture, then press it down firmly. Sprinkle with the sesame seeds and press them into the cake. Chill overnight and serve cut into thin slices.

Note: This is no empty snack! It's the kind of cake you might take with you when climbing mountains.

Caraway Cake

115g (4 oz)	margarine	½ cup
115g (4 oz)	sugar	⅔ cup
2 medium	free-range eggs, beaten	2 medium
225g (8 oz)	wholemeal (wholewheat) flour	2 cups
2 tsp	baking powder	2 tsp
4 tbs	milk	4 tbs
1 tbs	caraway seeds, or to taste	1 tbs

1 Cream together the margarine and sugar. When light and fluffy, gradually add the eggs, beating well after each addition.
2 In a separate bowl, sift together the flour and baking powder, then add to the first mixture. Stir in the milk and caraway seeds.
3 Turn into a small greased cake tin. Bake at 180°C/350°F (Gas Mark 4) for 1¼ hours, or until a sharp knife inserted in the centre comes out clean. Cool briefly in the tin, then transfer to a wire rack and leave to cool completely.

Note: This simple-to-make cake has a subtle and unusual flavour. You can use poppy seeds instead of the caraway seeds, increasing the quantity slightly.

Lemon Date Sponge

85g (3 oz)	wholemeal (wholewheat) flour	¾ cup
45g (1½ oz)	soya flour	a good ¼ cup
1½ tsp	baking powder	1½ tsp
140ml (¼ pt)	milk	⅔ cup
2 tbs	vegetable oil	2 tbs
2 tbs	vegan lemon curd (see page 114)	2 tbs
1 tbs	lemon juice	1 tbs
55g (2 oz)	sugar	1⅓ cups
85g (3 oz)	dates, chopped	½ cup
	extra lemon curd, optional	

1 Sift together the two flours and baking powder. Whisk together the soya milk and oil, then add to the dry ingredients with the lemon curd, lemon juice, sugar and dates. Make sure all the ingredients are well blended. If they seem very dry, add a little more lemon juice or milk.
2 Line a medium-sized sandwich tin with greased silver foil. Pour in the mixture. Bake at 200°C/400°F (Gas Mark 6) for 20 minutes, or until the centre feels springy when pressed with your fingertips.
3 Set aside to cool, then remove carefully from the tin. You may like to cut the cake in half diagonally and sandwich with extra lemon curd.

Note: To make a chocolate sponge cake, use the same recipe but substitute two tbs cocoa for the lemon curd, mixing it well with 2 tbs of water and proceeding as above.

Battenburg

170g (6 oz)	margarine	¾ cup
170g (6 oz)	caster sugar	1 cup
3 medium	free-range eggs	3 medium
170g (6 oz)	unbleached white flour	1½ cups
1 tsp	baking powder	1 tsp
1 tbs	carob powder	1 tbs
1 tbs	hot water	1 tbs
1 tbs	lemon peel, finely grated	1 tbs
4-6 tbs	lemon curd	4-6 tbs
225g (8 oz)	marzipan	8 oz

1 Cream together the margarine and sugar and when well mixed add the eggs, one at a time, beating thoroughly between each addition. Sift together the flour and baking powder and add to the mixture.
2 Divide the mixture in half, putting half in each of two separate bowls. Stir together the carob powder and hot water and mix it to one portion of cake mix. Mix the lemon peel into the other portion.
3 Line and grease a medium-sized square cake tin and divide lengthways into two sections with a piece of folded foil. Pour half of the mixture into one section and half into the other. Bake at 160°C/325°F (Gas Mark 3) for 40 minutes or until cooked. Remove carefully and cool before cutting lengthways so that you have four long strips of cake. Use the lemon curd to stick the four strips together to make a chequered pattern.
4 Roll out the marzipan to make an oblong the same size as the cake, spread the cake with more lemon curd, place in the centre of the marzipan and roll up, pressing the edges together gently but firmly. Serve cut in slices.

Note: Because this cake depends on the contrast between pale and dark squares for effect, it is better to use unbleached white flour rather than wholemeal flour.

Marmalade and Molasses Cake

225g (8 oz)	wholemeal (wholewheat) flour	2 cups
2 tsp	baking powder	2 tsp
170g (6 oz)	margarine	¾ cup
55g (2 oz)	sugar	⅓ cup
3 tbs	molasses	3 tbs
4 tbs	orange juice	4 tbs
1 large	free-range egg, beaten	1 large
3 tbs	marmalade	3 tbs

1 Sift together the flour and baking powder and then use fingertips to rub in the margarine to make a crumb-like mixture. Stir in the sugar.
2 Heat together the molasses and orange juice and add to the first mixture. Add the beaten egg and finally the marmalade to make a thick, heavy mixture. If it seems too dry add extra orange juice.
3 Pour into a small, greased loaf tin, smooth the top and bake at 180°C/350°F (Gas Mark 4) for 50 minutes to 1 hour, or until cooked. Serve sliced, spread with butter.

Note: For a special occasion, brush the top with warmed marmalade and sprinkle with crushed granola, or chopped nuts.

Coconut Cake with Apple Cream Filling

Cake

115g (4 oz)	creamed coconut	4 oz
285ml (½ pt)	boiling water	1⅓ cups
2 tsp	baking powder	2 tsp
340g (12 oz)	wholemeal (wholewheat) flour	3 cups
170g (6 oz)	sugar	1 cup
2 tbs	apple juice	2 tbs
approx. 140ml (¼ pt)	vegetable oil	⅔ cup
2 tbs	desiccated coconut	2 tbs

Apple Cream

3	dessert apples, peeled and grated	3
1 tbs	lemon juice	1 tbs
55g (2 oz)	sugar	⅓ cup
approx. 140ml (¼ pt)	concentrated soya milk or soya cream	⅔ cup

1 Grate the coconut and then dissolve it in the boiling water to make a thick cream.
2 Sift together the baking powder and flour, add the sugar, dissolved coconut and apple juice. Gradually trickle in the oil, stirring well as you do so, adding just enough to make a thick moist mixture.

3 Transfer to a small, round, lightly-greased cake tin and smooth the top. Bake at 180°C/350°F (Gas Mark 4) for 45 minutes, or until a sharp knife inserted in the centre comes out clean. Cool slightly and then leave on a wire rack to cool completely.
4 To make the apple cream, simply put all the ingredients into a blender and whisk well until thick and creamy. As it should not be too moist, start by using less milk or cream, adding more if necessary. You may also need to adjust the sweetness depending upon the apples you use.
5 Cut the cake diagonally, carefully spread the bottom half with the apple cream, top with the remaining cake and serve at once, cut into thick wedges.

Note: This cake is equally delicious sandwiched with other fillings, such as red fruit purées, jams, coconut cream and so on.

Pineapple Swiss Roll

3 large	free-range eggs	3 large
85g (3 oz)	caster sugar	½ cup
85g (3 oz)	wholemeal (wholewheat) flour	¾ cup
1 tsp	baking powder	1 tsp
1 small can	pineapple in natural juice, drained and finely chopped	1 small can
	extra caster sugar	

1 Whisk together the eggs and sugar until light and fluffy. In a separate bowl, sift together the flour and baking powder. Fold together both mixtures using a metal spoon.
2 Line a Swiss roll tin with silver foil and grease well. Pour in the mixture and smooth the top. Bake at 220°C/425°F (Gas Mark 7) for 10 minutes or until the edges begin to pull away from the side of the tin.
3 Carefully turn out onto a sheet of silver foil dredged with sugar and spread the upper surface with the chopped pineapple pieces. Roll up the cooked cake tightly. Cool on a wire rack before cutting into thick slices.

Note: This basic Swiss roll recipe can be adapted in a wide variety of ways, either by adding different ingredients to the cake mix, such as carob powder, cocoa, ground nuts and almond essence, or by varying the fillings.

Banana Yogurt Tea Bread

55g (2 oz)	margarine	¼ cup
115g (4 oz)	sugar	⅔ cup
1 medium	free-range egg, lightly beaten	1 medium
2 medium	ripe bananas, mashed well	2 medium
225g (8 oz)	wholemeal (wholewheat) flour	2 cups
1 tsp	baking powder	1 tsp
1 tsp	vanilla essence	1 tsp
3-4 tbs	natural yogurt	3-4 tbs
55g (2 oz)	banana chips, coarsely crushed	2 oz

1 Cream together the margarine and sugar until light and fluffy, then stir in the egg and when well mixed, add the bananas.
2 Sift together the flour and baking powder and add to the first mixture with the vanilla essence and enough yogurt to make a thick dough. Turn the mixture into a small, well-greased loaf tin, smooth the top and sprinkle with the banana chips.
3 Bake at 180°C/350°F (Gas Mark 4) for 50 minutes to 1 hour or until cooked.

Note: This is delicious sliced and spread with apricot jam. Alternatively, add candied peel, nuts or whatever you like to the basic mixture.

Frosted Almond Carrot Cake

Cake

3 medium	free-range eggs, separated	3 medium
170g (6 oz)	sugar	1 cup
1 tsp	vanilla essence	1 tsp
85g (3 oz)	wholemeal (wholewheat) flour	¾ cup
1½ tsp	baking powder	1½ tsp
½ tsp	ground ginger	½ tsp
½ tsp	ground nutmeg	½ tsp
1 tsp	ground cinnamon	1 tsp
225g (8 oz)	carrots, peeled and grated	8 oz
115g (4 oz)	ground almonds	1 cup
2 tbs	milk	2 tbs

Frosting

225g (8 oz)	sugar	1⅓ cups
4 tbs	water	4 tbs
1 medium	free-range egg white	1 medium
55g (2 oz)	flaked roasted almonds - optional	½ cup

1 Beat the egg yolks and sugar together until light and fluffy, then add the vanilla essence.

2 Sift together the flour, baking powder and spices and add to the first mixture. Stir in the carrot, ground almonds and enough milk to make a thick moist mixture.
3 Whisk the egg whites until stiff and use a metal spoon to fold them into the first mixture. Grease a medium-sized square tin, spoon the mixture in, smooth the top and bake at 190°C/275°F (Gas Mark 5) for 30 to 40 minutes or until cooked. It should be firm to the touch. Leave to cook briefly, then carefully remove from tin and place on a wire rack.
4 To make the frosting, heat the sugar and water together, stirring until the sugar dissolves, then bring to the boil without stirring again and continue boiling until the mixture reaches firm ball stage (*see* introduction to Chapter 11). Whisk the egg white and, when stiff, add it to the syrup still stirring to make a thick, smooth mixture. Use a knife to spread the icing over the top and sides of the cake. Leave to cool completely. Sprinkle with extra nuts to taste.

Note: Although this topping is not particularly healthy, it goes perfectly with carrot cake. Use it for special occasions only. A very quick and delicious alternative is to simply spread the cake with crème fraîche just before serving.

Carrot Cake

7g (¼ oz)	dried yeast	1 tsp
1 tbs	vegetable oil	1 tbs
3 tbs	corn syrup	3 tbs
140ml (¼ pt)	warm water	⅔ cup
225g (8 oz)	wholemeal (wholewheat) flour	2 cups
1 tsp	ground cinnamon	1 tsp
1 tsp	ground mace	1 tsp
	extra water	
225g (8 oz)	carrots, peeled and grated	8 oz
2 tbs	finely-grated orange peel	2 tbs
85g (3 oz)	sultanas (golden seedless raisins)	½ cup

1 Mix together the yeast, vegetable oil, syrup and warm water and leave for 10 minutes. Add the flour and spices and, if necessary, a little more water so that you have a batter that is smooth and heavy.
2 Stir in the carrots, orange peel and sultanas. Transfer to a medium-sized, square, greased baking tin and leave to stand in a warm place for an hour. Bake at 180°C/350°F (Gas Mark 4) for 1 hour.

Note: You can use other syrups instead of corn syrup - maple syrup, for example. You can also use candied peel instead of the orange peel or add finely chopped nuts of any kind - walnuts are most often used in carrot cake, but roasted hazel nuts make an interesting change.

Large Cakes and Gateaux

Papaya Layer Cake

Cake

115g (4 oz)	wholemeal (wholewheat) flour	1 cup
2 tsp	baking powder	2 tsp
115g (4 oz)	margarine	½ cup
115g (4 oz)	sugar	⅔ cup
2 medium	free-range eggs, lightly beaten	2 medium
1 tbs	finely-grated lemon peel	1 tbs

Filling

1 large	ripe papaya, peeled, stoned and cut into chunks	1 large
70ml (⅛ pt)	fromage frais	¼ cup
1 tbs	honey or syrup	1 tbs
1 tsp	concentrated orange juice	1 tsp

1 Sift together the flour and baking powder. Use fingertips to mix in the margarine.
2 Use a spoon to beat in the sugar, then the eggs and, finally, the grated orange peel. The mixture should be thick and smooth.
3 Grease and line a shallow oblong tin. Pour in the mixture and smooth. Bake at 180°C/350°F (Gas Mark 4) for 30 minutes or until cooked. Cool briefly, then place on a wire rack to cool completely before cutting in half diagonally.
4 To prepare the filling, blend the papaya, fromage frais, sweetener and fruit juice. This should be as smooth as possible, but not too moist – you might prefer to omit the fruit juice. Spread half the mixture on one part of the cake, top with the second part and spread the final mixture on top of that. You can also decorate the top with extra slices of papaya.

Note: Papayas are also known as pawpaws and are widely available these days. However peaches may be used instead.

Upside-down Yogurt Cake

285g (10 oz)	wholemeal (wholewheat) flour	2½ cups
3 tsp	baking powder	3 tsp
70ml (⅛ pt)	vegetable oil	⅓ cup
170g (6 oz)	sugar	1 cup
1 tsp	vanilla essence	1 tsp
140ml (¼ pt)	natural yogurt	⅔ cup
2 medium	free-range eggs, separated	2 medium
55g (2 oz)	sugar	⅓ cup
1 small can	pineapple slices	1 small can

1 Sift together the flour and baking powder in a large bowl, add the oil, sugar, vanilla essence and yogurt. Stir in the egg yolks and mix well.
2 Beat the egg whites until stiff but do not over-beat them. Fold them into the first mixture.
3 Grease a medium-sized round cake tin, sprinkle the sugar on the bottom and arrange the well-drained pineapple slices on top of it to cover the base of the tin. Pour in the cake mixture.
4 Bake at 180°C/350°F (Gas Mark 4) for 40 minutes or until cooked. To test, a sharp knife inserted in the centre should come out clean when the cake is ready. Cool briefly, then place a plate over the top of the tin and tip the cake upside down so that the pineapple is on the top. Transfer to a wire rack and leave to cool completely. Serve cut into slices.

Note: To serve this cake as a dessert, simply top with more yogurt – thick Greek yogurt is ideal.

Fruit and Bran Loaf

225g (8 oz)	bran cereal	8 oz
4 tbs	Pear and Apple Spread	4 tbs
115g (4 oz)	dried apricots, chopped	⅔ cup
115g (4 oz)	raisins	⅔ cup
115g (4 oz)	dried apples, chopped	⅔ cup
200ml (⅓ pt)	milk	¾ cup
340g (12 oz)	wholemeal (wholewheat) flour	3 cups
2 tsp	baking powder	2 tsp
30g (1 oz)	sugar	2 tbsp
1 tsp	ground cinnamon	1 tsp

1 Put the bran cereal, Pear and Apple Spread, dried fruit and milk into a bowl and leave to soak for a couple of hours.
2 Sift together the flour and baking powder and add to the first mixture, stirring well. Grease a small loaf tin, pour in the mixture and top with a sprinkling of the sugar and cinnamon. Bake at 180°C/350°F (Gas Mark 4) for 1 hour or until a sharp knife inserted in the centre comes out clean. Cool on a wire rack and serve sliced.

Note: Any dried fruits can be used in this loaf or fresh fruits such as bilberries. Kelloggs All Bran is an ideal cereal to use in this, but do try it with your favourite brand.

Simnel Cake

170g (6 oz)	margarine	¾ cup
170g (6 oz)	sugar	1 cup
3 medium	free-range eggs, beaten	3 medium
225g (8 oz)	wholemeal (wholewheat) flour	2 cups
2 tsp	ground mixed spice	2 tsp
½ tsp	ground nutmeg	½ tsp
225g (8 oz)	currants	1⅓ cups
225g (8 oz)	sultanas	1⅓ cups
115g (4 oz)	chopped candied peel	⅔ cup
55g (2 oz)	flaked almonds	½ cup
1 tbs	lemon peel, finely grated	1 tbs
340g (12 oz)	marzipan	12 oz
2 tbs	apricot jam	2 tbs

1 Cream together the margarine and sugar until light and fluffy, then gradually add the beaten eggs a little at a time, beating well before adding any more.
2 Sift the bran out of the flour, mix the flour with the spices and add this to the first mixture. Add the bran that remains in the sieve.
3 Use a metal spoon to fold the dried fruit, almonds and peel into the first mixture, thoroughly but gently.
4 Grease and line a medium-sized, round cake tin, spoon in half of the prepared mixture and smooth the top. Roll out the marzipan, cut a third of it into a circle the same size as the cake and place this over the ingredients in the tin. Add the rest of the cake mix.
5 Bake at 170°C/325°F (Gas Mark 3) for 1 hour, then lower the heat to 150°C/300°F (Gas Mark 2) and cook for 2 more hours. Cool the cake and remove very carefully from the tin.
6 Roll out a third of the remaining marzipan, again making it the same size as the cake. Spread the cake with apricot jam, add the marzipan and press down gently. Use the remaining marzipan to decorate the top.

Note: This is a traditional Easter cake and is usually decorated with 11 small balls around the rim of the cake, to represent the Disciples – minus Judas.

Pear and Apple Sandwich Cake

115g (4 oz)	margarine, softened	½ cup
approx. 6 tbs	Pear and Apple Spread	8 tbs
115g (4 oz)	wholemeal (wholewheat) flour	1 cup
2 tsp	baking powder	2 tsp
2-3 tbs	apple juice	2-3 tbs
	icing sugar - optional	

1 Mix together the margarine and 4 tbs of the Pear and Apple Spread. Sift the flour and baking powder together and add to the first mixture, returning any bran that is left in the sieve. Stir in enough juice to make a thick, moist mixture.
2 Grease two small sandwich tins, pour in the mixture and smooth the top. Bake at 180°C/350°F (Gas Mark 4) for 20 minutes or until cooked. Remove the cakes from the tins and cool on a wire rack.
3 Cover one portion of cake generously with the remaining Pear and Apple Spread and sandwich with the other portion. Sprinkle the top with icing sugar, if liked, and serve cut into wedges.

Note: A subtly flavoured cake – add sugar if you like a sweeter cake. Other sweet spreads or jams can, of course, be used instead of the Pear and Apple Spread. For the filling you could use a well-drained, sweet apple purée. Vegetarians can add an egg for a lighter sponge.

Coconut and Carob Gateau

Gateau

285g (10 oz)	wholemeal (wholewheat) flour	2½ cups
30g (1 oz)	soya flour	¼ cup
2 tsp	baking powder	2 tsp
55g (2 oz)	carob powder	½ cup
115g (4 oz)	margarine	½ cup
2 tbs	syrup	2 tbs
280ml (½ pt)	water	1⅓ cups
1 tsp	bicarbonate of soda	1 tsp

Filling

55g (2 oz)	margarine	¼ cup
85g (3 oz)	caster sugar	½ cup
2 tbs	desiccated coconut	2 tbs

Topping

170g (6 oz)	coconut cream	6 oz
approx. 140ml (¼ pt)	boiling water	⅔ cup
55g (2 oz)	caster sugar	⅓ cup
85g (3 oz)	flaked coconut, lightly roasted	1 cup
	glacé cherries for decoration	

1 Sift together the flours, baking powder and carob powder.
2 In a small saucepan, melt together the margarine and syrup and add to the first mixture. Use 2 tbsp water to mix with the bicarbonate of soda and add this to the first mixture with the remaining water, mixing everything very well.
3 Grease two small, round cake tins and divide the mixture between them. Bake at 180°C/350°F (Gas

Mark 4) for 30 to 40 minutes or until a sharp knife inserted in the centre comes out clean. Set aside to cool.

4 Mix together the margarine and sugar to make a fairly soft cream, add the desiccated coconut, and spread this mixture over one half of the cake. Top with the other half of the cake.

5 To make the topping, put the grated coconut into a bowl, add the boiling water and sugar and stir to make a very thick, smooth mixture. Add extra water as necessary. Then, before it cools, spread this evenly over the top of the cake. Decorate with flaked coconut pieces and glacé cherries for colour.

Note: This unusual gateau will suit the vegans among your family and friends.

Summer Fruit Gateau with Cinnamon Cream

Gateau

115g (4 oz)	margarine	½ cup
115g (4 oz)	sugar	⅔ cup
2 medium	free-range eggs, beaten	2 medium
½ tsp	vanilla essence	½ tsp
170g (6 oz)	wholemeal (wholewheat) flour	1½ cups
1 tsp	baking powder	1 tsp
approx. 2 tbs	milk	approx. 2 tbs
455g (1 lb)	fresh fruit (e.g. raspberries, apricots, strawberries, cherries, redcurrants etc)	1 lb

Cream

200ml (⅓ pt)	whipping cream	¾ cup
2 tsp	caster sugar	2 tsp
1 tsp	cinnamon, or to taste	1 tsp

1 Cream together the margarine and sugar until light and fluffy, then gradually add both eggs, mixing well between each addition. Beat briefly.

2 Sift together the flour and baking powder and fold gently into the first mixture with just enough milk to make a soft mixture.

3 Lightly grease two round, medium-sized cake tins, pour some of the mixture into each and bake at 180°C/350°F (Gas Mark 4) for 30 minutes or until a sharp knife inserted in the centre comes out clean. Cool briefly before transferring to a rack and leaving to cool completely.

4 Meanwhile prepare the fruit. This should be clean and trimmed, with stones removed as necessary. Cut the larger fruits in half.

5 To prepare the cinnamon cream, whip the cream until

thick and add the sugar and cinnamon to taste. Spoon a little of this mixture over the fruit and mix well. Pile the fruit onto one half of the cake and top with the other half of the cake. Use the rest of the cream to make a decorative topping and sprinkle, if liked, with extra cinnamon.

Note: Freshly grated cinnamon is infinitely better in this recipe than the ready ground kind. Other gateaux can be made using the same basic sponge mix – for example you can add cocoa powder, spread the sponge with blackcurrant jam and top with cream and then some grated chocolate. Alternatively, mix in chopped nuts and flavour the sponge with lemon.

3
Biscuits and Bars

Always useful to have around, biscuits can be cooked in fairly large batches and stored in airtight containers where they will keep fresh for up to a week, or even longer, depending on the recipe.

Apart from being good with morning coffee or afternoon tea, many biscuits can be served with ice creams, sorbets, mousses and other desserts, where their crisp texture makes a good contrast.

If cooking bars to be added to lunch boxes, wrap them individually in foil as soon as they are cold, and before storing. This way they will stay crisp longer – and will be ready to pack when time is short.

Banana Wheatgerm Biscuits

55g (2 oz)	margarine	¼ cup
55g (2 oz)	sugar	⅓ cup
1 medium	free-range egg, beaten	1 medium
1 large	banana, mashed	1 large
115g (4 oz)	wholemeal (wholewheat) flour	1 cup
2 tbs	wheatgerm	2 tbs
1 tsp	baking powder	1 tsp
55g (2 oz)	sultanas (golden seedless raisins)	⅓ cup
1 tsp	ground cinnamon	1 tsp

1 Cream together the margarine and sugar, then stir in the egg and banana.
2 Sift together the flour, wheatgerm and baking powder. Combine both mixtures, then add the sultanas and ground cinnamon.
3 Divide the dough into about 12 small pieces and roll into balls. Flatten them slightly and arrange on an ungreased baking sheet, leaving room for them to spread. Bake at 180°C/350°F (Gas Mark 4) for 15 to 20 minutes. Cool on a wire rack.

Note: Replace the wheatgerm with bran for a change. You could also stir in some crushed banana chips.

Cherry Almond Cookies

115g (4 oz)	margarine	½ cup
55g (2 oz)	sugar	⅓ cup
115g (4 oz)	almonds, ground	1 cup
225g (8 oz)	quinoa flour	2 cups
few drops	almond essence	few drops
55g (2 oz)	glacé cherries, chopped	2 oz
55g (2 oz)	almonds, flaked	½ cup

1 Cream together the margarine and sugar. When light and fluffy, add the almonds, quinoa flour and almond essence to make a firm dough. Mix in the chopped cherries.
2 Divide into small pieces, roll into balls and flatten slightly. Arrange on greased baking sheets, top each one with a few flaked almonds and press down lightly.
3 Bake at 190°C/375°F (Gas Mark 5) for 10 minutes. Leave to cool briefly, then transfer to a wire rack and leave to cool completely.

Note: Quinoa flour can be made by powdering washed, dried quinoa grains in a grinder. Although they give a unique texture to these cookies, wheat flour may be used instead.

Inca Cookies

170g (6 oz)	quinoa flour	1½ cups
55g (2 oz)	roasted hazelnuts, ground	½ cup
1 tsp	ground mixed spice	1 tsp
55g (2 oz)	sugar	⅓ cup
6 tbs	vegetable oil	6 tbs
1 medium	free-range egg, lightly beaten	1 medium
55g (2 oz)	chocolate	2 oz

1 Sift together the flour, nuts and spice and stir in the sugar. Add the vegetable oil, using a wooden spoon to combine all the ingredients then add the egg. The mixture should be fairly moist so add a drop more oil if necessary.
2 Coarsely chop the chocolate and stir it into the dough, making sure it is evenly distributed.
3 Drop small teaspoons of the mixture onto a lightly greased baking sheet. Bake at 200°C/400°F (Gas Mark 6) for 15 minutes, or until crisp. Leave the cookies on the sheet briefly, then transfer them to a wire rack and leave until cold.

Note: While quinoa was originally grown by the Incas, the quinoa on sale at your local wholefood shop will probably have been grown in Britain. To make flour, simply grind the washed, dried grains in a food processor.

Pear and Peanut Bars

225g (8 oz)	dried pears, minced	1 cup
115g (4 oz)	peanuts, ground	1 cup
2-3 tbs	syrup	2-3 tbs
30g (1 oz)	peanuts, roasted and coarsely chopped	¼ cup
	rice paper	

1 Stir together the pears and ground peanuts, adding just enough syrup to make a soft, but not too moist, mixture. Add the chopped peanuts, distributing them evenly.
2 Spoon the mixture onto rice paper, then spread with a knife to make a fairly thin even layer. Top with more rice paper and press down. Leave for a few hours or overnight, then use a sharp knife to cut into bars.

Note: Use honey instead of syrup if you prefer. Hazelnuts can also be used instead of peanuts.

Coconut Macaroons

115g (4 oz)	desiccated coconut	1⅓ cups
115g (4 oz)	sugar	⅔ cup
55g (2 oz)	wholemeal (wholewheat) flour	½ cup
1 tsp	baking powder	1 tsp
3 small	free-range egg whites	3 small
	rice paper	
	glacé cherries, halved	
55g (2 oz)	chocolate bar, coarsely chopped	2 oz

1 Mix together the coconut and sugar, then add the flour and baking powder. Lightly beat the egg whites and add to the first mixture to make a paste.
2 Arrange the rice paper on baking sheets and drop small spoonfuls of the mixture onto these, allowing space between them. Top each one with a piece of glacé cherry.
3 Bake at 190°C/375°F (Gas Mark 5) for 15 minutes. Cool briefly, transfer to a wire rack to cool completely, then trim to remove excess rice paper.
4 Melt the chocolate in a double saucepan or bowl placed over a saucepan of hot water, stirring frequently. Decorate the tops of the macaroons by piping parallel lines of chocolate across the top of each one. (Alternatively, trickle the chocolate from a small spoon.) Leave to set before storing in an airtight container.

Note: As an alternative, add crushed pineapple, apple or dried fruit to the basic mix.

Sesame Oat Bars

170g (6 oz)	tahini	⅔ cup
85g (3 oz)	honey or syrup	¼ cup
85g (3 oz)	sunflower seeds	⅔ cup
170g (6 oz)	rolled oats	1½ cups
3 tbs	grated orange peel	3 tbs
	cold water - optional	
2 tbs	sesame seeds	2 tbs

1 Stir together the tahini and honey or syrup. Add the seeds, then the oats, sprinkling them in a spoonful or two at a time and mixing well before adding more. Stir in the orange peel. The mix should be fairly soft so, if necessary, stir in some cold water.
2 Press the mixture into a lightly greased Swiss roll tin, smooth the top and sprinkle with seeds. Bake at 190°C/375°F (Gas Mark 5) for 15 to 20 minutes. Mark into bars, then cool briefly on the sheet before transferring to a wire rack.

Note: This is an excellent treat for children's lunchboxes.

Honey Flapjacks

115g (4 oz)	margarine	½ cup
4 tbs	thick honey	4 tbs
115g (4 oz)	sugar	⅔ cup
225g (8 oz)	muesli	2 cups

1 Melt the margarine in a saucepan, add the honey and sugar and stir well before adding the muesli. Mix until all ingredients are thoroughly blended.
2 Transfer to a greased Swiss roll tin and press down gently and evenly. Bake at 190°C/375°F (Gas Mark 5) for 20 minutes, or until nicely browned. Use a sharp knife to mark into oblongs, then leave to cool completely before breaking apart.

Note: Vegans can use corn syrup instead of the honey in this recipe.

Millet Flake Flapjacks

115g (4 oz)	margarine	½ cup
2 tbs	barley malt syrup	2 tbs
55g (2 oz)	sugar	⅓ cup
225g (8 oz)	millet flakes	2 cups
85g (3 oz)	sultanas (golden seedless raisins)	½ cup

1 Melt the margarine in a small saucepan, stir in the syrup and sugar, and heat for a few minutes, stirring continually.
2 When the sugar has melted, add the millet flakes and sultanas.
3 Grease a Swiss roll tin. Spoon in the mixture and press down evenly, smoothing the top as you do so. Bake at 180°C/350°F (Gas Mark 4) for 20 to 30 minutes, or until nicely browned. Use a sharp knife to mark into slices, but leave to cool completely before cutting through.

Note: These flapjacks get their distinctive flavour from the barley malt, but you can use other syrups instead.

Three Seed Flapjacks

115g (4 oz)	margarine	½ cup
3 tbs	syrup	3 tbs
85g (3 oz)	sugar	½ cup
170g (6 oz)	rolled oats	1½ cups
30g (1 oz)	pumpkin seeds	2 tbs
30g (1 oz)	sunflower seeds	2 tbs
30g (1 oz)	poppy seeds	2 tbs

1 Melt the margarine and syrup in a saucepan, stirring well. Add the sugar and then the oats and seeds.
2 Spoon the mixture into a lightly-greased Swiss roll tin, pressing it down and smoothing the top. Bake at 170°C/325°F (Gas Mark 3) for 30 minutes. Mark into squares straight away, then set aside to cool when they will firm up. Cut through before storing.

Note: Use sesame seeds instead of poppy seeds, if preferred. You could also chop the pumpkin seeds coarsely rather than leaving them whole.

Granola Lemon Bars

115g (4 oz)	margarine	½ cup
85g (3 oz)	sugar	½ cup
3 tbs	syrup	3 tbs
455g (1 lb)	granola	1 lb
3 tbs	lemon peel, grated	3 tbs
85g (3 oz)	candied citron peel, chopped	½ cup

1 Combine the margarine, sugar and syrup in a saucepan and heat gently until melted. Add the granola, fresh and candied peel, and mix thoroughly.
2 Spoon into a greased Swiss roll tin and press down lightly. Mark into bars. Chill overnight then cut into pieces.

Note: Any crunchy oat cereal can be used in this recipe, home-made or shop bought (vegans should check that it does not contain honey). If using a variety that is already well sweetened you may need to reduce the sugar. Other flavourings can be added, for example, chopped dried apricots or prunes, mixed candied peel, roasted chopped nuts or seeds.

Florentines

115g (4 oz)	margarine	½ cup
115g (4 oz)	sugar	⅔ cup
55g (2 oz)	walnuts, coarsely chopped	½ cup
55g (2 oz)	almonds, coarsely chopped	½ cup
55g (2 oz)	glacé cherries, coarsely chopped	⅓ cup
55g (2 oz)	candied peel, chopped	⅓ cup
55g (2 oz)	sultanas (golden seedless raisins)	⅓ cup
115g (4 oz)	chocolate bar, coarsely chopped	4 oz

1 Melt the margarine, add the sugar and stir until it dissolves. Then boil the mixture briefly before stirring in the nuts, cherries, peel and sultanas, mixing well. Cool briefly.
2 Place silver foil on a baking sheet. Drop spoonfuls of the mixture onto this, allowing room for them to spread. Bake at 180°C/350°F (Gas Mark 4) for 10

minutes. Leave to cool briefly then use a sharp knife to cut off the edges to make neat rounds. Leave to cool completely.

3 Melt the chocolate in the top of a double boiler or basin over a saucepan of hot water. Use a knife to spread some of the chocolate evenly over each of the florentines and set aside until firm.

Note: Turn vanilla ice cream into a special dessert by serving it with finger-shaped florentines or by crumbling a few and sprinkling them over the top.

Jumbo Pineapple Cookies

115g (4 oz)	margarine	½ cup
85g (3 oz)	sugar	½ cup
1 small	free-range egg, lightly beaten	1 small
1 tsp	vanilla essence	1 tsp
225g (8 oz)	wholemeal (wholewheat) flour	2 cups
2 tsp	baking powder	2 tsp
1 ring	canned pineapple, drained and coarsely crushed	1 ring
1-2 tbs	sour cream	1-2 tbs

1 Beat together the margarine and sugar until light and fluffy. Add the egg and vanilla essence.
2 Sift together the flour and baking powder. Fold into the first mixture. Add the pineapple, mixing well, then stir in enough sour cream to make a thick, moist mixture.
3 Drop eight heaps onto greased baking sheets, leaving space between. Use a fork to flatten the heaps slightly. Bake at 190°C/375°F (Gas Mark 5) for 15 minutes. Cool the cookies slightly before transferring to a wire rack and leaving to cool.

Note: These cookies are almost like cake with a soft texture. Instead of pineapple, try flavouring your cookies with chopped almonds and candied peel, chopped ginger, carob chips, lemon peel with spices, and so on.

Old-fashioned Ginger Nuts

225g (8 oz)	wholemeal (wholewheat) flour	2 cups
3 tsp	baking powder	3 tsp
1 tsp	ground ginger	1 tsp
1 tsp	caraway seeds	1 tsp
85g (3 oz)	margarine	⅓ cup
3-4 tbs	molasses	3-4 tbs
1 tbs	lemon juice	1 tbs
1 tbs	lemon peel, grated	1 tbs

1 Sift together the flour, baking powder and ginger. Stir in the seeds.

2 Melt the margarine with the molasses and lemon juice and add the lemon peel. Mix in the dry ingredients to make a stiff dough.
3 On a floured board, roll the dough out thinly and cut into rounds. Arrange on well-greased baking sheets. Bake at 180°C/350°F (Gas Mark 4) for 15 to 20 minutes. The biscuits should still be soft. Cool briefly then transfer to wire racks to cool, when they will harden.

Note: These ginger nuts have a strong flavour. For a more subtle flavour, replace some or all of the molasses with syrup or honey, and omit the caraway seeds. If the mixture seems too sticky to roll out, either add more flour, or break off pieces, roll them into small balls and then flatten them.

Cashew Date Drops

85g (3 oz)	margarine	⅓ cup
85g (3 oz)	sugar	½ cup
3 tbs	Pear and Apple Spread	3 tbs
1 tsp	vanilla essence	1 tsp
170g (6 oz)	wholemeal (wholewheat) flour	1½ cups
½ tsp	baking powder	½ tsp
115g (4 oz)	dried dates, chopped	1 cup
115g (4 oz)	cashews, finely chopped	1 cup

1 Cream together the margarine and sugar and add the spread and vanilla essence.
2 Sift together the flour and baking powder and add to the first mixture. Blend thoroughly, then stir in the dates. Chill the mixture briefly.
3 Break off small portions of the mixture, roll them in the nuts and arrange on baking sheets. Use a fork to flatten them slightly. Bake at 200°C/400°F (Gas Mark 6) for 10 minutes. Cool on wire racks.

Note: For a change, use other dried fruits such as apricots, pears or raisins instead of the dates.

Easter Biscuits

170g (6 oz)	wholemeal (wholewheat) flour	1½ cups
55g (2 oz)	ground rice	¼ cup
2 tsp	ground mixed spice	2 tsp
115g (4 oz)	margarine	½ cup
2 medium	free-range egg yolks, lightly beaten	2 medium
	milk	
85g (3 oz)	currants	½ cup

1 Sift together the flour, rice and spice. In a separate bowl, cream together the margarine and sugar until light and fluffy before adding the egg yolks.

2 Use a metal spoon to fold the dry ingredients into the margarine and sugar. Gradually add just enough milk to make a soft dough and mix it well. Add the currants.

3 On a floured board, knead the dough gently for a few minutes, then roll out to about 5mm (¼ in) thickness. Cut the biscuits into large rounds. Arrange on a lightly greased baking sheet and bake at 170°C/325°F (Gas Mark 3) for 15 to 20 minutes or until golden. Allow to cool briefly then transfer to a wire tray and leave to cool completely.

Note: For children, mould biscuits into bunny or chick shapes.

Tofu Apple Slices

285g (10 oz)	tofu, well drained and coarsely chopped	2¼ cups
170g (6 oz)	margarine, melted	¾ cup
2 tbs	Pear and Apple Spread	2 tbs
115g (4 oz)	sugar	⅔ cup
225g (8 oz)	wholemeal (wholewheat) flour	2 cups
2 tsp	baking powder	2 tsp
1 tsp	ground mixed spice	1 tsp
½ tsp	ground nutmeg	½ tsp
2 small	apples, peeled, cored and grated	2 small
55g (2 oz)	hazelnuts, chopped	½ cup

1 Combine the tofu, margarine and Pear and Apple Spread in a blender. Stir in the sugar.

2 Sift together the flour, baking powder and spices and add to the first mixture. Add the grated apple and nuts.

3 Pour into a greased Swiss roll tin and bake at 190°C/375°F (Gas Mark 5) for 30 minutes. Mark into slices but leave to cool completely before cutting right through.

Note: This high-protein snack can be adapted to include other fruits, fresh and dried, and other nuts or seeds.

Double Chocolate Cookies

115g (4 oz)	margarine	½ cup
85g (3 oz)	sugar	½ cup
1 medium	free-range egg, lightly beaten	1 medium
½ tsp	vanilla essence	½ tsp
115g (4 oz)	wholemeal (wholewheat) flour	1 cup
2 tbs	cocoa or carob powder	2 tbs
1 tsp	baking powder	1 tsp
85g (3 oz)	chocolate bar, coarsely chopped	3 oz

1 Cream together the margarine and sugar. When thick and smooth, add the egg and vanilla essence.

2 Sift together the flour, cocoa or carob powder and baking powder. Add to the first mixture, blending well, then gently stir in the chopped chocolate.

3 Lightly grease two or three baking sheets. Drop heaped teaspoonfuls of the mixture onto them, leaving room for the cookies to spread.

4 Bake at 180°C/350°F (Gas Mark 4) for 10 minutes. Cool briefly, then remove with a spatula and leave to cool on a wire rack.

Note: Chocolate Nut Cookies can be made by omitting the cocoa and adding 55g/2 oz chopped walnuts.

Fig Rolls

170g (6 oz)	wholemeal (wholewheat) flour	1½ cups
85g (3 oz)	caster sugar	½ cup
115g (4 oz)	block margarine	½ cup
115g (4 oz)	dried figs, finely chopped	1 cup

1 Sift the flour into a bowl and stir in 55g/2 oz of the sugar. Cut the margarine into pieces and use your fingertips to rub it into the dry ingredients so that the mixture resembles fine breadcrumbs.

2 Gently press to make a fairly firm dough. Transfer it to a floured board and knead briefly before covering with foil and chilling for at least 30 minutes, preferably longer.

3 Roll out the dough to make a large square and cut into six long strips of equal width. Mash the figs and spoon them onto the centre of three of the strips, cover with the remaining pastry and press the edges together. Carefully transfer to a baking sheet, press down slightly and sprinkle with the remaining sugar.

4 Bake at 180°C/350°F (Gas Mark 4) for 20 minutes. Mark into short lengths and cool on wire racks. When cold cut right through.

Note: As an alternative to figs use a dry spiced apple purée to make Apple Rolls, or alternatively use mincemeat.

Coconut Vanilla Crisps

115g (4 oz)	margarine	½ cup
115g (4 oz)	sugar	⅔ cup
55g (2 oz)	desiccated coconut	⅔ cup
1 tsp	vanilla essence	1 tsp
1 tbs	soya flour	1 tbs
2 tbs	cold water	2 tbs
225g (8 oz)	wholemeal (wholewheat) flour	2 cups
1 tsp	baking powder	1 tsp

1 Cream together the margarine and sugar and add the coconut and vanilla essence.
2 In a small bowl, stir the soya flour into the water to make a smooth cream and add this to the first mixture, blending well.
3 Sift the flour and baking powder, combine with the first mixture and knead to make a fairly firm dough. If time allows, cover and chill briefly.
4 Roll out the pastry – it should be thin so that the biscuits are really crisp. Cut into circles and arrange on greased baking sheets. Bake at 180°C/350°F (Gas Mark 4) for 12 to 15 minutes. Allow to cool briefly before transferring to a wire rack to cool completely.

Note: Vegetarians can use an egg instead of the soya flour to bind the mixture.

Carob Digestive Biscuits

115g (4 oz)	wholemeal (wholewheat) flour	1 cup
½ tsp	baking powder	½ tsp
30g (1 oz)	rolled oats	¼ cup
30g (1 oz)	sugar	2 tbs
1-2 tbs	milk	1-2 tbs
85g (3 oz)	carob bar, coarsely chopped	3 oz

1 Mix together the flour and baking powder, then stir in the rolled oats and sugar. Add enough milk to make a fairly firm dough and knead briefly.
2 On a floured board, roll out the dough to a thickness of 5mm (¼ in). Cut into rounds, pricking each with a fork. Arrange on greased baking trays and bake at 180°C/350°F (Gas Mark 4) for 15 minutes, or until crisp. Leave to cool on the baking trays.
3 Melt the carob bar in the top of a double boiler or a bowl over a saucepan of hot water, stirring frequently. Spread one side of the biscuits with the carob, pattern with a fork and leave to cool completely.

Note: Use plain or milk chocolate instead of carob. Alternatively, leave the biscuits uncoated, perhaps adding some currants or chopped ginger to the basic mixture.

Candied Peel and Currant Cookies

115g (4 oz)	margarine	½ cup
115g (4 oz)	sugar	⅔ cup
55g (2 oz)	candied peel	⅓ cup
55g (2 oz)	currants	⅓ cup
115g (4 oz)	wholemeal (wholewheat) flour	1 cup
1 tsp	baking powder	1 tsp
115g (4 oz)	oatmeal	1 cup
3-4 tbs	milk	3-4 tbs

1 Cream together the margarine and sugar until light and fluffy. Gradually add the peel and currants. Sift together the flour and baking powder and stir into the first mixture, then add the oatmeal. Make sure everything is well mixed.
2 Add enough milk to make a fairly firm dough and knead this briefly before shaping into a roll. Wrap in foil and chill briefly. Cut into thin slices with a sharp knife, arrange on greased baking sheets, and bake at 180°C/350°F (Gas Mark 4) for 20–30 minutes. Cool briefly then transfer to wire racks and leave to cool completely.

Note: This simple basic mix can be varied in many ways. For example, instead of the peel and currants try adding nuts, seeds, chocolate chips or chopped prunes.

Sticky Fingers

115g (4 oz)	wholemeal (wholewheat) flour	1 cup
115g (4 oz)	oatmeal	1 cup
½ tsp	bicarbonate of soda	½ tsp
115g (4 oz)	margarine	½ cup
115g (4 oz)	sugar	⅔ cup
3-4 tbs	marmalade	3-4 tbs

1 Mix together the flour, oats and bicarbonate of soda.
2 In a small saucepan, heat the margarine and sugar until the sugar dissolves, then stir in the marmalade. Remove from the heat and add to the first mixture, blending well.
3 Spoon the mixture into a greased shallow baking tin, pressing down gently and smoothing the top. Bake at 180°C/350°F (Gas Mark 4) for 20 minutes. Mark into fingers but leave to cool before cutting through.

Note: Honey or syrup may be used instead of the marmalade.

Semolina Shortbread

115g (4 oz)	margarine or butter	½ cup
55g (2 oz)	caster sugar	⅓ cup
115g (4 oz)	wholemeal (wholewheat) flour	1 cup
55g (2 oz)	semolina	½ cup
30g (1 oz)	sunflower seeds	2 tbs

1 Beat together the fat and sugar until smooth and creamy.
2 Combine the flour and semolina and work into the first mixture, pressing it together to make a dough. Knead this briefly then press into a small, round, greased cake tin, smoothing the top. Prick the dough, sprinkle with the seeds and press them in lightly.
3 Bake at 150°C/300°F (Gas Mark 2) for 45 to 50 minutes, or until cooked. Leave to cool briefly, then mark into triangles and leave to cool completely before removing. Break into triangles to store.

Note: A loose bottomed tin is ideal for shortbread as it makes it easier to remove. For a finer textured shortbread use 81% flour, or for a crunchier biscuit, use polenta which is coarser in texture than semolina. Other seeds may be used instead of sunflower – or add chopped nuts.

Ginger Cream Shortbread Fingers

55g (2 oz)	cornflour	⅓ cup
115g (4 oz)	wholemeal (wholewheat) flour	1 cup
55g (2 oz)	caster sugar	⅓ cup
1 tsp	ground ginger	1 tsp
1 tsp	ground mixed spice	1 tsp
55g (4 oz)	block margarine or butter	½ cup
140ml (¼ pt)	crème fraîche	⅔ cup
2 tbs	preserved ginger, finely chopped	2 tbs
	drop of syrup – optional	

1 Sift together the flours and add the sugar and spices. Cut the fat into pieces, then use fingertips to mix it into the dry ingredients. Press to bind together, transfer to a floured board and knead to make a dough. Cover with foil and chill for 30 minutes.
2 Roll out the dough as thinly as possible and cut into small, even-sized rectangles. Place on a baking sheet and bake at 180°C/350°F (Gas Mark 4) for 20 to 30 minutes. Leave to cool.
3 When ready to serve the biscuits, mix the crème fraîche with the ginger and, if liked, a tiny drop of the syrup in which the ginger was preserved. Use this to sandwich the biscuits together and serve at once.

Note: The creamy filling makes a lovely contrast to the crisp shortbread. If, however, you prefer a more conventional biscuit cream filling, mix 55g (2oz) margarine with 115g (4 oz) caster sugar. This has a firmer texture and will keep well.

Peanut Butter Cookies

115g (4 oz)	margarine	½ cup
115g (4 oz)	sugar	⅔ cup
140g (5 oz)	peanut butter	⅔ cup
½ tsp	vanilla essence	½ tsp
140g (5 oz)	wholemeal (wholewheat) flour	1¼ cups
½ tsp	bicarbonate of soda	½ tsp
30g (1 oz)	peanuts, coarsely chopped	¼ cup

1 Cream together the margarine and sugar until light and fluffy. Add the peanut butter and vanilla essence.
2 Sift together the flour and bicarbonate of soda, and use a wooden spoon to stir into the first ingredients, making sure that everything is well blended.
3 Lightly grease two or three baking sheets. Break off even-sized pieces of the dough, roll into balls and then flatten slightly. Arrange them on the baking sheets, sprinkle with some of the nuts and press them down lightly.
4 Bake at 180°C/350°F (Gas Mark 4) for 15 minutes. Cool slightly before removing from the trays, then leave on a wire rack to cool completely.

Note: You can use either smooth or crunchy peanut butter for this recipe, but look out for additives and extra sweetening.

Mincemeat Squares

115g (4 oz)	margarine	½ cup
85g (3 oz)	sugar	½ cup
1 medium	free-range egg, lightly beaten	1 medium
225g (8 oz)	wholemeal (wholewheat) flour	2 cups
225g (8 oz)	vegetarian mincemeat (see page 115)	8 oz
1 tbs	caster sugar	1 tbs

1 Beat together the margarine and sugar until light and fluffy. Gradually add the egg, then the flour, mixing to make a pliable but soft dough. If necessary, use a little more flour. Knead for a few minutes before wrapping in foil to chill for 30 minutes.
2 Divide the dough in half. Roll out one piece and use it to line a lightly-greased shallow tin. Bake at 190°C/375°F (Gas Mark 5) for 10 minutes, then cool briefly.

3 Spread with the mincemeat, roll out the second piece of dough and lay this on top of the mincemeat. Brush with water, sprinkle with sugar. Return to the oven and cook for 20 minutes more, or until the pastry is cooked. Cool before cutting into squares.

Note: Other spreads to be used instead of mincemeat include low sugar fruit jams, lemon curd and marmalade. Alternatively, try a mix of honey and chopped nuts.

Nut-topped Caramel Cookies

Cookies

170g (6 oz)	wholemeal (wholewheat) flour	1½ cups
55g (2 oz)	caster sugar	⅓ cup
115g (4 oz)	block margarine	½ cup

Topping

30g (1 oz)	blanched almonds	¼ cup
30g (1 oz)	walnut halves	¼ cup
30g (1 oz)	hazelnuts	¼ cup
55g (2 oz)	sugar	⅓ cup
3 tsp	glucose syrup	3 tsp
1 tbs	water	1 tbs
2 tbs	cream	2 tbs

1 Mix together the flour and sugar. Use a knife to cut the margarine into small pieces, add to the flour, then use fingertips to rub it in to make a crumb-like mixture. Press this together to make a dough, transfer to a floured board and knead briefly. Wrap in silver foil and chill for 30 minutes.

2 Roll the dough out on a floured board and cut into small rounds (preferably with a fluted cutter). Place on a baking sheet and bake at 180°C/350°F (Gas Mark 4) for 20 minutes. Cool slightly then transfer to a wire tray to cool completely.

3 Lightly roast the nuts for a few minutes until just beginning to colour. In a small saucepan, combine the sugar, glucose syrup and water, stirring gently over a medium heat until the sugar dissolves. Then bring the mixture to the boil and continue boiling for 2 minutes.

4 Remove from the heat, stir in the cream and then the nuts. Drop spoonfuls onto the tops of the biscuits and leave until firm.

Note: The nuts can be chopped, but they especially look attractive if left whole. These plain little biscuits can also be topped with jam, or with icing sugar coloured with vegetable dyes, making them ideal for children's parties.

No-bake Carob Oatmeal Bars

170g (6 oz)	sugar	1 cup
2-3 tbs	carob powder	2-3 tbs
55g (2 oz)	margarine	¼ cup
3 tbs	milk	3 tbs
½ tsp	vanilla essence	½ tsp
170g (6 oz)	oatmeal	1½ cups

1 Combine the sugar, carob powder, margarine, milk and vanilla essence in a heavy saucepan. When it comes to the boil, continue boiling gently for a few minutes more, then remove from the heat.

2 Stir in the oatmeal, mixing well.

3 Line a shallow oblong tin with silver foil, spoon in the mixture and smooth the top. Mark into bars, then leave to cool completely before cutting through.

Note: To make these bars even more scrumptious, coat one side with a melted carob bar.

4
Chilled Desserts

There's nothing like a dish of home-made ice cream on a hot day, except perhaps a home-made sorbet, or some frozen yogurt.

Making your own ice cream is easy if you simply follow a few rules. Set the freezer controls for fast freezing before you start. Put the prepared mixture into a freezing tray or polythene tub, freeze until it starts to become firm around the edges, then whip well to get air into it before returning to a clean tray and refreezing. The more times you beat it, the lighter the results will be. (If you prefer, use an electric blender for this.) When finished, return the fridge to its usual settings.

Both colour and flavour are diminished by coldness, so keep this in mind when adding either.

Transfer your ice cream or sorbet to the fridge about 30 minutes before you intend to serve it to allow it to defrost.

Candied Peel Ice Cream

115g (4 oz)	candied peel, chopped	4 oz
1 tsp	vanilla essence	1 tsp
285ml (½ pt)	whipping cream	1⅓ cups
30g (1 oz)	caster sugar	2 tbs
30g (1 oz)	hazelnuts, lightly roasted and finely chopped	¼ cup

1 Place the peel in a bowl, cover with the essence, and leave to soak for 15 minutes.
2 Whip the cream until thick and smooth, then gradually fold in the caster sugar. Add the nuts, mixing them well and, finally, stir in the candied peel, making sure it is evenly distributed.
3 Turn the mixture into a freezing tray, and leave in the freezer for three to four hours or until set firm.

Note: This ice cream is also delicious when chopped almonds are used instead of hazelnuts. Alternatively, or as well, replace the vanilla essence with almond essence.

Maple Pecan Ice Cream

285ml (½ pt)	milk	1⅓ cups
4 tbs	maple syrup	4 tbs
2 large	free-range eggs	2 large
200ml (⅓ pt)	thick yogurt	¾ cup
85g (3 oz)	pecan nuts, coarsely chopped	¾ cup
	extra maple syrup and/or *pecan nuts to serve - optional*	

1 Gently heat the milk and syrup in a heavy saucepan until almost boiling, then set aside for 15 minutes.
2 Separate one of the eggs, add the yolk to the other and keep the white to one side. Whisk together lightly and then add the milk. In a clean saucepan, bring the mixture to the boil slowly, stirring continually. When the custard is thick enough to coat the back of a wooden spoon lightly, remove from the heat and leave to cool.
3 Whisk the remaining egg white. Add this, the yogurt and nuts to the custard, mixing gently but well.
4 Transfer to a freezing tray and freeze until needed. On special occasions serve with a spoonful of syrup over the top and a scattering of chopped nuts.

Note: Using eggs makes this a rich and very smooth ice cream. To reduce the fat content use semi-skimmed milk.

Banana Cottage Cheese Ice Cream

445g (1 lb)	cottage cheese, sieved	2 cups
200ml (⅓ pt)	thick yogurt	¾ cup
2 large	ripe bananas, peeled and mashed	2 large
1 tbs	lemon juice	1 tbs
115g (4 oz)	caster sugar	⅔ cup
55g (2 oz)	banana chips, coarsely crushed	2 oz
	extra banana chips - optional	

1 Beat together the cheese and yogurt, then gradually add the mashed bananas, making sure they are well mixed in. Stir in the lemon juice and then the sugar.
2 Transfer the mixture to a freezing tray and freeze until it begins to go mushy around the edges. Beat it again to lighten, then add the banana chips. Return to the freezing tray and freeze until firm.
3 Serve individual scoops of the ice cream, topping each with extra crushed banana chips if liked.

Note: Although the taste is delicious, this is a very pale looking ice cream, so if you like a little more colour in your food, add a few drops of natural yellow colouring. For those who are not worried about calories, serve with chocolate sauce!

Cinnamon Brown Bread Ice Cream

45ml (¾ pt)	whipping cream	2 cups
85g (3 oz)	sugar	½ cup
1-2 tsp	ground cinnamon	1-2 tsp
115g (4 oz)	fresh wholemeal (wholewheat) breadcrumbs	2 cups
2 medium	free-range egg whites	2 medium
	extra cinnamon red berry purée (see page 109) or other sauce to serve - optional	

1 Whip the cream until thick and smooth, then gradually fold in the sugar and cinnamon. When well mixed, add the breadcrumbs.
2 Beat the egg whites until stiff, then use a metal spoon to fold these into the first mixture. Freeze for a few hours or until firm. If liked, beat to add more air although this is not strictly necessary.
3 Serve sprinkled with extra cinnamon to taste or top with either a warm or chilled fruit purée.

Note: This traditional ice cream is simple, inexpensive and popular with everyone. Remember that when ingredients are frozen the taste is diminished so adjust it according to taste - the cinnamon flavour should be noticeable.

Praline Ice Cream

285ml (½ pt)	whipping cream	1⅓ cups
2 medium	free-range egg yolks	2 medium
55g (2 oz)	caster sugar	⅓ cup
1 tsp	vanilla essence	1 tsp
115g (4 oz)	praline, crushed (see page 96)	4 oz

1 Whip the cream until thick. Stir together the egg yolks, sugar and vanilla, then fold the mixture into the cream.
2 Spoon the mixture into a freezing tray and freeze until mushy, then beat well again before adding most of the crushed praline. Return the mixture to the tray, and freeze until firm. Serve in scoops, sprinkled with remaining praline.

Note: You can use any nut brittle - home-made or shop bought - instead of praline.

Orange and Lemon Ice Cream

2 medium	oranges	2 medium
2 medium	lemons	2 medium
570ml (1 pt)	single cream	2½ cups
4 medium	free-range egg yolks	4 medium
115g (4 oz)	caster sugar	⅔ cup

1 Squeeze and set aside the juice from the fruit. Remove the peel, finely grate it, then put it into a bowl with the cream and leave to soak for a while.
2 Beat together the egg yolks and sugar and combine with the cream and peel. (This is best done in a blender.)
3 Put the mixture into a bowl over a pan of hot water and heat gently, stirring continually with a wooden spoon. When the mixture is thick enough to coat the back of the spoon, remove it from the heat and leave to cool briefly before adding 3 tablespoons of the fresh orange juice and 1 of lemon juice.
4 Transfer the mixture to a freezer tray and freeze until mushy. Beat well again before returning it to the freezer, then leave until firm.

Note: Make sure you buy fruit that has not been polished or waxed, and wash it well before use. You can decorate ice cream servings with orange and lemon slices.

Vanilla Yogurt Ice Cream with Hot Blueberry Sauce

Ice Cream

500ml (1 pt)	yogurt	2½ cups
115g (4 oz)	caster sugar	⅔ cup
2 tsp	vanilla essence	2 tsp
140ml (¼ pt)	whipping cream	⅔ cup
2 medium	free-range egg whites	2 medium

Sauce

225g (8 oz)	fresh blueberries	8 oz
85g (3 oz)	sugar	½ cup
2-3 tbs	water	2-3 tbs

1 Mix together the yogurt, sugar and vanilla essence. Whip the cream until thick and fold into the first mixture.
2 Pour into a freezing tray and freeze until mushy around the edges, then beat well. Whisk the egg whites until stiff and fold these into the mixture, returning it to the freezer until firm.
3 To make the sauce, combine the cleaned blueberries, sugar and water in a saucepan and bring to the boil, then simmer very gently for 15 minutes or until the blueberries have broken up to make a purée. Adjust the flavour as necessary.
4 Serve the ice cream with a little hot sauce poured over each serving.

Note: Although other sauces can be used instead of blueberry, this really is a delicious combination.

Chestnut Ice Cream

85g (3 oz)	caster sugar	½ cup
340g (12 oz)	chestnut purée	12 oz
2 tbs	rum	2 tbs
285ml (½ pt)	crème fraîche	1⅓ cups

1 Mix together the sugar, chestnut purée and rum, making sure they are well blended. Add the crème fraîche.
2 Turn into a freezing tray and freeze until beginning to firm up, then beat well before returning to tray and freezing until firm.

Note: Simple to make, this ice cream has a deliciously subtle taste and creamy texture. Instead of rum, use brandy, or if you prefer to avoid alcohol, orange juice. Those who like ginger might like to stir in a couple of tablespoons of chopped stem preserved ginger before the final freezing. You may also prefer to use thick yogurt instead of crème fraîche.

Avocado Ice Cream

3 medium	avocados, peeled and stoned	3 medium
85g (3 oz)	sugar	½ cup
4 tbs	lemon juice	4 tbs
1 tbs	lemon peel, finely chopped	1 tbs
285ml (½ pt)	whipping cream fresh fruit purée to serve - optional	1⅓ cups

1 Cut the avocado flesh into cubes and mix with the sugar and lemon juice (use a blender to make it really smooth). Stir in the lemon peel.
2 Whip the cream until stiff and add to the first mixture before turning into a freezing tray and leaving to freeze until the mixture becomes mushy. Beat well again and freeze until firm. Serve topped with a spoonful or two of fresh fruit purée.

Note: Vegans could use tofu instead of the cream, following the same method as described above. For a crunchier ice cream, add chopped nuts such as roasted almonds.

Rosewater and Pistachio Ice Cream

340ml (⅔ pt)	concentrated soya milk	1½ cups
115g (4 oz)	sugar	⅔ cup
2 tbs	vegetable oil	2 tbs
4 tbs	rosewater	4 tbs
1 tsp	agar agar	1 tsp
55g (2 oz)	pistachio nuts, coarsely chopped	½ cup

1 Blend together the soya milk, sugar and oil, heating gently to dissolve the sugar. In another small saucepan heat the rosewater, sprinkle in the agar agar, and continue simmering gently, stirring continually, until the mixture begins to boil. Cook gently for 2 more minutes, then add this mixture to the first one.
2 Turn into a freezing tray and chill until mushy. Beat well before adding the chopped pistachio nuts. Return to the tray and freeze until firm.

Note: This unusual ice cream has a rather exotic taste. As flavours fade when frozen, you might need to adjust the amount of rosewater used. Using agar agar when making ice cream is an easy way to improve its texture – follow the same method using other ingredients such as strawberry purée. Vegetarians can replace the soya milk with single cream.

Pineapple Sorbet

1 small	pineapple, peeled	1 small
1 large	orange, peeled	1 large
200ml (⅓ pt)	orange juice	¾ cup
1-2 tbs	syrup	1-2 tbs
2 medium	free-range egg whites	2 medium

1 Chop the pineapple and orange finely and mix with the orange juice and syrup.
2 Transfer to a freezing tray and freeze until the mixture becomes mushy.
3 Whisk the egg whites until peaks form and fold them into the fruit mixture carefully. Return to a clean tray and freeze until firm.

Note: An attractive way of serving this sorbet is to pile it into pineapple halves before freezing. If fresh pineapple is unavailable you can use the canned variety, preferably packed in natural juice. In this case, use the juice to replace some or all of the orange juice in the recipe.

Mango Water-ice with Chocolate Curls

3 large	ripe mangoes	3 large
1 tbs	lemon juice	1 tbs
4 tbs	orange juice	4 tbs
2 tbs	syrup or to taste	2 tbs
170g (6 oz)	chocolate	6 oz

1 Peel the mangoes and use a sharp knife to slice off the flesh. Either mash or blend this together with the lemon and orange juice and syrup, then, when well mixed, turn into a freezing tray and freeze until the mixture becomes mushy.
2 Beat well before returning to the tray and freezing until firm.
3 When ready to serve, transfer the water-ice to the fridge and leave for half an hour to soften slightly. Meanwhile, use a potato peeler to make curls of chocolate.
4 Serve scoops of the water-ice in serving bowls, topped with the chocolate curls.

Note: When making the chocolate curls, use chocolate that is at room temperature or even slightly warmer. If, however, you do not intend to serve them at once, store them in the fridge so that they hold their shape.

Creamy Lemon Lollipops

3 tbs	syrup, or to taste	3 tbs
200ml (⅓ pt)	lemon juice	¾ cup
570ml (1 pt)	water	2½ cups
2 tbs	lemon peel, grated - optional	2 tbs
4-6 tbs	concentrated soya milk	4-6 tbs

1 Heat together the syrup, lemon juice and water, in a small saucepan, continuing to heat and stir until the syrup melts. Add the peel if using it. Remove from heat and stir in the soya milk.
2 Pour the mixture into ice-lolly moulds inserting a stick into each one. Freeze until set.

Note: This recipe is quick, easy and great for children. You can use plain yogurt instead of soya milk.

Blackberry and Apple Sorbet

340g (12 oz)	fresh blackberries, cleaned	12 oz
2 medium	apples, peeled and sliced	2 medium
2 tbs	lemon juice	2 tbs
85g (3 oz)	sugar	½ cup
2 medium	free-range egg whites single cream or fromage frais - optional	2 medium

1 Cook the blackberries, apples, lemon juice and sugar in a covered saucepan with just a few spoonfuls of water until the fruit is soft. Check that it does not burn, adding more water if necessary.
2 Drain the fruit and turn into a freezing tray. Freeze until the mixture becomes mushy.
3 Whisk the egg whites until stiff, then use a metal spoon to fold them into the fruit. Return the mixture to a clean freezing tray and freeze until firm.
4 Serve in scoops with a spoonful or two of cream or fromage frais, if liked.

Note: The sugar may be replaced with 3 tablespoons of Pear and Apple Spread if preferred. Other sorbets can be made in exactly the same way - water melon flesh, for example, makes a wonderfully refreshing sorbet.

Cranberry Sorbet

225g (8 oz)	fresh cranberries, trimmed	8 oz
3 tbs	water	3 tbs
3 tbs	orange juice	3 tbs
1 tbs	orange peel, finely chopped	1 tbs
85g (3 oz)	sugar, or to taste	½ cup
2 large	free-range egg whites extra cranberries to decorate - optional crispy biscuits to serve - optional	2 large

1 Cook the cranberries with the water, juice, peel and sugar, using just enough water to stop them from burning – you may need to add a little more during the cooking process, but do keep this to the minimum.

2 When soft, beat the cranberries together with the syrup to make a thick smooth purée, or purée them in a blender. Turn the mixture into a freezing tray and freeze until mushy.

3 Whisk the egg whites until stiff, then fold them into the cranberry mixture and return to a freezing tray until quite firm.

4 Serve the sorbet with extra cranberries sprinkled on top and accompanied with crispy biscuits if liked.

Note: This unusual sorbet gives these sharp flavoured American berries a whole new image. For an especially smooth textured sorbet, sieve the purée before freezing. You may need to adjust the sugar according to the sweetness you require – cranberries can vary enormously in taste depending on how ripe they are. Fresh cranberries are available from November to January but at other times of the year use frozen ones. Canned cranberries may also be used although they are often highly sweetened so, again, adjust the sugar accordingly.

Passion Fruit Sorbets in Meringue Shells

Sorbet

4 large	passion fruits	4 large
55g (2 oz)	sugar	1⅓ cups
1 tbs	lemon juice	1 tbs
4 tbs	water	4 tbs

Meringue shells

4 medium	free-range egg whites	4 medium
¼ tsp	cream of tartar	¼ tsp
2 tsp	syrup	2 tsp
1 tsp	vanilla extract	1 tsp

1 Cut the passion fruits in half and use a spoon to scoop out the flesh and seeds. In a small saucepan, stir together the sugar, lemon juice and water until the sugar has dissolved. Bring to the boil, then lower the heat and simmer for a few minutes. Add the passion fruit flesh, stir and simmer for a few more minutes. Spoon into a freezing tray and freeze until mushy, then beat again and leave to freeze until quite firm.

2 To make meringues, beat the egg whites until they begin to thicken, then gradually add the cream of tartar, syrup and vanilla extract and continue beating until the mixture is stiff.

3 Drop onto a greased and floured baking sheet to make four to six even-sized mounds, using a spoon to mark a dip in the centre of each. Bake at 130°C/250°F (Gas Mark ½) for 3 hours or until firm and golden. Cool briefly then carefully remove to a wire rack and leave to cool completely.

4 When ready to serve, simply drop scoops of sorbet into the meringue shells and take to the table at once.

Note: Some people prefer to sieve out the passion fruit seeds first; others like the slightly crunchy texture they give to a sorbet – the choice is yours. As the meringues take so long to make it is worth preparing double the quantity and storing unused meringue shells in an airtight jar or polythene bag.

Double Chocolate Ice Milk

2 large	free-range eggs, beaten	2 large
6 tbs	syrup or honey	6 tbs
2 tbs	cornflour	2 tbs
850ml (1½ pts)	milk	3¾ cups
3 tsp	chocolate sauce (see Carob Sauce page 112)	3 tsp
55g (2 oz)	chocolate bar, coarsely grated	2 oz

1 Beat together the eggs and syrup or honey.

2 Add a little of the water to the cornflour and stir to make a smooth paste. Put this into a saucepan with 285ml/½ pint of the milk and heat gently, stirring continually until the sauce thickens. Whisk some of the hot sauce into the eggs and add them, with the remainder of the milk, to the saucepan. Continue heating gently until the mixture is thick and smooth. Stir in the chocolate sauce.

3 Turn the mixture into a freezing tray and freeze until mushy. Then beat well, add the grated chocolate and return to a freezing tray. Freeze until frozen solid.

Note: This is lower in fats and calories than ice cream. When making the sauce you may, if you prefer, use a double pan or a bowl over a saucepan of hot water, to reduce the chance of curdling. For an unusual looking chocolate ice milk, add grated white chocolate instead of the raw cane chocolate.

Raspberry Buttermilk Ice

2 medium	free-range eggs, well beaten	2 medium
4 tbs	syrup	4 tbs
425ml (¾ pt)	buttermilk	2 cups
225g (8 oz)	raspberries, hulled and chopped	8 oz
1 tbs	lemon juice	1 tbs

1 Stir together the beaten eggs, syrup and buttermilk.
2 Blend and then sieve the raspberries to remove the pips, add the lemon juice and stir into the first mixture.
3 Turn into a freezing tray and freeze until mushy. Beat well before returning to the freezer and leaving to get completely firm.

Note: Although buttermilk contains less fat than cream, it has a very creamy taste – try this recipe and judge for yourself. This is also a good way to use up less than perfect raspberries, or you may use frozen ones.

Coconut Ice Cream

115g (4 oz)	desiccated coconut	1⅓ cups
4 tbs	maple syrup, or to taste	4 tbs
200ml (⅓ pt)	soya cream or concentrated soya milk	¾ cup

1 Stir together the coconut and maple syrup, then gradually add the soya cream or concentrated soya milk and mix well. Turn into a freezing tray and leave until the mixture starts to become firm.
2 Beat well, then return the mixture to the freezing tray and freeze until quite firm.

Note: This rich, creamy ice cream is best served in small quantities and is ideal as a topping for an exotic fruit salad. Alternatively, serve packed into coconut shells (which can be used more than once if carefully cleaned each time). Follow the same recipe to make other vegan ice creams, for example, using dried apricots which have been soaked and then puréed with maple syrup. Adjust the sweetener according to taste and vary the flavour by using other syrups.

Raisin Almond Ice Cream

455g (1 lb)	silken tofu, well drained	2 cups
4 tbs	maple or corn syrup	4 tbs
few drops	vanilla essence	few drops
55g (2 oz)	raisins	⅓ cup
30g (1 oz)	roasted almonds, chopped	¼ cup
	extra syrup - optional	

1 Blend together the tofu, syrup and vanilla essence until smooth. Pour into a freezing tray and freeze for 2 hours, or until mushy.

2 Beat the mixture to lighten and stir in the raisins and nuts. Freeze until firm. Serve in scoops with a little extra syrup poured over each portion.

Note: Any fruit can be added to this basic recipe. Instead of syrup, try adding a few spoonfuls of your favourite liqueur.

Fruit Salad Ice Cream with Tofu

340g (12 oz)	fruit salad	12 oz
1 tsp	vanilla essence	1 tsp
285g (10 oz)	silken tofu, well drained	1¼ cups
4 tbs	sugar, or to taste	4 tbs

1 Blend together the fruit salad, vanilla essence, tofu, and sugar to make a thick, smooth purée.
2 Pour into a freezing tray and freeze until just beginning to become firm, then beat well or blend again. Freeze until needed.

Note: This ice cream benefits by being half frozen and then beaten again a couple of times to lighten the mixture, although this is not absolutely necessary. It is a perfect way to use up leftover fruit salad! The amount of sugar needed will depend on the sweetness of the fruit you use.

Coffee Ice Cream

4 tbs	syrup, or to taste	4 tbs
570ml (1 pt)	soya (soy) milk	2½ cups
2-3 tbs	strong coffee	2-3 tbs
5 tbs	vegetable oil	5 tbs

1 Blend together the syrup, soya (soy) milk, coffee and vegetable oil – you might need to adjust the sweetness depending on the strength of the coffee you use.
2 Pour into a freezing tray and freeze until it becomes mushy, then beat well and return to the freezer. Freeze until quite firm.

Note: To adapt this to make mocha ice cream, chop a 55g/2 oz carob or chocolate bar into small pieces, and stir these into the mixture after the first freezing. Serve scoops topped with a sprinkling of carob or cocoa powder.

Strawberry Ice Cream

525g (⅞ pt)	*carton of strawberry flavoured soya dessert*	*2⅓ cups*
140ml (¼ pt)	*soya 'cream'* or *concentrated milk*	*⅔ cup*
225g (8 oz)	*fresh strawberries, cleaned and hulled*	*8 oz*
1 tbs	*syrup - optional*	*1 tbs*

1 Pour the soya dessert into ice cube trays and freeze until solid.
2 In a blender, quickly combine the ice cubes, soya 'creem' and fresh strawberries. When the mixture is thick add syrup, if liked. Use a scoop to divide the ice cream between four bowls and serve immediately.

Note: Make sure the cubes are completely frozen or the ice cream will be runny. To make the ice cream richer, add a few spoonfuls of vegetable oil. This instant ice cream can be made using other flavoured soya desserts and other fruits.

Frozen Yogurt

140ml (¼ pt)	*cherry fruit spread*	*⅔ cup*
55g (2 oz)	*sugar, or to taste*	*⅓ cup*
¼ tsp	*almond essence*	*¼ tsp*
285ml (½ pt)	*plain yogurt*	*1⅓ cups*

1 Stir together all the ingredients, making sure they are well blended, then put into a freezing tray and freeze until they start to become firm.
2 Beat well, then re-freeze until set.

Note: This unusual recipe for frozen yogurt is easy to make. Adapt it by using other fruit spreads or jams, fruit purées, nuts, dried fruit etc. (When using jams and spreads, try to buy low sugar or sugar free ones - you may be surprised at the varieties available.)

Though low in calories, frozen yogurt is not as nutritious as yogurt at room temperature as the freezing process kills the valuable bacteria for which it is famous.

Nectarine and Apricot Sundae

4 medium	*nectarines, peeled and stoned*	*4 medium*
6	*apricots, stoned*	*6*
115g (4 oz)	*caster sugar*	*⅔ cup*
570ml (1 pt)	*water*	*2½ cups*
2 tbs	*orange juice*	*2 tbs*
200ml (⅓ pt)	*whipping cream*	*¾ cup*
225g (½ pt)	*vanilla ice cream*	*1⅓ cups*
55g (2 oz)	*coconut flakes, roasted*	*⅔ cup*
	extra nectarines or *apricots*	

1 Start by making a nectarine and apricot water ice. Either mash the fruit together with the sugar, or blend in a food processor. Add the water and orange juice, stirring well.
2 Turn the mixture into a freezing tray, freeze for 2 hours, then beat well. Return to the freezer and leave until firm.
3 When ready, whisk the whipping cream until stiff. Put a scoop of vanilla ice cream into the base of 4 tall glasses and top with 2 scoops of the water ice. Add cream and a sprinkling of coconut flakes. Use sliced fruit to garnish the sundaes and serve at once.

Note: Use apricot purée instead of fresh apricots if preferred or, for Nectarine and Apricot Ice Cream, add whipped cream or concentrated soya milk before freezing.

Pear and Ginger Sundae

2 large	*dessert pears, peeled and quartered*	*2 large*
2 tbs	*lemon juice*	*2 tbs*
2 tbs	*syrup*	*2 tbs*
140ml (¼ pt)	*water*	*⅔ cup*
115g (4 oz)	*ginger biscuits, coarsely crushed*	*4 oz*
285g (½ pt)	*frozen yogurt*	*1⅓ cups*
4 pieces	*preserved stem ginger, chopped*	*4 pieces*

1 In a saucepan, cook the pears in the lemon juice, syrup and water until just tender. Set aside to cool, then chill.
2 Put some of the biscuits in the base of each of 4 tall glasses, then top with a small scoop of frozen yogurt. Add the pears, followed by another scoop of frozen yogurt.
3 Top with a sprinkling of chopped stem ginger, adding a spoonful or two of the liquid in which the ginger was preserved, if liked. Serve at once.

Note: Other fruit or fruit purées may be used instead of pears.

Cassata Dessert

455g (1 lb)	ricotta cheese	2 cups
55g (2 oz)	caster sugar	⅓ cup
2 tbs	single cream or fromage frais	2 tbs
2-4 tbs	orange flower water	2-4 tbs
55g (2 oz)	candied peel	2 oz
55g (2 oz)	chocolate	2 oz
55g (2 oz)	roasted hazelnuts, coarsely chopped	½ cup

1 Press the cheese through a strainer to remove excess moisture, then beat well to make a thick smooth cream. Add the cream, sugar and orange flower water, and beat well.
2 Fold in the candied peel. Chop the chocolate and add with the nuts. Cover and chill for at least 1 hour. Divide between four glasses and serve at once.

Note: While not frozen, this does need to be well chilled. This unusual dessert can be adapted by replacing the orange flower water with an orange flavoured liqueur, and the hazelnuts with pistachio nuts.

Christmas Ice Pudding

285ml (½ pt)	whipping cream	1⅓ cups
115g (4 oz)	sugar	⅔ cup
2 tsp	vanilla essence	2 tsp
4 tbs	single cream	4 tbs
140ml (¼ pt)	yogurt	⅔ cup
approx. 8 tbs	vegetarian mincemeat (see page 115)	approx. 8 tbs
55g (2 oz)	almonds, roasted and coarsely chopped	½ cup
2-3 tbs	sherry glacé cherries and angelica for decoration - optional	2-3 tbs

1 Whip the whipping cream until stiff, then stir in the sugar and vanilla essence. Gradually add the single cream and yogurt making sure that everything is well blended. Turn the mixture into a freezing tray and freeze until it becomes mushy.
2 Beat the mixture well and stir in the vegetarian mincemeat, together with the almonds and sherry. Spoon the mixture into a pudding mould and press down firmly. Freeze until set.
3 When ready to serve, dip the bowl into warm water for a few seconds to loosen the ice cream, then cover with a plate and invert it. Quickly decorate the top of the pudding with glacé cherries and angelica to represent holly, (or, if liked, use a sprig of real holly!)

Note: This is a delicious and light alternative to the heavier Christmas pudding. The amount of mincemeat you use depends on how strongly you wish to flavour the ice cream. You can also stir in extra dried fruit, spices, nuts etc.

Icebox Banana Swirl Cake

225g (8 oz)	wholemeal digestive biscuits, crushed	8 oz
85g (3 oz)	margarine, melted	⅓ cup
285ml (½ pt)	whipping cream	1⅓ cups
55g (2 oz)	sugar	⅓ cup
2 large	ripe bananas, peeled and mashed	2 large
1 tbs	lemon juice	1 tbs
1 tsp	banana essence - optional	1 tsp
200ml (⅓ pt)	apricot sauce (see page 110) extra cream and/or banana slices to decorate	¾ cup

1 Oil a loaf tin and line it with silver foil. Blend together the biscuits and margarine and, when well mixed, spoon half the mixture into the tin, pressing down to form a firm base. Freeze this briefly.
2 Whip the cream until thick, add the sugar, turn into a freezing tray and freeze until the mixture begins to set. Beat well again. Mix the bananas with the lemon juice and essence if using it, and add these to the first mixture, blending thoroughly. Spoon this into the prepared tin before stirring in the apricot sauce, using a fork to create a swirl effect and taking care not to over-mix. Smooth, then top with the remaining crumbs, pressing down gently.
3 Freeze again until set, preferably overnight or longer. Use the foil to carefully lift the cake out of the tin and serve cut into slices. Pipe a decoration with whipped cream along the length of the cake, and dot with banana slices, if liked.

Note: Use a berry purée instead of an apricot one, or chocolate sauce, or, for a complete change, stir crushed oat biscuits into the cream and banana mixture. You can also use other biscuits, wholemeal breadcrumbs or even crumbled, stale cake for the base.

Carob Nut Sundae

6 tbs	carob spread	6 tbs
200ml (⅓ pt)	hot water or soya milk	¾ cup
4 scoops	coffee ice cream	4 scoops
4 scoops	strawberry ice cream	4 scoops
55g (2 oz)	hazelnuts, roasted and coarsely chopped	½ cup
	glacé cherries	

1 To make the carob sauce, stir the spread into the hot water or milk, and heat very gently until you have a thick sauce. You may need to use more spread or less milk to get the desired consistency - adjust this as you go along. Allow to cool briefly.

2 In four tall sundae glasses, put a scoop of coffee ice cream, top with a scoop of strawberry ice cream, then pour some of the carob sauce over each. Sprinkle immediately with hazelnuts, dot with cherries and serve at once.

Note: Carob spread can be bought at your local wholefood or healthfood shop. Other sundaes can be made in the same way, using a variety of different flavoured ice creams, or combining ice creams and water ices or sorbets. Different sauces may be used instead of the carob (butterscotch is particularly good), or other nuts or even fresh fruit in whatever combinations you like. The art of making sundaes is one that every ice cream lover should master!

5
Pancakes

Perhaps because pancakes are considered fiddly to make, they are rarely served as a dessert. However, try some of these recipes here and you will soon discover they are nowhere near as complicated as you might imagine.

Whisk the batter well to work in lots of air and leave to stand for a while before using to soften any bran. Plain flour has a higher gluten content than self-raising and if using wholemeal flour you may like to sift the bran out. Milk or cream gives a richer batter; for a lighter one use water or soya milk. Remember that the thinner the batter, the lighter the results will be. Stirring a tablespoon of oil into the batter will make it crisper.

When making pancakes, add a drop of oil to a heavy-based pan (or use a brush to lightly coat the surface with oil), heat, then pour in one or two spoonfuls of batter. (A jug makes it easier to control the amount you are adding.) Tip the pan so that the batter spreads evenly, shaking the pan occasionally to prevent sticking, and cook until just brown underneath. Flip the pancake, or turn it with a spatula and cook the other side. Keep cooked pancakes warm either in a barely warm oven or by piling them on a plate over a pan of boiling water and covering with another plate.

It is worth making extra pancakes when you have time, layering them with greaseproof paper, and freezing wrapped in foil. They will also keep for up to a week in a plastic box in the fridge.

Finally, for the difference between pancakes and crêpes . . . pancakes are generally bigger and thicker, while crêpes tend to be smaller, lighter and crisper. In truth, however, they are interchangeable!

Lemon Spiced Pancakes with Bananas

115g (4 oz)	wholemeal (wholewheat) flour	1 cup
1 tsp	baking powder	1 tsp
1 tsp	ground cinnamon	1 tsp
1 tsp	ground mixed spice	1 tsp
30g (1 oz)	soya flour	2 tbs
30g (1 oz)	sugar	2 tbs
140ml (¼ pt)	soya milk	⅔ cup
3 tbs	lemon juice	3 tbs
2 tbs	lemon peel, grated	2 tbs
2 large	bananas, mashed	2 large
2 tbs	syrup	2 tbs
	vegetable oil for frying	

1 Sift together the flour, baking powder, spices and soya flour. Stir in the sugar. Gradually whisk in the milk to make a batter, then add 2 tbs of the lemon juice and the peel.
2 Mix the bananas with the remaining lemon juice and the syrup and set aside.
3 Heat a little oil in the pan, add 2 tbs of the batter, tipping the pan so that it spreads evenly. Cook until lightly browned, then flip or turn with a spatula and cook the other side. Keep the pancakes warm while using the rest of the batter in the same way.
4 Serve the pancakes at once, folding each one over a spoonful of banana.

Note: Other fruits can, of course, be used in these simple pancakes.

Buttermilk Pancakes

285ml (½ pt)	buttermilk	1⅓ cups
2 medium	free-range eggs, beaten	2 medium
115g (4 oz)	wholemeal (wholewheat) flour	1 cup
½ tsp	bicarbonate of soda	½ tsp
1 tbs	sugar	1 tbs
55g (2 oz)	margarine, melted	¼ cup
55g (2 oz)	roasted hazelnuts, coarsely chopped	½ cup
	vegetable oil for frying	

1 Combine the buttermilk and eggs.
2 Sift together the flour and soda and add to the first mixture, together with the sugar and melted margarine. Beat well until the batter is thick and smooth, then stir in the nuts.
3 Heat a drop of oil in a heavy-based pan and add 2 tbs of the batter. Cook until brown then either flip or turn with a spatula and cook the other side. Keep the pancakes warm while using the rest of the batter in the same way.

Note: These American-style pancakes are thicker and softer than you might be used to. If you cannot get buttermilk, try using yogurt instead.

Chestnut Purée Pancakes

Batter

115g (4 oz)	wholemeal (wholewheat) flour	1 cup
2 medium	free-range eggs, beaten	2 medium
285ml (½ pt)	milk and water	1⅓ cups
	vegetable oil for frying	

Filling

425g (15 oz)	can chestnut purée	15 oz
small piece	stem ginger, finely chopped	small piece
30g (1 oz)	margarine	2½ tbs
55g (2 oz)	sugar	⅓ cup
2 tbs	cream	2 tbs

Topping

200ml (⅓ pt)	crème fraîche	¾ cup
2 tbs	syrup in which ginger was preserved	2 tbs

1 Sift the flour into a bowl, add the eggs and stir briefly, then gradually add the liquid, stirring continually to blend in the flour and remove any lumps. Beat energetically until you have a smooth, creamy batter. If possible chill for half an hour before using.
2 Heat the chestnut purée gently, then stir in the ginger, margarine and sugar, continuing to heat until the mixture is well blended. Add the cream but do not let the mixture boil.

3 Heat some of the oil in a large pan, add a few spoonfuls of batter, and cook the pancake until it is beginning to brown underneath. Flip or turn with a spatula and cook the other side. Keep the pancakes warm while using the remainder of the batter in the same way.
4 Fill each pancake with some of the chestnut purée, then fold. Top with a spoonful or two of crème fraîche, into which you have mixed the ginger syrup. Serve at once.

Note: If the purée you are using has been sweetened, you may not need to add any further sugar.

Nectarine Pancakes

Batter

115g/4 oz	wholemeal (wholewheat) flour	1 cup
1 large	free-range egg, lightly beaten	1 large
285ml (½ pt)	milk and water	1⅓ cups
	vegetable oil for frying	

Filling

170g (6 oz)	ricotta cheese	¾ cup
2 tbs	caster sugar	2 tbs
2 tsp	lemon peel, finely grated	2 tsp

Topping

2 large	nectarines, sliced	2 large
1 tbs	lemon juice	1 tbs

1 Put the flour into a bowl, then gradually add the egg. Stir in the liquid and continue mixing until you have a smooth batter. Beat energetically for a few minutes, and, if possible, chill in the fridge for half an hour before using.
2 Meanwhile, beat together the cheese, caster sugar and lemon peel. Brush the nectarines with the lemon juice so they do not go brown.
3 Heat some of the vegetable oil in a heavy-based pan, add a few spoonfuls of the batter, and cook gently until brown underneath. Flip or turn with a spatula and cook the other side. Use the remaining batter in the same way, keeping the pancakes warm while you do so.
4 Fill each pancake with some of the cheese, fold and top with slices of nectarine arranged decoratively. Serve at once.

Note: Crème fraîche or quark may be used instead of the ricotta and peaches instead of the nectarines.

Chilled Apple Crêpes with Coconut Nut Cream

Batter

115g (4 oz)	wholemeal (wholewheat) flour	1 cup
1 large	free-range egg, lightly beaten	1 large
285ml (½ pt)	milk	1⅓ cups
	vegetable oil for frying	

Filling

8 tbs	apple purée (see page 110)	8 tbs
55g (2 oz)	raisins	⅓ cup
55g (2 oz)	flaked coconut, lightly roasted	⅔ cup

Cream

55g (2 oz)	cashew pieces, ground	½ cup
1-2 tbs	syrup	1-2 tbs
2-3 tbs	coconut powder	2-3 tbs
	cold water to mix	

1 Put the flour into a bowl, add the egg, then gradually beat in the milk to make a thick, smooth batter. If possible, leave to chill for 30 minutes before using.
2 Make the apple purée as instructed. Fold in the raisins and flaked coconut.
3 To make the cream, simply blend together the cashews, syrup and coconut powder with enough cold water to make a fairly thick cream.
4 Heat a little oil in a heavy-based pan and add two spoonfuls of the batter. Cook gently until it is beginning to brown underneath, then flip or turn the crêpe with a spatula and cook the other side. Use the rest of the batter in the same way. You should have approximately 8 small crêpes.
5 Fill each crêpe with a spoonful of the apple purée, fold in half and then in half again to make a triangle. Chill briefly on a baking sheet.
6 Serve topped with a spoonful or two of the cream.

Note: Vegans can use a vegan batter with this recipe (see Cherry Crêpes opposite).

Sunflower Honey Pancakes

85g (3 oz)	sunflower seeds, ground to a meal	¾ cup
85g (3 oz)	wholemeal (wholewheat) flour	¾ cup
1 tsp	baking powder	1 tsp
½ tsp	bicarbonate of soda	½ tsp
2 medium	free-range eggs, beaten	2 medium
30g (1 oz)	margarine, melted	2½ tbs
2 tbs	honey	2 tbs
340g (⅔ pt)	buttermilk or milk	1½ cups
	vegetable oil for frying	
	strawberry or other jam to serve	

1 Sift together the sunflower seed meal, wholemeal flour, baking powder and bicarbonate of soda.
2 In a small saucepan, warm the margarine and honey, then remove from the heat, cool briefly and add the eggs. Add the dry ingredients and then the buttermilk, beating to lighten the batter.
3 Heat a drop of oil in a small pan, then add a few spoonfuls of the batter and cook for 2 minutes. Turn the pancakes and cook the other side. Keep the cooked pancakes warm while using the remainder of the batter in the same way. Serve sprinkled with sugar and topped with a spoonful of jam.

Note: These pancakes, which are similar to small cakes, are popular in America. Serve them at teatime or for breakfast. They can also be topped with other ingredients, for example, mashed bananas, syrup and tahini.

Cherry Crêpes

Batter

115g (4 oz)	wholemeal (wholewheat) flour	1 cup
55g (2 oz)	soya flour	½ cup
2 tsp	baking powder	2 tsp
285ml (½ pt)	water or half water, half milk	2 tbsp
	vegetable oil for frying	

Filling

225g (8 oz)	fresh black cherries	8 oz
3 tbs	blackcurrant juice	3 tbs
1 tsp	arrowroot	1 tsp
2 tbs	Kirsch - optional	2 tbs
30g (1 oz)	blanched almonds, coarsely chopped	¼ cup

Topping

170g (6 oz)	silken tofu, well drained	¾ cup
1 tbs	vegetable oil	1 tbs
½ tsp	vanilla essence	½ tsp
1 tbs	sugar	1 tbs
	milk to mix	

1 Sift together the flour, soya flour and baking powder, then gradually whisk in the liquid and oil and continue whisking until the batter is thick and smooth. Chill if possible.
2 Put the cherries and blackcurrant juice into a saucepan, bring to the boil and then cook for just a few minutes until the cherries begin to soften. Remove the fruit with a slotted spoon. Add the arrowroot to a little of the juice in a small bowl and return this to the pan,

heating gently until the sauce thickens. Add the Kirsch if using it. Return the cherries to the sauce with the almonds and set aside.

3 Make the cream by blending together the tofu, vegetable oil, vanilla essence and sugar, adding just enough soya milk to make a thick cream.

4 When ready, heat a little vegetable oil in a heavy-based pan and add 2 spoonfuls of the batter. Cook until just beginning to colour underneath, then flip or turn the crêpe and cook the other side. Keep warm while using the rest of the batter in the same way.

5 When ready, spread a little of the cherry and nut mixture across each of the crêpes, roll up and serve topped with the tofu cream.

Note: Lemon juice may be used instead of the liqueur.

Buckwheat Pancakes with Kumquat Sauce

115g (4 oz)	buckwheat flour	1 cup
30g (1 oz)	sugar	2 tbs
1 large	free-range egg, beaten	1 large
approx. 200ml (⅓ pt)	water	¾ cup
	kumquat sauce (see page 110)	
	vegetable oil for frying	

1 Sift the flour into a bowl and stir in the sugar and egg. Gradually add water to make a batter the consistency of thick cream.

2 Beat the batter well to let in as much air as possible. Cover and chill for 30 minutes, or longer if possible.

3 Meanwhile prepare the kumquat sauce and keep this warm.

4 Heat a drop of oil in a heavy-based pan, pour in a spoonful or two of the batter, tipping to spread it. Cook until brown underneath, then flip or turn with a spatula and cook the other side. Use the rest of the batter in the same way.

5 Serve the pancakes folded (twice) into triangles, with some of the sauce poured over the top of each.

Note: Buckwheat flour is very high in protein. These pancakes have a stronger, more interesting flavour than those made with wholemeal flour, although they also have a heavier texture. For a lighter pancake, add a little more water, or a few spoonfuls of dry cider. For a quick dessert serve with syrup and lemon juice.

Orange and Quark Pancakes

Batter

115g (4 oz)	wholemeal (wholewheat) flour	1 cup
1 medium	free-range egg, beaten	1 medium
140ml (¼ pt)	water	⅔ cup
140ml (¼ pt)	orange juice	⅔ cup
30g (1 oz)	sugar	2 tbs
1 tbs	orange peel, finely chopped	1 tbs

Filling

170g (6 oz)	Quark	¾ cup
1 tbs	honey or syrup	1 tbs
1 tsp	vanilla essence	1 tsp
½ tsp	ground cinnamon	½ tsp
2 large	oranges, peeled and cut into segments	2 large

Topping

30g (1 oz)	sugar extra ground cinnamon	2 tbs

1 Put the flour into a bowl, add the egg, then gradually add the water and juice, mixing well so that the batter is smooth and well aerated. Stir in the sugar and orange peel. If possible, leave in the fridge for 30 minutes.

2 Mix together the Quark, sweetener, vanilla essence and orange segments.

3 Heat a drop of oil in a heavy-based pan and add a few spoonfuls of the pancake batter. Cook gently until brown underneath, then flip or turn with a spatula and cook the other side. Keep warm while using the rest of the batter in the same way.

4 Put a spoonful of the Quark and orange mixture onto each pancake, fold and sprinkle with sugar and extra cinnamon. Serve at once.

Note: Use fresh ground cinnamon if possible – it really does make all the difference in this recipe.

Crêpes Belle Hélène

Batter

85g (3 oz)	wholemeal (wholewheat) flour	¾ cup
1½ tbs	cocoa powder	1½ tbs
1 large	free-range egg, beaten	1 large
285ml (½ pt)	milk	⅓ cup
	vegetable oil for frying	

Filling

4 medium	pears, peeled, cored and quartered	4 medium
200ml (⅓ pt)	water	¾ cup
1 tsp	lemon juice	1 tsp
1 tsp	grated lemon peel	1 tsp
55g (2 oz)	sugar	⅓ cup

Topping

170g (6 oz)	plain chocolate broken into pieces	6 oz
6-8 tbs	undiluted milk	6-8 tbs

1 Sift together the flour and cocoa powder. Add the egg and then gradually add the milk, beating well between each addition. Stand the batter in the fridge for 30 minutes.

2 Meanwhile, put the pears into a saucepan with the water, lemon juice, lemon peel and sugar. Bring to the boil then cover the pan and simmer for about 15 minutes or until the pears are just cooked, turning them occasionally.

3 At the same time, drop the chocolate into a bowl over a saucepan of hot water, and stir until it melts. Stir in enough milk to make a fairly thin cream.

4 Add a little oil to a heavy-based pan and add two spoonfuls of the batter. Cook gently until it begins to brown underneath, then toss or flip with a spatula and cook the other side. Keep warm while using the rest of the batter in the same way.

5 To serve, fill each crêpe with some of the pear mixture, then fold and top with a spoonful or two of the chocolate sauce. Serve immediately.

Note: As an alternative to chocolate sauce as a topping, try a few spoonfuls of yogurt, or crème fraîche.

Tropical Fruit Crêpes

Batter

85g (3 oz)	wholemeal (wholewheat) flour	¾ cup
30g (1 oz)	desiccated coconut	⅓ cup
285ml (½ pt)	milk	1⅓ cups
1 medium	free-range egg, lightly beaten	1 medium
	vegetable oil for frying	

Filling

1 small	mango, peeled and sliced	1 small
½ small	pineapple, cubed	½ small
1	star fruit, thinly sliced	1
1 medium	banana, peeled and sliced	1 medium
1-2	passion fruits	1-2
1-2 tbs	fruit juice	1-2 tbs
	caster sugar - optional	

1 Whisk together the flour and coconut, add the milk and the egg and continue beating until the batter is smooth and free from lumps. Leave to stand in the fridge for 30 minutes.

2 Meanwhile, stir together the mango, pineapple, star fruit and banana slices. Halve the passion fruits, scoop out the pulp and mix with the fruit juice. Add the prepared fruit and mix well.

3 When ready, heat a drop of oil in a small pan, add a few spoonfuls of batter and tip the pan so that it spreads evenly. Cook until lightly browned underneath, then toss or flip with a spatula and cook the other side. Use the rest of the batter in the same way, keeping the cooked crêpes warm.

4 Fill each crêpe with some of the fruit, fold, and sprinkle with a little of the sugar if using it. Serve at once.

Note: This is a perfect dessert for any weight watchers in the family! Although simple, it tastes indulgent. If you cannot get passion fruit, try flavouring the fruit juice with a pinch of ground coriander instead.

American-style Pancakes with Maple Cream

Batter

225g (8 oz)	wholemeal (wholewheat) flour	2 cups
3 tsp	baking powder	3 tsp
1 tbs	sugar	1 tbs
2 medium	free-range eggs, beaten	2 medium
285ml (½ pt)	milk	1⅓ cups
85g (3 oz)	blueberries	3 oz
	vegetable oil for frying	

Maple cream

140ml (¼ pt)	maple syrup	⅔ cup
3-4 tbs	tahini	3-4 tbs
3-4 tbs	hot water	3-4 tbs

1 Sift together the flour and baking powder, then add the sugar and the eggs. Gradually add the milk, beating well between each addition, then stir in the blueberries. Chill for 30 minutes.

2 Stir together the maple syrup, tahini and water to make a smooth cream. Adjust the flavour to taste, adding more tahini for a more subtle taste or extra maple syrup if you prefer a sweeter taste. Adjust the consistency.

3 Heat a small amount of oil in a heavy-based pan. Use a large spoon to drop in some of the batter to make a small circle, then repeat so that you are cooking a number of pancakes at the same time, leaving space between them. When brown underneath, use a spatula to flip them and cook the other side. Keep warm while using the rest of the batter in the same way.

4 Pile 2 or 3 pancakes onto each of 4 small places, top with some of the maple cream, and serve at once.

Note: These delicious little pancakes can be flavoured with raisins or other dried fruits, or other berries such as blackberries.

Christmas Banana Crêpes

Batter

115g (4 oz)	wholemeal (wholewheat) flour	1 cup
55g (2 oz)	soya flour	½ cup
2 tsp	baking powder	2 tsp
285ml (½ pt)	water	1⅓ cup
2 tbs	vegetable oil	2 tbs
	vegetable oil for frying	

Filling

8 tbs	vegetarian mincemeat (see page 115)	8 tbs
2 large	bananas, coarsely chopped	2 large
1 tbs	brandy or rum	1 tbs

Topping

30g (1 oz)	caster sugar	2 tbs

1 Sift together the flours and baking powder. Gradually add the water and then the oil, beating well so that the batter is smooth and well aerated. If possible, chill for 30 minutes.

2 Stir together the mincemeat and bananas. Add the alcohol, if using.

3 Heat a little oil in a heavy-based frying pan and add a few spoonfuls of the batter. Cook gently until it starts to brown underneath, then flip or turn with a spatula and cook the other side. Keep warm while using the rest of the batter in the same way.

4 Fill each crêpe with some of the mincemeat and banana mix, roll up and sprinkle with a little of the sugar. Serve at once.

Note: These crêpes are also delicious topped with custard.

Ice Cream Crêpes with Melba Sauce

Batter

115g (4 oz)	wholemeal (wholewheat) flour	1 cup
1 medium	free-range egg, beaten	1 medium
285ml (½ pt)	milk and water	1⅓ cups
	vegetable oil for frying	

Sauce for filling

225g (8 oz)	raspberries, fresh or frozen	8 oz
55g (2 oz)	sugar	⅓ cup
200ml (⅓ pt)	water	¾ cup
1 tbs	arrowroot	1 tbs

Topping

8 scoops	vanilla ice cream (see page 40)	8 scoops
55g (2 oz)	chopped roasted nuts	⅓ cup

1 Sift the flour into a bowl, beat in the egg, then gradually add the milk and water. Beat well, then chill for 30 minutes.

2 Meanwhile, make the sauce. In a saucepan combine the raspberries, sugar and most of the water, bring to the boil then lower the heat and simmer for 10 minutes. Mix the remaining water with the arrowroot, add it to the pan, and cook until the sauce thickens. Add a drop more water if liked.

3 Heat a little oil in a heavy-based frying pan and add a few spoonfuls of the batter. Cook until it starts to brown underneath, then flip or turn with a spatula and cook the other side. Keep warm while you use the rest of the batter in the same way.

4 Spread each of the crêpes with some of the sauce, roll up, top with a scoop of ice cream and sprinkle with nuts. Serve at once.

Note: Other sauces may be used instead of Melba Sauce, for example, Butterscotch Sauce (*page 111*) or Apricot Sauce (*page 110*). In an emergency, spread with jam. Also experiment with different flavoured ice cream.

Pineapple and Ginger Crêpes

Batter

115g (4 oz)	wholemeal (wholewheat) flour	1 cup
55g (2 oz)	soya flour	½ cup
2 tsp	baking powder	2 tsp
285ml (½ pt)	water and milk	1⅓ cups
2 tbs	vegetable oil	2 tbs
	vegetable oil for frying	

Filling

395g (14 oz) can	pineapple in natural juice	14 oz can
170g (6 oz)	vegan wholemeal (wholewheat) ginger biscuits	6 oz
1 tsp	ground ginger	1 tsp
30g (1 oz)	margarine, melted	2½ tbs

1 Sift together the flours and baking powder. Gradually add the water and milk, beating well after each addition. Add the oil then chill the batter for 30 minutes.

2 Drain the pineapple (reserving the juice) and then chop it coarsely. Crumble two-thirds of the biscuits and mix with the pineapple. Stir the ginger into a few spoonfuls of the reserved juice and use this to moisten the fruit and biscuit mixture.

3 Crumble the remaining biscuits and mix with the melted margarine.

4 Add a drop of oil to a heavy-based frying pan and then pour in two spoonfuls of the batter. Cook gently until the pancake begins to brown underneath, then flip or turn with a spatula and cook the other side. Keep warm while using the rest of the batter in the same way.

5 Fill each crêpe with some of the pineapple and ginger, fold in half and then in half again to make a triangle. Sprinkle with the remaining crumbs and heat under a hot grill for a few minutes before serving.

Note: For ginger freaks, add a little finely chopped stem ginger to the pineapple and biscuit mixture.

Pancake Lemon Pie

Batter

115g (4 oz)	wholemeal (wholewheat) flour	1 cup
2 large	free-range eggs, separated	2 large
285ml (½ pt)	milk and water	1⅓ cups
	vegetable oil for frying	

Filling

4-6 tbs	lemon curd	4-6 tbs
4 tbs	thick yogurt	4 tbs
1 tbs	lemon peel, finely chopped	1 tbs
55g (2 oz)	flaked almonds, lightly roasted	½ cup

1 Sift the flour into a bowl, then stir in the egg yolks, milk and water. Beat well and chill briefly.

2 Stir together the lemon curd, yogurt and lemon peel.

3 Whisk the egg whites until stiff and use a metal spoon to fold them into the batter. At the same time, heat some oil in a heavy-based pan. Add about a quarter of the batter and cook until puffed up on top and lightly browned underneath, then turn and cook the other side. Keep warm while making three more pancakes in the same way.

4 Spread each pancake with some of the lemon curd and yogurt mixture, and use this to sandwich them together to make a pie, finishing with a generous layer on the top pancake. Sprinkle with nuts and serve at once, cut into wedges.

Note: This is an unusual way of serving pancakes. Other fillings could include puréed or fresh fruits with dairy or tofu cream.

6
Soufflés, Mousses, Whips and Creams

Baby food, comfort food, or the most sophisticated of desserts – however you think of them, all the dishes in this chapter are easy to eat, and make the perfect ending to a heavy meal.

When making soufflés, remember that the more air you whip into the egg whites, the lighter the results will be. Try not to knock the dish when transferring it from table to oven, do not bang the oven door when checking on cooking (this is one time when having a glass door on the oven really is a boon), and of course, take the soufflé to the table as soon as it is ready. Cooking your soufflé in a small dish so that it rises well above the rim makes it look especially impressive. To do this, make a collar of double greaseproof paper or foil that stands 5cm (2 in) above the rim, wrap it around the outside of the soufflé dish then tie or seal it so that it stays in place. (This method can be used with cooked or chilled soufflés). When ready to serve, peel the paper off carefully to avoid damaging the soufflé.

The other recipes in this chapter are both simple and quick to prepare. However, they may need a few hours in the fridge to reach the desired consistency.

Souffléd Oranges

4 large	oranges	4 large
1 tbs	orange peel, finely grated	1 tbs
4 medium	free-range eggs, separated	4 medium
55g (2 oz)	sugar	⅓ cup
1 tbs	concentrated orange juice	1 tbs

1 Halve the oranges and use a sharp knife to remove the flesh, being careful not to damage the shells. Put them aside. Stir the grated orange peel into a tablespoon or two of water and cook gently to soften, then drain well.
2 Press as much juice as possible from the flesh, pour into a saucepan and heat gently to reduce.
3 Beat together the egg yolks and sugar until thick and smooth. Add the orange peel, warm orange juice and concentrated juice, mixing well.
4 Whisk the egg yolks until stiff, then carefully fold them into the first mixture using a metal spoon. Divide between the eight orange shells, place on a baking sheet, and bake at 220°C/425°F (Gas Mark 7) for 8 to 10 minutes, or until puffed up and golden. Serve at once.

Note: For the extra orange peel, either reserve some from another orange or trim a thin ring of peel from the top of each of the shells. The soufflés may then rise above the shells but that can look even more attractive. As an alternative to concentrated orange juice, use a liqueur such as Grand Marnier.

Gooseberry and Elderflower Soufflé

115g (4 oz)	gooseberries, washed and trimmed	4 oz
2 tbs	water	2 tbs
55g (2 oz)	sugar, to taste	⅓ cup
1	elderflower head	1
85g (3 oz)	margarine	⅓ cup
55g (2 oz)	wholemeal (wholewheat) flour	½ cup
285ml (½ pt)	milk	1⅓ cups
3 large	free-range eggs, separated	3 large

1 Cook the gooseberries, water and sugar in a saucepan for 15 minutes or until soft. Sieve, add the elderflower, and leave the purée to cool.
2 In a separate saucepan, melt the margarine, stir in the flour, and cook briefly. Add the milk and continue heating until the sauce thickens. Remove the elderflower head before stirring the purée into the sauce.
3 Whisk the egg whites until stiff then use a metal spoon to fold them into the first mixture. Grease a medium soufflé dish, add the mixture, and bake at 190°C/375°F (Gas Mark 5) for 40 to 50 minutes. Serve at once.

Note: Elderflowers give gooseberries a lovely flavour, but don't worry if you can't get any – the end result is equally delicious.

Lemon Soufflés with Nut Brittle Topping

6 tbs	lemon juice	6 tbs
2 tbs	water	2 tbs
2 tsp	agar agar	2 tsp
3 large	free-range eggs, separated	3 large
115g (4 oz)	sugar	⅔ cup
2-3 tbs	lemon peel, finely grated	2-3 tbs
285ml (½ pt)	thick yogurt	1⅓ cups
85g (3 oz)	peanut brittle, powdered in grinder	3 oz
	whipped cream - optional	

1 In a saucepan, stir together the lemon juice and water, sprinkle with the agar agar, and bring to the boil, stirring continually. Heat gently for 3 minutes more, then leave to cool slightly.
2 Combine the egg yolks and sugar, mixing until thick and smooth. Add the lemon peel and stir into the first mixture. Add the yogurt and set aside.
3 When the mixture begins to thicken, use a metal spoon gently to fold in the stiffly whisked egg whites. Divide between four small, greased soufflé dishes or ramekins. Chill well until set firm.
4 When ready to serve, sprinkle the soufflés with the powdered nut brittle and, if liked, decorate with whipped cream. Serve at once.

Note: Sour cream or crème fraîche may be used instead of yogurt.

Chilled Apricot Soufflé

225g (8 oz)	dried apricots, soaked overnight	8 oz
3 tbs	orange juice	3 tbs
2 tsp	agar agar	2 tsp
3 medium	free-range egg whites	3 medium
55g (2 oz)	hazelnuts, roasted and coarsely chopped	½ cup

1 Cook the apricots in fresh water and when soft, drain well before blending or mashing well to make a thick purée.
2 In a small saucepan, heat the orange juice, sprinkle with agar agar, and bring to the boil. Simmer gently for a few minutes before adding to the apricots and mixing well.
3 Whisk the egg whites until stiff and stir into the first mixture.
4 Spoon into a medium sized soufflé dish. Chill well until set. Serve decorated with the chopped hazelnuts.

Note: This low calorie, low cholesterol soufflé is quick and easy to make. While the apricots should be sweet enough as they are, add extra sugar if necessary. Other fruit purées can be combined with agar agar and beaten egg whites to produce a wide range of soufflés.

Coconut Vanilla Soufflé

1 medium	free-range egg	1 medium
3 tbs	milk	3 tbs
2 tbs	honey, or to taste	2 tbs
170g (6 oz)	cottage cheese	¾ cup
1 tsp	vanilla essence, or to taste	1 tsp
30g (1 oz)	desiccated coconut	⅓ cup
2 large	free-range egg whites	2 large

1 Blend together the egg, milk and honey, then add the cottage cheese, vanilla essence and desiccated coconut.
2 Whisk the egg whites until stiff and gently fold into the first mixture.
3 Lightly grease a medium-sized soufflé dish, spoon in the mixture. Stand in another larger tin and pour in enough hot water to come half way up the side of the soufflé dish. Bake at 350°C/180°F (Gas Mark 4) for 35 to 45 minutes, or until well risen.

Note: This subtly flavoured soufflé is perfect for the dieters in the family. It is also delicious sweetened with vanilla flavoured sugar instead of honey.

Raspberry Soufflettes

455g (1 lb)	raspberries, cleaned	1 lb
2 tbs	honey or sugar	2 tbs
1 tbs	lemon juice	1 tbs
4 large	free-range egg whites	4 large

1 Press the raspberries through a sieve, or blend to make a purée. Stir in the honey or sugar and lemon juice.
2 Whisk the egg whites until stiff. Use a metal spoon to gently fold them into the raspberry purée.
3 Divide the mixture between 4 small, lightly-greased ramekins. Bake at 180°C/350°F (Gas Mark 4) for 15 minutes or until well risen. Serve at once.

Note: Use frozen raspberries in winter for a taste of summer - defrost them and use as described above. Strawberries may be used instead.

Chocolate Soufflé with Macaroons

30g (1 oz)	margarine	2½ tbs
30g (1 oz)	wholemeal (wholewheat) flour	¼ cup
200ml (⅓ pt)	milk	¾ cup
55g (2 oz)	chocolate	2 oz
55g (2 oz)	sugar	⅓ cup
½ tsp	vanilla essence	½ tsp
3 large	free-range eggs, separated	3 large
55g (2 oz)	macaroons (see page 31), crumbled	2 oz
30g (1 oz)	cocoa powder	¼ cup

1 Melt the margarine, stir in the flour, add the milk and bring gently to the boil, stirring continually, until the sauce thickens.
2 Grate the chocolate and stir into the sauce with the sugar and vanilla essence. Set aside to cool briefly, then add the egg yolks.
3 Whisk the egg whites until stiff. Use a metal spoon to fold them gently into the other ingredients.
4 Grease a medium-sized soufflé dish. Sprinkle the biscuits across the base, then spoon the chocolate mixture over the top of them. Bake at 200°C/400°F (Gas Mark 6) for 10 minutes, then reduce the temperature to 180°C/350°F (Gas Mark 4) and cook for a further 20 minutes, or until the soufflé is well risen. Dust with cocoa powder and serve at once.

Note: For a change use peppermint essence instead of vanilla, or add chopped nuts or orange peel.

Almond Soufflé

3 medium	free-range eggs, separated	3 medium
85g (3 oz)	sugar	½ cup
285ml (½ pt)	fromage frais	1⅓ cups
½ tsp	almond essence	½ tsp
85g (3 oz)	almonds, ground	¾ cup
2 tbs	candied peel, finely chopped	2 tbs
30g (1 oz)	almond flakes, roasted - optional	¼ cup

1 Beat together the egg yolks and sugar until thick and smooth. Add the fromage frais, almond essence, almonds and peel, making sure everything is well mixed.
2 Whisk the egg whites until stiff and use a metal spoon to fold them into the first mixture.
3 Transfer the mixture to a medium, greased soufflé dish, standing this in another ovenproof dish and pouring hot water into the bigger dish so that it comes half way up the side of the soufflé dish. Bake at 190°C/375°F (Gas Mark 5) for 40 minutes, or until set. Serve at once.

Note: This rich, heavy, soufflé dessert is best served at the end of a light meal.

Lime and Mango Mousse

3 tbs	lime juice	3 tbs
3 tbs	water	3 tbs
2 tsp	agar agar	2 tsp
1 large	mango, peeled	1 large
140ml (¼ pt)	fromage frais	⅔ cup
55g (2 oz)	caster sugar	⅓ cup
2 large	free-range egg whites chocolate to decorate - optional	2 large

1 In a small saucepan, whisk together the lime juice, water and agar agar. Bring gently to the boil then simmer for a few minutes before setting aside to cool slightly.
2 Use a sharp knife to remove as much mango flesh from the stone as possible. Blend to make a thick, smooth purée and add to the first mixture. Stir in the fromage frais and caster sugar.
3 Whisk the egg whites until stiff, then carefully fold into the lime and mango mix. Spoon into four small bowls or glasses and chill well before serving. Top, if liked, with some grated chocolate.

Note: Yogurt or sour cream may be used instead of fromage frais. Other fruits and juices can also be used in the same way - try lemon juice with apple purée, orange juice with strawberry, and so on.

Creamy Yogurt Ring

4 tbs	cold water	4 tbs
1 tbs	agar agar	1 tbs
200ml (⅓ pt)	crème fraîche	¾ cup
4 tbs	maple syrup, or to taste	4 tbs
285ml (½ pt)	thick yogurt	1⅓ cups
	kumquat sauce	
	(see page 110)	

1 In a small saucepan, stir together the cold water and agar agar, bring gently to the boil, then simmer for a few minutes. Cool briefly before adding the crème fraîche and maple syrup.
2 Whisk in the yogurt, making sure all the ingredients are well blended. Pour into a small, lightly-greased ring mould and chill until set firm.
3 Make the sauce.
4 When almost ready to serve, dip the mould into hot water for a few seconds only. Put a plate over the top, then invert the mould and shake it slightly to loosen. Chill the ring again before serving with kumquat sauce spooned into the centre and over the top.

Note: Mildly flavoured, cool and creamy, this is a lovely summer's day dessert. As an alternative to kumquat sauce, fill the ring with fresh berries moistened with orange juice or a few spoonfuls of liqueur. For a really impressive dish, line the ring mould with thin slices of kiwi fruit before pouring in the yogurt mix and leaving to set.

Mocha Mousse

170g (6 oz)	chocolate bar	6 oz
2 tbs	strong coffee	2 tbs
4 medium	free-range eggs, separated	4 medium
2 tbs	rum	2 tbs
285ml (½ pt)	whipping cream	1⅓ cups
	ratafia biscuits to serve	

1 Break the chocolate into small pieces. In the top of a double boiler (or a bowl over a pan of boiling water), gently melt the chocolate with the coffee, stirring to make a thick smooth sauce.
2 Beat the egg yolks and add to the sauce with the rum. Whip the egg whites and fold into the sauce, then whip the cream until thick and add this too.
3 Spoon the mousse into four glasses and chill thoroughly. Serve with biscuits.

Note: Use a carob bar instead of chocolate if you prefer.

Dried Fruit Syllabub

115g (4 oz)	dried apricots	¾ cup
115g (4 oz)	dried prunes	¾ cup
285ml (½ pt)	apple juice	1⅓ cups
115g (4 oz)	silken tofu, well drained	½ cup
30g (1 oz)	roasted hazelnuts, chopped	¼ cup

1 Soak the fruit in the apple juice overnight. In the morning, remove the stones from the prunes, then blend the fruit and juice into a smooth purée.
2 Blend in the tofu. Divide between four glasses and chill well. Serve sprinkled with the nuts.

Note: Although the fruit should be sweet enough, add a spoonful of syrup or concentrated apple juice if you need extra sweetening. This recipe can be made with cream instead of tofu.

Honey Syllabub

570ml (1 pt)	whipping cream	2½ cups
140ml (¼ pt)	white wine	⅔ cup
6 tbs	runny honey	6 tbs
3 tbs	lemon juice	3 tbs
1 tbs	grated lemon rind	1 tbs
	biscuits to serve	

1 Lightly whip the cream and set aside.
2 Combine the wine, honey, lemon juice and rind. Gradually add the cream and continue whisking to make a stiff froth.
3 Spoon into individual glasses and chill well. Serve with biscuits such as shortbread or macaroons.

Note: This is a rich dessert. For a lighter version, replace some of the cream with whipped egg whites. Alternatively, use it as a topping for fresh fruit salad.

Apple Pumpkin Mousse

1.15 kilos (2 lbs)	pumpkin, peeled and seeded	2 lbs
680g (1½ lbs)	dessert apples, peeled and cored	2 lbs
2 tbs	vegetable oil	2 tbs
140ml (¼ pt)	cold water	⅔ cup
1 tsp	ground cinnamon	1 tsp
½ tsp	ground nutmeg	½ tsp
30g (1 oz)	almonds, coarsely chopped	¼ cup
55g (2 oz)	raisins	2 tbs
30g (1 oz)	margarine	2½ tbs

1 Chop the pumpkin and apples into small pieces. Heat the oil in a heavy based pan and sauté the pumpkin and apples for 5 minutes, stirring frequently. Add the

water, cover the pan, and cook gently for 15 minutes, or until everything is well cooked. You may need to add more water, but keep this to the minimum so that the mixture is dry and creamy.

2 Add the spices and beat well (or blend) until smooth.

3 Rinse four glasses with cold water and divide the mixture between them. Chill briefly.

4 Meanwhile, lightly fry the nuts and raisins in the margarine. Divide between the four glasses and serve at once.

Note: This subtly flavoured dish gets its mousse–like texture from the pumpkin. Add sweetening to taste.

Apricot and Banana Crunch

285ml (½ pt)	apricot sauce (see page 110)	1⅓ cups
425ml (¾ pt)	banana flavoured soya milk	2 cups
2 tsp	cornflour	2 tsp
few drops	banana essence - optional	few drops
170g (6 oz)	granola (see page 62)	6 oz

1 Make the apricot purée and set aside.

2 Pour most of the banana flavoured soya milk into a small saucepan and heat gently. Stir together the remaining milk and cornflour to make a paste, and add slowly to the milk in the pan, stirring continually. Continue heating to make a thick custard. Add flavouring if liked. Leave to cool.

3 Spoon some of the apricot sauce into the base of four tall glasses, then add a sprinkling of granola and some of the banana custard. Repeat to use all of the ingredients. Chill briefly before serving.

Note: If you cannot find banana flavoured soya dessert, either flavour plain milk, or simply use mashed bananas.

Chocolate Mint Swirls

200ml (⅓ pt)	whipping cream	¾ cup
140ml (¼ pt)	Greek yogurt	⅔ cup
115g (4 oz)	plain chocolate	4 oz
½ tsp	peppermint essence, or to taste	½ tsp
4	fresh cherries to garnish - optional	4

1 Whip the cream until stiff, fold in the yogurt and set aside.

2 Put the chocolate into a bowl over a pan of hot water and stir until melted. Remove from the heat then stir half the cream and yogurt mixture into it until well blended.

3 Flavour the remaining cream with peppermint essence.

4 Spoon some of the mixture into the base of four sundae glasses, add some of the chocolate mix, and repeat until all the ingredients are used. As you do so, use a fork to make a swirling pattern. Chill well before serving, topping with the cherries to add colour.

Note: This recipe is quick, easy and not as calorie laden as it appears. You could use glacé cherries instead of fresh ones.

Strawberry and 'Cream' Jellies

455g (1 lb)	strawberries, cleaned	1 lb
2 tbs	syrup	2 tbs
1 tbs	agar agar	1 tbs
2 tbs	orange juice	2 tbs
140ml (¼ pt)	soya 'cream'	⅔ cup

1 Set aside 4 strawberries to garnish, then blend or sieve the rest to make a thick purée. Stir in the syrup. (For a smoother texture sieve out the pips, although they do give an interesting texture.) Stir in the syrup.

2 In a small saucepan, sprinkle the agar agar onto the orange juice, stir well, bring to the boil, then lower the heat and simmer for 3 minutes. Allow to cool briefly.

3 Whisk together the strawberry purée and agar agar and add the soya 'cream'. Spoon into four tall glasses and chill well until set. Top each one with a strawberry before serving.

Note: This is a traditional combination of strawberries and cream with a new slant. Use frozen strawberries if fresh are not available, or tinned, using the juice instead of orange juice. The cream could be replaced with puréed tofu, or - for vegetarians - yogurt or crème fraîche.

Spiced Apple Whips with Tofu

285g (10 oz)	silken tofu, well drained	1¼ cups
2-4 tbs	syrup	2-4 tbs
225g (½ pt)	apple purée (see page 110)	1⅓ cups
1 tsp	ground cinnamon	1 tsp
½ tsp	ground cardamom	½ tsp
55g (2 oz)	sultanas (golden seedless raisins)	⅓ cup
30g (1 oz)	hazelnuts, roasted and coarsely chopped	¼ cup

1 Combine the tofu and syrup in a blender, then add the apple purée and spices. Stir in the sultanas.

2 Spoon into four bowls and chill. Serve sprinkled with the nuts.

Note: Other fruit purées may be used instead of apple.

Cottage Cheese Puddings

455g (1 lb)	cottage cheese, drained	2 cups
1 tbs	orange peel, finely grated	1 tbs
1 tbs	lemon juice	1 tbs
3-4 tbs	marmalade, or to taste	3-4 tbs

1 Blend the cottage cheese or push through a sieve. Stir in the orange peel, lemon juice and enough marmalade to flavour the cheese lightly.
2 Spoon into four bowls and chill.

Note: To make these puddings more substantial, spoon the mixture over squares of Marmalade and Molasses Cake (*see page 25*). Or, for something completely different, use lemon curd instead of the marmalade.

Chestnut Crunch Maple Mousse

140ml (¼ pt)	whipping cream	⅔ cup
140ml (¼ pt)	yogurt	⅔ cup
255g (9 oz) can	chestnut purée, unsweetened	9 oz can
3 tbs	maple syrup, or to taste	3 tbs
30g (1 oz)	pumpkin seeds, coarsely chopped	¼ cup
30g (1 oz)	almonds, coarsely chopped	¼ cup
½ tsp	ground ginger	½ tsp
1 tbs	margarine, melted	1 tbs

1 Whip the cream until just beginning to stiffen, then stir in the yogurt, mixing well. Add the chestnut purée and maple syrup. Spoon into four small bowls and chill.
2 Mix together the pumpkin seeds, almonds and ginger, and cook briefly in the melted fat for a few minutes, stirring continually. Add the sugar and sprinkle the mixture over the chestnut mousses. Serve at once.

Note: Make sure the chestnut purée is unsweetened or the flavour of the maple syrup will be lost.

Rainbow Jellies

½ packet	vegetarian strawberry jelly	½ packet
½ packet	vegetarian greengage jelly	½ packet
½ packet	vegetarian lemon jelly	½ packet
55g (2 oz)	almonds, ground	½ cup
	soya 'cream' to serve - optional	

1 Make up the strawberry jelly according to instructions, divide between four tall glasses and leave to set.
2 Make up the greengage jelly, allow to cool briefly, then pour the mix on top of the first jelly and leave to set.

3 Make up the lemon jelly, stir in the nuts and leave to cool slightly. Spoon the mixture over the other jellies, smooth the tops and leave to set firm. Serve, if liked, with some soya 'cream' poured over the top.

Note: You can, of course, make up your own jellies using fresh fruit juice and agar agar, but you may also need to add some colouring – it's the contrast between the bands of red, yellow and a creamy white that make these jellies so pretty. For fun, tip the glasses slightly (rest one side on a mat) so that the stripes are sloped.

Coconut Tofu Dessert

170g (6 oz)	creamed coconut, grated	6 oz
115g (4 oz)	sugar	⅔ cup
1-2 tsp	vanilla essence or rosewater	1-2 tsp
340g (12 oz)	silken tofu, drained	1½ cups
2 tbs	coconut flakes, lightly roasted	2 tbs

1 In a small saucepan, stir together the coconut and sugar, keeping the heat low and stirring continually. When melted, add the vanilla essence or rosewater.
2 Blend the tofu and add to the coconut cream.
3 Turn into four small bowls, sprinkle with the coconut flakes, and serve at once.

Note: For a firmer textured dish, chill briefly. This is a very rich mixture; if it is *too* rich for your taste, use it in smaller quantities as a topping for a fresh fruit salad.

Prune Whip

340g (12 oz)	prunes, soaked overnight cold water	2¼ cups
2 tbs	lemon peel, coarsely chopped	2 tbs
4 tbs	tahini, or to taste	4 tbs
2 tbs	concentrated apple juice	2 tbs
	biscuits to serve	

1 Drain the prunes, then cover with cold water, add the lemon peel, and cook until just tender.
2 Drain them well, remove the stones, then blend or sieve the flesh to make a purée. Add a drop of the water in which they were cooked if necessary, but keep this to a minimum.
3 Mix the tahini into the apple juice, then stir this into the prune purée, mixing well. Spoon into four small bowls and chill before serving with crisp biscuits.

Note: Despite having no added sugar, this whip should be sweet enough as the prunes and apple juice are both high in natural sugar.

Lemon Creams

140ml (¼ pt)	whipping cream	⅔ cup
425ml (¾ pt)	yogurt	2 cups
4-6 tbs	lemon curd	4-6 tbs
55g (2 oz)	candied lemon peel, chopped	2 oz

1 Whip the cream until just beginning to thicken. Mix in the yogurt and lemon curd.
2 Divide between four dishes or glasses. Top with chopped peel. Chill well before serving.

Note: For a lighter textured dessert, reduce the yogurt and add two whisked egg whites to extend the mixture. It is also delicious topped with grated chocolate or carob instead of candied lemon.

Quick Crème Brulée with Ginger

425ml (¾ pt)	made-up custard	2 cups
140ml (¼ pt)	whipping cream	⅔ cup
1 tbs	chopped preserved ginger, or to taste	1 tbs
55g (2 oz)	sugar	⅓ cup

1 Turn the custard into a bowl, whip the cream until thick and add to the custard, mixing well. Stir in the ginger, divide between four small pots or dishes, and chill.
2 When ready to serve, sprinkle each one with some of the sugar and heat under a hot grill for just a few minutes, or until the sugar melts. Cool briefly then serve.

Note: Alternatively chill the cremes again so that the topping sets and becomes crunchy! Use ready made custard for speed, either from a packet, or left over from a previous meal. A vegan version can be made by combining a carton of vanilla flavoured soya dessert with 115g/4 oz drained and puréed tofu, some vanilla essence, and then following the same method.

Carob Orange Pots

200ml (⅓ pt)	carob sauce (see page 112)	¾ cup
3 tbs	concentrated orange juice	3 tbs
170g (6 oz)	ricotta cheese	¾ cup
4 slices	orange	4 slices

1 Make up the sauce and stir in the orange juice and then the ricotta cheese, making sure everything is thoroughly blended.

2 Spoon into four small pots, smooth the top and chill well.
3 Cut the orange slices into quarters and arrange these on top of the pots. Serve at once.

Note: This is a healthier version of the better known chocolate pots. You could of course use chocolate instead of carob, and other soft cheeses (such as Quark) instead of ricotta.

Banana Mousse

2 medium	free-range eggs, separated	2 medium
30g (1 oz)	sugar	2 tbs
1 tbs	lemon juice	1 tbs
2 tbs	orange juice	2 tbs
2 tsp	agar agar	2 tsp
3 medium	bananas	3 medium
200ml (⅓ pt)	whipping cream	¾ cup
1 tsp	banana essence	1 tsp
	granola or chopped nuts to garnish	

1 Mix together the egg yolks and sugar. Put the lemon and orange juice into a small saucepan, stir in the agar agar, bring to the boil and simmer for a few minutes.
2 Combine the first two mixtures, adding the peeled and mashed bananas. Put into a heavy saucepan (or a bowl over a pan of hot water) and stir, heating gently, until the mixture is thick enough to coat the back of a spoon. Cool slightly.
3 Whip the cream and add half of it to the mixture with the banana essence. Whisk the egg whites and carefully fold them into the other ingredients.
4 Transfer to a small soufflé dish or to individual glasses. Smooth the top and chill well. When ready to serve decorate with the remaining cream and sprinkle with granola or nuts.

Note: This mixture is also ideal for using to fill flan cases.

Ginger Preserve Creams

30g (1 oz)	arrowroot	1½ tbs
570ml (1 pt)	milk	2½ cups
1 tbs	vanilla essence	1 tbs
55g (2 oz)	sugar	⅓ cup
2 tbs	stem ginger, finely chopped	2 tbs
3 tbs	ginger preserve	3 tbs
55g (2 oz)	flaked almonds, lightly roasted	½ cup

1 Mix the arrowroot with a few spoonfuls of milk. Put the remaining milk into a saucepan, heat gently, add the arrowroot paste and stir well. Add the essence and sugar then continue heating until the mixture comes to the boil and thickens. Set aside until cold.

2 Mix the chopped ginger and ginger preserve into the custard. Divide between four small bowls, smooth the tops and chill. Serve sprinkled with the nuts.

Note: For an extra creamy custard, use concentrated soya milk. Alternatively, use dairy instead of soya milk, or stir a few spoonfuls of whipped cream into the custard. Vegans should make sure the ginger preserve is free from animal derived ingredients.

Home-made Yogurt

570ml (1 pt)	milk	2½ cups
1 good tbs	natural yogurt, or packet yogurt culture flavouring as required	1 good tbs

1 Place the milk in a clean saucepan, bring to the boil, then leave to cool to just above body temperature. (To test, dip a clean finger into the milk which should be comfortably warm).

2 Whisk in the yogurt or yogurt culture, making sure it is thoroughly mixed. Pour at once into glass jars, a thermos flask or an electric yogurt maker, cover or seal. Leave undisturbed until set. Yogurt made in glass jars (wrapped in towels and left in a warm spot such as an airing cupboard) or in a flask will take between 6 and 12 hours. If using an electric yogurt maker, check the manufacturer's instructions for timing.

3 Transfer the yogurt to the fridge and leave to thicken. If flavouring, add the chosen ingredients before putting it in the fridge or, alternatively, just before it is served. Eat within 4 to 6 days, reserving a few spoonfuls of the yogurt to start your next batch.

Note: For thicker yogurt, either boil the milk for a while first to reduce it, or add 2 tbs powdered milk to each 570ml/1 pint milk. Another method is to use a creamy sterilized milk (which will not need to be boiled first as – unlike fresh milk – it will contain no bacteria). Alternatively, pour the finished yogurt into a clean piece of muslin and leave to drain for a while, until you are left with a thick white cream – not unlike a soft cheese. You can vary both the flavour and texture of your yogurt by combining different types of milk. Flavourings you might like to add include honey, maple syrup, sugar, cinnamon sugar, fruit purées, chopped dried or fresh fruit, chopped nuts, lemon curd, low sugar jams, chocolate or carob syrup, chopped stem ginger with some syrup, orange flower or rosewater, crushed melon or pineapple, etc. Yogurt cultures are available from health food and wholefood shops. Vegans can use soya milk, and should make extra sure that the culture they are buying is suitable – or use a commercially made soya yogurt (that specifies it is suitable for vegans) as a starter.

Yogurt Brulée

340g (12 oz)	fresh berries (e.g. strawberries, raspberries etc.)	12 oz
140ml (¼ pt)	yogurt	⅔ cup
85g (3 oz)	sugar	½ cup

1 Clean the berries and, if necessary, chop so that they are all similar in size. Mix with the yogurt and divide between four small, heatproof dishes.

2 Sprinkle the tops with sugar, place under a hot grill until they bubble and leave to cool. Transfer to the fridge and chill, preferably overnight.

Note: Use other fruits or fruit combinations as liked.

Cinnamon Yogurt Ramekins

570ml (1 pt)	yogurt	2½ cups
3 large	free-range eggs, lightly beaten	3 large
2 tbs	honey, or to taste	2 tbs
3 tsp	ground cinnamon	3 tsp

1 Stir together the yogurt, eggs and honey. Divide between four ramekins, sprinkle with nutmeg, bake at 170°C/325°F (Gas Mark 3) for 30 to 40 minutes, or until set. Serve at once.

Note: Quick to prepare, this dessert is delicious, made even tastier by the fresh cinnamon. If liked, add a layer of fruit or fruit purée beneath the yogurt mixture.

7
Wholesome Nibbles

These are the kind of things you could put on a buffet table, or eat in front of the TV. Some of them you could take with you in your back-pack, or to the beach.

Nibbling is a habit we have all acquired, but if we eat nutritious foods it can do no harm. All the following are full of good things! Use them to inspire you to think up ideas of your own.

Note: Because they are completely natural and have not been cooked, these snacks will keep only for a short time. Eat them soon after they are prepared to enjoy them at their best.

Maple Halvah

115g (4oz)	sesame seeds, ground	¾ cup
55g (2 oz)	almonds, ground	½ cup
approx. 4 tbs	maple syrup	approx. 4 tbs
30g (1 oz)	soya flour	¼ cup

1 Mix together the sesame seeds and almond meal.
2 Add just enough maple syrup to bind the ingredients together – do not make them too wet. Add the soya flour and mix thoroughly. Spread across the base of a small tin, cover and chill. Serve cut into squares.

Note: This vegan version of halvah (which often contains honey) is also softer and moister although you'll find the taste very much like the real thing.

Spicy Granola

455g (1 lb)	rolled oats	4 cups
115g (4 oz)	hazelnuts, coarsely chopped	1 cup
115g (4 oz)	coconut flakes	1 cup
55g (2 oz)	pumpkin seeds	½ cup
55g (2 oz)	sesame seeds	½ cup
1 tsp	ground cinnamon	1 tsp
1 tsp	ground ginger	1 tsp
½ tsp	ground cloves	½ tsp
70ml (⅛ pt)	vegetable oil	¼ cup
70ml (⅛ pt)	honey or corn syrup	¼ cup
2 tbs	orange peel, grated	2 tbs
85g (3 oz)	raisins	½ cup
85g (3 oz)	dried apples, chopped	½ cup

1 Stir together the oats, hazelnuts, coconut flakes, seeds and spices.
2 Whisk together the oil and honey *or* syrup. Add the peel, pour over the dry ingredients and mix well.
3 Spread the mixture across the base of one or two baking sheets. Bake at 200°C/400°F (Gas Mark 6) for 45 minutes, or until crisp and golden. Stir the mixture occasionally.
4 Remove from the oven, add the raisins and apples and leave to cool completely. Store in an airtight container. Eat as an energy-packed nibble, with dairy or soya milk for breakfast, or use to top ice cream, yogurt, or in other dessert dishes.

Note: Cook the granola for longer if you like an extra rich flavour – you can also do this in a saucepan on the cooker top. Vary the nuts and fruits as you like.

Honey Sesame Popcorn

2 tbs	vegetable oil	2 tbs
85g (3 oz)	popping corn	½ cup
2 tbs	honey, or to taste	2 tbs
2 tbs	sesame seeds	2 tbs

1 Heat the oil in a large, heavy-based saucepan. Stir in the corn and cover with a well-fitting lid.
2 Continue cooking over a medium heat, shaking the pan every now and again. When the popping noises stop the corn is ready to eat.
3 Stir in the honey and seeds and leave over the heat for just a minute more, then tip the mixture into a bowl. This popcorn can be eaten hot, warm or cold.

Note: Chopped nuts can be stirred into the popcorn instead of the seeds. For a vegan version, use syrup instead of honey, or for a savoury version, salt.

Mocha Popcorn

2 tbs	vegetable oil	2 tbs
85g (3 oz)	popping corn	½ cup
30g (1 oz)	margarine	2½ tbs
1 tbs	syrup	1 tbs
½ tsp	vanilla essence	½ tsp
½ tsp	carob powder	½ tsp
¼ tsp	instant coffee	¼ tsp

1 Heat the oil in a large, heavy-based saucepan. Stir in the corn and cover with a well-fitting lid. Continue cooking over a medium heat, shaking the pan occasionally until the popping stops.
2 Meanwhile, in another saucepan, combine the margarine, syrup and vanilla essence. Stir until melted. Add the carob powder and coffee and continue heating and stirring for a few more minutes.
3 When the popcorn is ready, tip it into the mocha mixture, stir well, and serve at once.

Dried Fruit Truffles

225g (8 oz)	mixed dried fruit (i.e. raisins, sultanas, currants)	1¼ cups
85g (3 oz)	wholemeal cake crumbs	1½ cups
85g (3 oz)	mixed nuts, finely chopped	¾ cup
4 tbs	milk	4 tbs
	desiccated coconut	
	carob powder	

1 Wash the fruit, pat dry, then chop finely. Mix with the cake crumbs, nuts and milk, and set aside for 10 minutes. The mixture should be fairly firm, but moist enough to bind together - add a little more milk if necessary.

2 Break into small even-sized pieces, shape into balls and roll half of them in coconut, the other half in carob powder. Put into paper cases and chill briefly before serving.

Note: For sweeter truffles, stir in some honey *or* syrup and reduce the milk accordingly.

Chocolate Banana Chips

85g (3 oz)	chocolate	3 oz
225g (8 oz)	banana chips	8 oz

1 Break the chocolate into small pieces. Drop it into a bowl over a pan of hot water and stir until melted.
2 Add the banana chips and stir well. Use a spoon to drop in small mounds onto a baking sheet. Leave to cool then store in an airtight container.

Note: A carob bar can be used instead of the chocolate, or alternatively, use white chocolate. Vegans should use plain chocolate, and check that the banana chips have not been sweetened with honey.

Candied Peel and Coconut Cakes

85g (3 oz)	candied peel	3 oz
85g (3 oz)	desiccated coconut	1 cup
3 tbs	soya flour	3 tbs
½ tsp	ground cardamom	½ tsp
3 tbs	maple syrup	3 tbs
	rice paper	

1 Chop the peel as finely as possible, then combine with the coconut, soya flour and cardamom. Stir in enough maple syrup to bind the ingredients to make a fairly firm mixture.
2 Roll pieces into balls, flatten them between sheets of rice paper and trim the edges.

Note: These will keep for approximately a week if stored in an airtight container in the cool. Chopped apricots or other dried fruits can be used instead of candied peel.

Walnut Bites

85g (3 oz)	walnuts, ground	¾ cup
85g (3 oz)	caster sugar	½ cup
1 tbs	margarine	1 tbs
2 tbs	strong coffee	2 tbs

1 Put the walnuts into a bowl, add the sugar and margarine and mix well. Stir in the coffee.
2 Divide the mixture into small even–sized pieces and roll into balls. (If the mixture is too sticky to handle, coat hands with extra caster sugar or add some more nuts to the basic mixture.) Chill the balls for several hours. Eat within a couple of days.

Note: Use black coffee or, if you prefer, concentrated fruit juice.

Almond Apricot Slices

140g (5 oz)	dried apricots, soaked overnight	1 cup
55g (2 oz)	almonds, ground	½ cup
1 tbs	finely-grated orange peel	1 tbs
1-2 tbs	concentrated orange juice	1-2 tbs
30g (1 oz)	almonds, flaked, lightly crushed	¼ cup

1 Drain the apricots well, then chop and mash them to make a coarse purée. (If they seem very firm, cook briefly first.)
2 Mix together the apricots, ground almonds and peel, adding enough juice to bind the ingredients. Divide into two pieces and shape into small sausage shapes, rolling them in the almond flakes. Wrap each one in cling–film and chill well. Serve cut into slices.

Note: These are also delicious made with dried pears.

Tahini Treats

175g (8 oz)	tahini	⅔ cup
3 tbs	honey or syrup	3 tbs
85g (3 oz)	sunflower seeds, ground	½ cup
85g (3 oz)	raisins	½ cup
1 tsp	banana essence	1 tsp
55g (2 oz)	wheatgerm	½ cup
55g (2 oz)	banana chips, lightly crushed	⅔ cup

1 Blend together the tahini, sweetener, sunflower seeds, raisins and banana essence, mixing well. Add enough wheatgerm to firm up the mixture.
2 Break off into small pieces, roll into balls and coat with banana chips. Chill before serving.

Note: For a change, try replacing the wheatgerm with desiccated coconut, then rolling the balls in more crushed roasted coconut flakes.

Brazilian Mix

115g (4 oz)	Brazil nuts, coarsely chopped	1 cup
55g (2 oz)	cashew pieces	½ cup
55g (2 oz)	banana chips	⅔ cup
55g (2 oz)	preserved pineapple, chopped	⅓ cup
55g (2 oz)	dried mangoes, chopped	⅓ cup
115g (4 oz)	raisins	⅔ cup
30g (1 oz)	pumpkin seeds	2 tbs

1 Simply mix all the ingredients together and store in an airtight container until needed. This snack is lovely to pick at when hungry, to put in children's lunchboxes, or to take when out walking. It can also be sprinkled over sorbets, fruit crumbles, and so on.

Note: Although Brazil nut pieces can be purchased, and are usually cheaper than whole nuts, make sure they are fresh before buying – once cut these fatty nuts can easily lose their taste. Make up other mixes using any fruits and nuts you have handy.

Peanut Sugar Puffs

55g (2 oz)	peanuts	3½ tbs
1 large	free-range egg white	1 large
85g (3 oz)	caster sugar	½ cup

1 Remove the skins from the peanuts. If this is difficult, roast them briefly in the oven so that the skins brown and shrivel.
2 Beat the egg white until just beginning to stiffen, then stir in enough powdered sugar so that the mixture is the right consistency for coating the back of a spoon.
3 Cover a baking sheet with foil. Use a spoon to dip some of the nuts into the egg and sugar mixture, then place them on the sheet in a mound. Repeat, using the remaining ingredients. Bake at 180°C/350°F (Gas Mark 4) for 5 minutes, or until the coating is lightly browned. Allow to cool on the tray, then transfer to an airtight container. Eat within a few days.

Note: Other nuts can be used in the same way.

Peppermint Cream Carob Truffles

55g (2 oz)	carob bar, broken up	2 oz
2 tbs	crème fraîche	2 tbs
½-1 tsp	peppermint essence	½-1 tsp
115g (4 oz)	caster sugar	⅔ cup
	carob powder to coat	

1 Put the carob pieces into the top of a double boiler, or a bowl over a saucepan of boiling water, and stir until melted.
2 Remove from the heat, stir in the crème fraîche, peppermint essence to taste and sugar. Mix well before transferring the mixture to a plate and leaving to cool.
3 Break into small even-sized pieces, roll into balls and dip in the carob powder. Place in paper cases and chill well.

Note: Although a good alternative to the more conventional truffles, these are very rich. Serve with after-dinner coffee. As an alternative, use a peppermint flavoured carob bar and omit the peppermint essence. However, the flavour will be milder.

Stuffed Dates

20	whole dried dates	20
4	Brazil nuts	4
8	hazelnuts	8
small piece	marzipan	small piece
2 tbs	desiccated coconut	2 tbs
1 tbs	honey or syrup	1 tbs
30g (1 oz)	low fat cream cheese	2 tbs
	caster sugar - optional	

1 Wipe the dates clean, then pat dry. Carefully split them and remove the stones.
2 Use the Brazil nuts to stuff four of the dates, put two hazelnuts together in each of four more. Cut the marzipan into four small chunks and use to stuff four more dates.
3 Mix the coconut with the honey or syrup and pile into four more dates, then divide the cheese between the remaining dates. If liked, roll all the dates lightly in the sugar before arranging them on a plate and chilling briefly. Eat within a day of preparation.

Note: For an even more attractive display, use a variety of other dried fruits as well as dates. Figs are good, and whole apricots will add colour.

Granola Balls

55g (2 oz)	butter or margarine	¼ cup
170g (6 oz)	dates, chopped	1 cup
1 tsp	ground cinnamon	1 tsp
115g (4 oz)	granola, shop bought or home-made (see page 62)	4 oz
55g (2 oz)	pecan nuts, coarsely chopped	½ cup

1 In a saucepan, melt the fat and stir in the dates and cinnamon, continuing to simmer and stir until you have a thick purée. Set aside to cool.
2 Add the granola and nuts, mixing well. Break off pieces and roll into balls. Set aside until firm.

Note: If liked, coat in desiccated coconut.

Peanut Butter Balls

3 tbs	peanut butter	3 tbs
2 tbs	skimmed milk powder	2 tbs
2 tbs	honey or syrup	2 tbs
30g (1 oz)	bread or cake crumbs	½ cup
1 tbs	finely-grated orange peel	1 tbs
30g (1 oz)	sesame seeds	¼ cup

1 Place the peanut butter in a bowl and mix well with the skimmed milk powder and sweetener. Add the crumbs to make a thick, dry mixture, similar to dough. Add the peel, making sure it is evenly distributed.
2 Break off small pieces and roll into balls. Coat with the seeds. Chill briefly before eating.

Note: To vary these high protein snacks, mix in raisins or use different coatings such as cocoa, carob or wheatgerm. For lunchboxes, press the mixture between sheets of rice paper and cut into bars.

Fruit and Nut Chocolate Fingers

115g (4 oz)	prunes	¾ cup
115g (4 oz)	apricots	¾ cup
115g (4 oz)	raisins	⅔ cup
115g (4 oz)	hazelnuts, roasted	¾ cup
1 medium	free-range egg white	1 medium
55g (2 oz)	chocolate	2 oz

1 Wipe the fruit clean, pat dry and remove the stones from the prunes. Chop all the fruit and nuts as finely as possible.
2 Lightly beat the egg white and use as much as is necessary to bind the fruit and nut mixture together. Press down into a small shallow tin that has been lined with foil, then smooth the top.

3 Break the chocolate into small pieces. Place in the top of a double boiler or a bowl over a pan of boiling water and stir until it melts to make a thick sauce. Use a knife to spread the chocolate evenly over the fruit mixture.
4 Set aside for at least 1 hour, then cut into fingers.

Note: To make these bars more substantial, add cake crumbs to the fruit mixture.

Pear 'Fudge'

115g (4 oz)	dried pears, chopped	1 cup
2 tbs	lemon juice	2 tbs
140ml (¼ pt)	water	⅔ cup
30g (1 oz)	margarine	2½ tbs
30g (1 oz)	gram flour	¼ cup

1 Combine the pears, lemon juice and water in a saucepan, bring gently to the boil and continue cooking, stirring continually, for 5 minutes or until the pears become mushy.
2 In another pan, melt the margarine, add the gram flour, stir, and cook for a few minutes. Remove from the heat, add the pears, and use a wooden spoon to mix thoroughly.
3 Spoon into a small shallow tin, smooth the top, and leave to cool completely. Cut into squares to serve.

Note: This is an ideal sweet for lunch boxes, or to take backpacking. Gram flour is made from dried pulses, so adds protein as well as a distinctive flavour. For a sweeter flavoured 'fudge' add a spoonful or two of syrup or honey.

Pineapple Jelly Cubes

30g (1 oz)	agar agar	2 tbs
285ml (½ pt)	pineapple juice	1⅓ cups
	caster sugar	

1 Mix the agar agar with a drop of the pineapple juice. Put the rest into a small saucepan and bring to the boil gently, then add the agar agar and stir well. Heat gently, stirring continually, until the mixture reaches boiling point, then continue boiling for a few more minutes. Set aside to cook.
2 Pour the mixture into a shallow tray (wet it first, then pour off any excess water). Leave until cool and firm. Cut into squares and roll in the sugar. Keep cool and eat within a week, preferably sooner.

Note: Use only pure, unsweetened pineapple juice – or other juices such as grape or apple. These little sweets are quick and easy to make.

Banana Popsicles

2 large	bananas	2 large
1 tbs	lemon juice	1 tbs
2 tbs	rice syrup	2 tbs
2 tbs	desiccated coconut	2 tbs

1 Peel the bananas and cut in half to make four short chunks. Press a popsicle stick into each one, then brush the banana lightly with syrup and roll in the coconut.
2 Place on a sheet of foil on a baking sheet and leave in the freezer until firm. If they are to be left for some time, wrap individually in silver foil once they are firm.

Note: These are like a cross between fruit and ice cream. The rice syrup gives them their special flavour, but you can use other syrups or honey instead. Alternatively, coat the bananas with sugar instead of coconut. Choose bananas that are almost ripe, but still firm.

8
Suet and Other Winter Puddings

Cold days are a perfect excuse for the sweet and stodgy puddings so many of us grew up with. Yet, while the recipes that follow may appear to be rich in calories and fats, most of them are not. Instead, they contain good, nourishing ingredients to keep you going, as well as a combination of flavours and textures that will satisfy the sweetest tooth.

One secret is the use of vegetarian suet which gives similar results to beef suet, yet is derived entirely from vegetable sources.

When steaming puddings, make sure that the saucepan doesn't boil dry, and if you need to top up do so with freshly boiled water. Suet and steamed puddings taste best served piping hot.

Ricotta Pudding

285 (10 oz)	ricotta cheese	1¼ cups
55g (2 oz)	sugar	⅓ cup
85g (3 oz)	almonds, ground	¾ cup
2 tbs	grated orange peel	2 tbs
4 large	free-range egg whites	4 large
55g (2 oz)	wholemeal (wholewheat) breadcrumbs fruit or chocolate sauce (see page 110)	1 cup

1 Press the cheese through a strainer into a bowl. Stir in the sugar, almonds and peel. Lightly whisk the egg whites and add to the other ingredients.
2 Pour into a lightly-greased, medium-sized ovenproof dish. Scatter with the breadcrumbs. Bake at 190°C/350°F (Gas Mark 4) for 30 minutes, or until firm. Serve hot, cut into squares and topped with a sauce of your choice.

Note: Curd cheese may be used instead of ricotta.

Exotic Rice Pudding

85g (3 oz)	sweet brown rice	⅓ cup
570ml (1 pt)	soya milk	2½ cups
2 tbs	rosewater	2 tbs
30g (1 oz)	sugar - optional	2 tbs
55g (2 oz)	sultanas (golden seedless raisins)	⅓ cup
55g (2 oz)	pistachio nuts, coarsely chopped	½ cup

1 Drop the rice into a pan of boiling water and cook for 10 minutes, then drain well.
2 Grease a medium-sized ovenproof dish. Stir together the drained rice, milk, rosewater, sugar, sultanas and nuts and spoon into the prepared dish, smoothing the top.
3 Bake at 150°C/300°F (Gas Mark 2) for 45 to 60 minutes, or until browned on top. Serve hot.

Note: Sweet brown rice is especially suitable when you want to reduce the amount of sugar used in a dish and can be found in wholefood shops. Brown short grain rice may be used instead, but you might need to add a little more sweetening.

Creamed Rice with Wild Apricot Sauce

115g (4 oz)	sweet brown rice	½ cup
425ml (¾ pt)	soya milk	2 cups
55g (2 oz)	sugar, or to taste	⅓ cup
1 tbs	margarine	1 tbs
½ tsp	ground nutmeg	½ tsp
1 tsp	ground cinnamon	1 tsp
6 tbs	Wild Apricot Spread (see page 113)	6 tbs
	warm water or orange juice	

1 Add the rice to boiling water and cook for 10 minutes, then drain well.
2 In another saucepan, gently heat the milk until almost boiling, then stir in the rice and cook gently for 10 more minutes.
3 Add the sugar, margarine and spices and continue cooking until the rice is soft.
4 Meanwhile, stir together the Wild Apricot Spread and water or orange juice to make a sauce of pouring consistency. If liked, heat this gently.
5 Divide the rice between four small bowls and stir in a little of the Wild Apricot Sauce to give a marbled effect. Serve at once.

Note: For note on rice *see* previous recipe. Any fruit spread or purée may be used instead of the one suggested. Creamed rice is also good served cold, topped with whipped cream and roasted flaked almonds.

Fruit and Nut Bread Pudding

170g (6 oz)	wholemeal (wholewheat) breadcrumbs	3 cups
285ml (½ pt)	milk	1⅓ cups
1 tsp	almond essence	1 tsp
2 tbs	vegetable oil	2 tbs
115g (4 oz)	mixed dried fruit (e.g. raisins, apricots, dates, etc.)	⅔ cup
1 tbs	orange peel, finely chopped	1 tbs
55g (2 oz)	flaked almonds	½ cup

1 Place the breadcrumbs in a bowl, pour over the milk, and leave to soak for 30 minutes or until the milk has been absorbed.
2 Stir in the almond essence, vegetable oil, fruit and peel, mixing well.
3 Grease a small, square tin, spoon in the mixture and smooth the top. Sprinkle with the flaked almonds. Bake at 200°C/400°F (Gas Mark 6) for 20 minutes, or until firm to touch.
4 Serve warm, cut into squares or transfer to a wire rack and leave to cool.

Note: Bread pudding is usually accompanied by custard but is also lovely with crème fraîche. As it is traditionally made with eggs, one or two may be added with the dried fruit for a firmer texture.

Spotted Dick

85g (3 oz)	wholemeal (wholewheat) flour	¾ cup
1 tsp	baking powder	1 tsp
85g (3 oz)	wholemeal (wholewheat) breadcrumbs	1½ cups
85g (3 oz)	vegetarian suet, grated	⅓ cup
55g (2 oz)	sugar	⅓ cup
115g (4 oz)	currants	⅔ cup
55g (2 oz)	mixed peel - optional	⅓ cup
	cold water to mix	
	vanilla soya dessert to serve	

1 Mix together the flour, baking powder, breadcrumbs, suet and sugar. Add the currants and peel with enough water to make a fairly firm dough. Wrap in foil and chill for 30 minutes.
2 Roll this out onto a floured board to make a large rectangle, and dot with the currants (and peel if using it) before rolling up lengthways. Lay this on a piece of silver foil and fold the foil around it securely but loosely, fastening the ends.
3 Steam the roll for 1½–2 hours making sure that the water does not boil dry. Serve hot, cut into generous slices. A packet of vanilla soya dessert, warmed, makes a quick and tasty topping.

Note: Use chopped dates instead of currants for a change.

Sussex Pond Pudding

225g (8 oz)	wholemeal (wholewheat) flour	2 cups
½ tsp	baking powder	½ tsp
½ tsp	ground mixed spice	½ tsp
85g (3 oz)	vegetarian suet, grated	⅓ cup
85g (3 oz)	sugar	½ cup
1 large	lemon, well scrubbed	1 large

1 Sift together the flour, baking powder and spices. Stir in the suet. Add enough cold water to bind to a fairly firm dough, wrap in foil and chill for 30 minutes. Roll out to make a large circle.
2 Grease a small pudding basin, then use the dough to line it, letting the excess dough hang over the edge temporarily.

3 Dry the lemon and prick it all over with a needle or fine skewer. Sprinkle half of the sugar into the hollow in the dough, add the lemon and sprinkle with the remaining sugar. Carefully fold the dough across the top and press gently but firmly to seal.

4 Cover with greased foil and tie down. Stand in a large saucepan, filled with enough boiling water to come half way up the bowl and cover. Steam for 2 hours, making sure that the water doesn't boil dry.

5 When cooked, serve cut into wedges. Make sure everyone has some of the lemon, and the lemony sauce that will ooze out once the pastry is cut.

Note: Although traditionally made with lemon, orange, grapefruit or lime may be used for a change.

Steamed Ginger Puddings with Cream

55g (2 oz)	wholemeal (wholewheat) breadcrumbs	1 cup
115g (4 oz)	wholemeal (wholewheat) flour	1 cup
1 tsp	baking powder	1 tsp
1 tsp	bicarbonate of soda	1 tsp
1 tsp	ground ginger	1 tsp
115g (4 oz)	sugar	⅔ cup
115g (4 oz)	vegetarian suet, grated	½ cup
200ml (⅓ pt)	milk	¾ cup
1-2 tbs	preserved stem ginger, chopped	1-2 tbs
2 tbs	syrup in which ginger was preserved	2 tbs
140ml (¼ pt)	whipping cream	⅔ cup

1 Stir together the breadcrumbs, flour, baking powder, bicarbonate of soda, ginger and sugar. Add the suet then stir in the milk to make a heavy, moist mixture. Add the chopped ginger together with 1 tablespoon of the syrup.

2 Grease four small ramekins or heatproof dishes, spoon in the mixture and cover each one with foil. Place in a large saucepan and pour in hot water to reach half way up the ramekins. Cover and steam for 1 hour or until the puddings are firm, making sure that the water doesn't boil dry.

3 Whip the cream together with the remaining tablespoon of ginger syrup. Serve with the hot puddings.

Wheat Berry Dessert

170g (6 oz)	wholewheat berries	¾ cup
285ml (½ pt)	milk	1⅓ cups
1 tsp	ground cinnamon	1 tsp
115g (4 oz)	dried apricots, finely chopped	1 cup
2 tbs	honey	2 tbs

1 Rinse the berries well, then add to a pan of water, bring to the boil, cover, and leave to stand for an hour. Drain well.

2 Stir together the grains, milk, cinnamon, apricot pieces and sweetener. Cook in a saucepan for 30 minutes or until the grains are tender, making sure they do not boil dry. Alternatively, turn into a greased ovenproof dish and bake at 180°C/350°F (Gas Mark 4) for 45 minutes or until cooked.

Note: This is rather like rice pudding but with a much chewier texture. Use other dried fruit instead of the apricots, if liked, and adjust the sweetness as necessary. Syrup may be used instead of honey.

Aduki and Apple Pie

Pastry

225g (8 oz)	wholemeal (wholewheat) flour	2 cups
115g (4 oz)	margarine	½ cup
2-3 tbs	cold water	2-3 tbs

Filling

225g (8 oz)	cooked aduki beans, drained	8 oz
2 medium	apples, cored and coarsely chopped	2 medium
85g (3 oz)	raisins	½ cup
85g (3 oz)	walnuts, chopped	¾ cup
1 tbs	lemon peel, grated	1 tbs
2-3 tbs	Pear and Apple Spread	2-3 tbs

1 Put the flour into a bowl, rub in the fat to make a mixture like fine crumbs, then add just enough water to bind to a dough. Wrap in foil and chill for 30 minutes. Set aside a quarter of the dough, roll out the rest and use to line a shallow pie or flan dish.

2 Mix together the beans, apples, raisins, walnuts, lemon peel and spread. If necessary, add one or two spoonfuls of water to moisten the mixture, but make sure it's not too wet or it will seep through the pastry. Turn into the prepared base.

3 Roll out the remaining pastry and use to make a topping, pressing the edges together gently but firmly. Prick the top lightly with a fork.

4 Bake at 200°C/400°F (Gas Mark 6) for 20 minutes or until the pastry is cooked. Serve at once.

Note: This is an unusual but very tasty combination. Remember, you can use previously cooked, frozen or canned aduki beans.

Lemon Suet Puddings

115g (4 oz)	81% wholemeal (wholewheat) flour	1 cup
1 tsp	baking powder	1 tsp
55g (2 oz)	vegetarian suet, shredded	¼ cup
30g (1 oz)	sugar	2 tbs
1 tbs	lemon peel, grated	1 tbs
2 tbs	lemon juice	2 tbs
1 medium	free-range egg, beaten	1 medium
3 tbs	milk	3 tbs
	Hot Lemon Sauce to serve (see page 111)	

1 Sift the flour into a bowl, then stir in the suet, sugar and lemon peel.
2 Whisk together the lemon juice, egg and milk, and add to the first mixture, stirring well. The resulting mix should have a soft dropping consistency – if necessary, add a little more milk.
3 Lightly grease 4 individual soufflé dishes or old cups. Divide the mixture between them and cover each with greased foil. Stand in a large heavy-based saucepan and pour in enough boiling water to come half way up the sides of the dishes. Cover the pan and steam the puddings for 30 minutes, making sure that the saucepan does not boil dry.
4 Meanwhile, make the sauce. Carefully remove the puddings from the dishes, put each one on a small plate, and either top with some of the sauce or serve it in a jug for everyone to help themselves.

Note: Although you can use 100% wholemeal flour, 81% flour gives these puddings a lighter texture. Other sauces can be used instead of the Hot Lemon Sauce, or, for an instant sauce, simply add hot water to Lemon Curd.

Macaroni Bake

115g (4 oz)	wholemeal (wholewheat) macaroni	1 cup
570ml (1 pt)	milk	2½ cups
55g (2 oz)	sugar	⅓ cup
1 large	free-range egg, lightly beaten	1 large
30g (1 oz)	wholemeal (wholewheat) breadcrumbs	½ cup
30g (1 oz)	margarine, melted	2½ tbs

1 Place the macaroni, milk and half the sugar in a saucepan, bring to the boil and cook for a few minutes.
2 Add the egg and transfer the mixture to an ovenproof dish. Stir together the breadcrumbs, margarine and remaining sugar and sprinkle over the macaroni. Bake at 180°C/350°F (Gas Mark 4) for 30 minutes or until the macaroni is tender.

Note: A really nourishing winter pud, this may be made in the same way with rice, semolina, tapioca or other grains.

Ginger Biscuit Log

285ml (½ pt)	crème fraîche or Quark	1⅓ cups
225g (8 oz)	wholemeal (wholewheat) ginger biscuits	8 oz
	fresh fruit (e.g. grapes, crushed pineapple etc.)	

1 Beat the crème fraîche until thick and smooth. Use it to bind the biscuits to form a log, spreading any extra cream along the outer edges. Wrap in silver foil and chill well, preferably overnight.
2 Before serving, cut diagonally into chunks and top with fresh fruit – grapes and pineapple make a pleasing contrast.

Note: Serve this easy and inexpensive dish at the end of a light meal – although not hot it's certainly rich and filling! For special occasions, top with exotic fruit such as kiwi and Cape gooseberries moistened with a little liqueur.

Apple Dumplings

4 medium	dessert apples	4 medium
55g (2 oz)	dates, chopped	⅓ cup
1 tbs	concentrated apple juice	1 tbs
225g (8 oz)	wholemeal (wholewheat) flour	2 cups
115g (4 oz)	margarine	½ cup
1 tbs	sugar	1 tbs
2-3 tbs	cold water	2-3 tbs
	soya 'creem' to serve	

1 Use a sharp knife to remove the cores from the apples, then cut a shallow line around the outside (this stops them bursting). Stir together the dates and juice and use the mixture to fill the centres of the apples.
2 Use fingertips to rub the fat into the flour to make a crumb-like mixture, then add enough water to make a dough. Wrap in foil and chill for 30 minutes.
3 Break the dough into 4 even-sized pieces and roll them out into large circles. Place an apple on each, then mould the dough around the fruit, dampening and pressing the edges together to make neat parcels.
4 Transfer to a baking sheet. Bake at 200°C/400°F (Gas Mark 6) for 30 minutes. Serve hot with soya 'creem'.

Note: Other fillings such as fruit, nuts, candied peel etc may be used, moistened with syrup, honey or melted margarine. For a simpler dish, cook the apples without pastry at a lower oven temperature, basting the fruit with a syrup occasionally.

Sweet Yorkshire Puddings

115g (4 oz)	wholemeal (wholewheat) flour	1 cup
1 medium	free-range egg, lightly beaten	1 medium
285ml (½ pt)	milk and water Dried Fruit Compôte (see page 86)	1⅓ cups
55g (2 oz)	Brazil nuts, coarsely chopped custard to serve	½ cup

1 Sift the flour into a bowl, make a hollow in the centre then add the egg and stir. Add some of the milk and water and stir to make a paste, then add the rest and whisk to make a thick smooth sauce. Leave to stand in the cool for 30 minutes.
2 Combine the dried fruit and chopped nuts. Drain off any excess liquid.
3 Lightly grease four Yorkshire pudding tins. Divide the batter between them and add some of the fruit mixture to each. Bake at 200°C/425°F (Gas Mark 7) for 5 minutes or until beginning to rise, then lower the heat to 180°C/350°F (Gas Mark 4) and cook for about 10 more minutes. Serve at once with custard.

Note: For a sweeter batter replace the milk and water with apple juice. Fresh fruit may be used instead of dried.

Coconut Brown Betty

85g (3 oz)	margarine	⅓ cup
170g (6 oz)	wholemeal (wholewheat) breadcrumbs	3 cups
2 large	apples, cored and sliced	2 large
2 large	bananas, peeled and sliced	2 large
55g (2 oz)	sugar	⅓ cup
1 tsp	ground mixed spice	1 tsp
85g (3 oz)	desiccated coconut	1 cup
4 tbs	orange juice	4 tbs
4 tbs	water	4 tbs

1 Melt 55g/2 oz of the margarine, add the breadcrumbs and mix well.
2 Grease a pie or soufflé dish and sprinkle with some of the crumbs. Make alternate layers of the fruit and crumbs, sprinkling each one with some of the sugar, spice and coconut. Finish with a layer of crumbs. Combine the orange juice and water and sprinkle over the dish, then dot with knobs of the remaining margarine.
3 Bake at 180°C/350°F (Gas Mark 4) for 45 minutes, or until the apple is cooked and the crumbs browned. Serve hot.

Note: Traditionally this dish is steamed – but allow about 1½ hours to cook it this way. Other fruits may be used instead of the apples and bananas, such as stewed rhubarb or plums but drain them well first.

Pumpkin Creams

2½ lbs	pumpkin, peeled and seeded	2½ lbs
3 tbs	vegetable oil	3 tbs
3 tbs	honey	3 tbs
½ tsp	ground nutmeg	½ tsp
½ tsp	ground ginger	½ tsp
1 tsp	ground mixed spice	1 tsp
3 tbs	tahini	3 tbs
2 medium	free-range eggs, lightly beaten	2 medium
3 tbs	candied peel, chopped dairy or soya cream to serve	3 tbs

1 Cut the pumpkin into small pieces and steam until tender. Drain well, mash to a purée, then drain again.
2 Stir together the pumpkin, vegetable oil, honey, spices, tahini, eggs and peel. Lightly grease four small heatproof dishes and divide the mixture between them.
3 Bake at 180°C/350°F (Gas Mark 4) for 40 to 50 minutes, or until just set – do not overcook. Serve with single cream.

Note: Smooth, subtly flavoured, and easy to eat, these may be flavoured with vanilla essence instead of spice or a tablespoon of ground almonds instead of tahini.

Blueberry Cobbler with Soya Custard

55g (2 oz)	sugar	⅓ cup
140ml (¼ pt)	orange juice	⅔ cup
12 oz	blueberries, cleaned	12 oz
1 tbs	arrowroot	1 tbs
55g (2 oz)	wholemeal (wholewheat) flour	½ cup
1 tsp	baking powder	1 tsp
3 tbs	vegetable oil cold water	3 tbs
1 tbs	sugar	1 tbs
285ml (½ pt)	soya custard	1⅓ cups
3 tbs	soya 'cream', optional	3 tbs

1 Stir together the sugar and orange juice, then simmer until the sugar dissolves. Add the blueberries and cook briefly until just tender. Stir the arrowroot into a tablespoon of water to make a paste then add to the blueberries and continue cooking until the sauce thickens. Transfer to a small ovenproof dish.

2 Make a dough by sifting together the flour and baking powder, then stirring in the oil and enough cold water to bind. Wrap in foil and chill for 30 minutes.

3 Roll out the dough to make a circle and cut into wedges. Arrange these on top of the fruit and sprinkle with the extra sugar. Bake at 220°C/425°F (Gas Mark 7) for 20 to 30 minutes, or until the pastry is brown. Serve at once topped with hot custard.

Note: If adding soya 'cream' to the custard, do so away from the heat.

Carrot and Almond Pudding

Pudding

2 medium	carrots, peeled and grated	2 medium
55g (2 oz)	wholemeal (wholewheat) breadcrumbs	1 cup
55g (2 oz)	wholemeal flour	½ cup
55g (2 oz)	almonds, ground	½ cup
½-1 tsp	ground cardamom	½-1 tsp
2 tbs	milk	2 tbs
2 medium	free-range eggs, separated	2 medium
30g (1 oz)	almonds, flaked	¼ cup

Sauce

285ml (½ pt)	orange juice	1⅓ cups
1 tbs	syrup	1 tbs
1 flat tbs	cornflour	1 flat tbs

1 Mix together the grated carrot, breadcrumbs, flour, almonds, spice, milk and egg yolks. Whisk the egg whites until stiff and use a metal spoon to fold them into the first mixture.

2 Pour into a greased, medium-sized pudding basin, cover with greased foil, and stand in a large saucepan. Pour enough hot water into the pan to come half way up the basin, cover the pan and steam for 1½ hours.

3 Make the sauce by combining most of the orange juice and syrup in a small saucepan and bringing gently to boiling point. Stir the cornflour with the remaining juice and add to the pan. Heat, stirring continually, until the sauce thickens.

4 Serve cut into slices and topped with a few spoonfuls of sauce.

Note: Both crème fraîche and sour cream make quick toppings which go well with this pudding. Alternatively, use a nut cream (see page 109), making a pouring consistency by mixing it with warmed orange juice.

Semolina and Date Pudding

570ml (1 pt)	milk	2½ cups
30g (1 oz)	margarine	2 tbs
115g (4 oz)	sugar	⅔ cup
55g (2 oz)	semolina	½ cup
85g (3 oz)	dates, chopped	½ cup
1 tsp	ground cinnamon	1 tsp
30g (1 oz)	walnuts, coarsely chopped	½ cup

1 Bring the milk to the boil, add the margarine and half the sugar, and stir until dissolved. Whisk in the semolina and then heat gently, stirring continually, until the mixture thickens.

2 Stir in the dates. Transfer the mixture to a small ovenproof dish. Mix the remaining sugar, spice and walnuts and scatter over the top. Bake at 140°C/275°F (Gas Mark 1) for 30 minutes or until cooked.

Note: Semolina can also be cooked in a saucepan but it has a better flavour and texture when cooked for longer and at a lower temperature, as described above. Unrefined semolina can be found in wholefood and healthfood shops.

Steamed Chocolate Sponge Pudding

Pudding

55g (2 oz)	wholemeal (wholewheat) flour	½ cup
1 tsp	baking powder	1 tsp
2 tbs	cocoa powder	2 tbs
55g (2 oz)	wholemeal (wholewheat) breadcrumbs	1 cup
55g (2 oz)	sugar	⅓ cup
55g (2 oz)	vegetarian suet, grated	¼ cup
½ tsp	vanilla essence	½ tsp
55g (2 oz)	hazelnuts, roasted and ground	½ cup
2-4 tbs	soya milk	2-4 tbs

White sauce

1 tbs	cornflour	1 tbs
285ml (½ pt)	soya milk	1⅓ cups
30g (1 oz)	sugar	2 tbs
½ tsp	vanilla essence, or to taste	½ tsp

1 Sift together the flour, baking and cocoa powders. Add the breadcrumbs, sugar, suet, vanilla essence, ground nuts, plus enough soya milk to make a mixture with a soft sticky consistency.

2 Grease a medium-sized pudding basin, add the mix and cover with foil. Stand in a large pan, pour in hot water to come half way up the basin, cover the saucepan.

Steam for 1 to 1½ hours, or until just cooked. Add extra boiling water as necessary.

3 Meanwhile, make the sauce. Stir the cornflour into a spoonful of the milk. Put the rest of the milk into a saucepan, bring to the boil, then add the cornflour and vanilla essence and continue heating gently until the sauce thickens.

4 Serve the pudding in slices, topped with the hot sauce.

Note: To make a carob sponge, replace the cocoa with carob powder.

Coconutty Baked Bananas

2 tbs	lemon juice	2 tbs
4 tbs	orange juice	4 tbs
2 tbs	maple syrup	2 tbs
2 tbs	coconut powder, or to taste	2 tbs
4 medium	bananas, peeled and halved lengthways	4 medium
2 tbs	flaked coconut soya cream to serve	2 tbs

1 Stir together the lemon and orange juices and the maple syrup, and heat gently. Whisk in the coconut powder.

2 Put the bananas, cut side down, in a shallow heatproof dish and spoon on the prepared syrup. Sprinkle with flaked coconuts. Bake at 180°C/350°F (Gas Mark 4) for 15 minutes, or until heated right through, basting with the juice several times while cooking.

3 Serve hot with cool, smooth cream for a contrast.

Note: To make the sauce thicker and more coconutty, use more powder, but do not make it too thick or the bananas will be unable to absorb it.

Quinoa with Pineapple and Mint

115g (4 oz)	quinoa	½ cup
340ml (⅔ pt)	water	1½ cups
200ml (⅓ pt)	pineapple juice	¾ cup
½ tsp	ground nutmeeg	½ tsp
½ tsp	ground cinnamon	½ tsp
4 slices	pineapple, crushed fresh mint to garnish	4 slices

1 Rinse and drain the quinoa. Combine the water and pineapple juice, bring to the boil, then stir in the quinoa, cover the pan, and simmer for 30 minutes. The quinoa should be creamy smooth and all the liquid should have been absorbed (if not, drain it).

2 Add the crushed pineapple and leave for just a few minutes to heat through. Divide between four bowls and serve at once, garnished with sprigs of fresh mint.

Note: Quinoa is an unusual grain with a distinctive look and subtle taste. For a crunchier texture, cook it for half the time and reduce the liquid slightly. Use dairy or soya milk instead of water, and add other fruits or fruit purées as an alternative to pineapple.

Soufflé Omelette

6 medium	free-range eggs, separated	6 medium
4 tbs	water	4 tbs
55g (2 oz)	sugar	⅓ cup
2 tbs	pecan nuts, coarsely chopped	2 tbs
	vegetable oil for frying	
	extra sugar	
	raw cane sugar jam - optional	

1 Beat the egg yolks, water and sugar together. Whisk the egg whites and use a metal spoon to fold them into the first mixture, adding the nuts at the same time.

2 Heat a small amount of oil in a large, heavy–based pan. Pour in the mixture, tip the pan so that it spreads and cook gently until it is just beginning to set underneath.

3 Put the pan under a grill and continue cooking until the top is lightly browned and the omelette set. Sprinkle with sugar, cut into wedges, and serve at once.

Note: A spoonful of jam tastes surprisingly good with this sweet omelette.

Plum Upside-down Pudding

225g (8 oz)	plums, cleaned, halved and stoned	8 oz
115g (4 oz)	margarine	½ cup
115g (4 oz)	caster sugar	⅔ cup
2 medium	free-range eggs, lightly beaten	2 medium
115g (4 oz)	wholemeal (wholewheat) flour	1 cup
1 tsp	baking powder	1 tsp
140ml (¼ pt)	whipping cream	⅔ cup

1 Grease a medium–sized soufflé or other heatproof dish. Arrange the plum halves across the base, cut side down.

2 Cream together the margarine and sugar until light and fluffy. Gradually add the eggs, then the flour and baking powder. Carefully pour the mixture over the fruit and smooth the top.

3 Bake at 180°C/350°F (Gas Mark 4) for 50 minutes, or until set. Meanwhile, whip the cream.

4 To remove the pudding, run a knife around the side of the dish to loosen it, cover with a plate, then tip upside down. Serve with cream.

Note: A vegan version can be made by arranging the fruit in the same way, then topping with a grain such as couscous or rice mixed with fruit juice, and cooking as above. The pudding will have a less firm texture but will still taste delicious.

Marmalade Roll

225g (8 oz)	wholemeal (wholewheat) flour	2 cups
2 tsp	baking powder	2 tsp
115g (4 oz)	vegetarian suet, grated	½ cup
55g (2 oz)	sugar	⅓ cup
3-4 tbs	cold water	3-4 tbs
4-8 tbs	marmalade	4-8 tbs

1 Sift the flour and baking powder together into a bowl, then use a knife to stir in the suet before adding enough cold water to make a stiff pastry. Knead briefly then wrap in foil and chill for 30 minutes.

2 Roll out thinly to make an oblong and spread with the marmalade, leaving a small gap along the edges. Turn in the side edges (to keep the marmalade from spilling out) and roll up lightly to form a roll. Transfer to a greased baking sheet.

3 Bake at 200°C/400°F (Gas Mark 6) for 20 minutes, then at 180°C/350°F (Gas Mark 4) for 15 minutes more.

Note: As an alternative to marmalade, fill with jam, mincemeat, thick fruit purée - whatever you fancy.

Pear Pie with Puff Pastry

4 medium	pears, peeled, cored and sliced	4 medium
3 tbs	lemon juice	3 tbs
1 tbs	lemon peel, grated	1 tbs
3 tbs	syrup, or to taste	3 tbs
3 tbs	raisins	3 tbs
225g (8 oz)	frozen puff pastry, defrosted	8 oz
	soya milk - optional	

1 Lightly grease a shallow, medium-sized heatproof dish, and arrange the pears across the base. Sprinkle with lemon juice and peel, trickle the syrup over the fruit and add the raisins.

2 Roll out the pastry and use to cover the other ingredients, pressing the edges against the dish, lightly but firmly. Decorate with any extra pieces. If liked, brush with milk. Bake at 200°C/400°F (Gas Mark 6) for 40 minutes, or until the pastry is cooked. Serve at once.

Note: The sweeter the pears, the less syrup you will need. You can also stir in a spoonful or two of tahini.

Gooseberry Almond Sponge

Sponge

455g (1 lb)	gooseberries, cleaned and trimmed	1 lb
2 tbs	honey	2 tbs
2 tbs	water	2 tbs

Topping

85g (3 oz)	margarine	⅓ cup
85g (3 oz)	sugar	½ cup
1 large	free-range egg, lightly beaten	1 large
115g (4 oz)	wholemeal (wholewheat) flour	1 cup
1 tsp	baking powder	1 tsp
1-2 tbs	lemon juice	1-2 tbs
5g (2 oz)	blanched almonds	½ cup
	thick yogurt or crème fraîche to serve	

1 Place the gooseberries in a heatproof dish, mix the honey and water and pour over the fruit.

2 Cream together the margarine and most of the sugar until light and smooth then add the egg. Sift together the flour and baking powder and fold into the first mixture, adding lemon juice to moisten.

3 Spoon the mixture over the gooseberries and smooth the top. Dot with the nuts and sprinkle with the remaining sugar. Bake at 180°C/350°F (Gas Mark 4) for 40 to 50 minutes, or until the sponge is just firm. Serve with yogurt or crème fraîche.

Note: Use other fruit or fruit combinations for variation.

Couscous Layer Pudding

570ml (1 pt)	apple or grape juice	2½ cups
115g (4 oz)	couscous	⅔ cup
1 tsp	ground cinnamon	1 tsp
455g (1 lb)	rhubarb, cleaned and cut into small pieces	1 lb
3-4 tbs	Pear and Apple Spread	3-4 tbs
1 tbs	lemon juice	1 tbs

1 Bring the fruit juice to the boil gently, add the couscous and cinnamon, lower the heat and cook for 5 minutes or until the grains are soft and all the liquid has been absorbed.

2 Meanwhile, cook the rhubarb with the Pear and Apple Spread and lemon juice, stirring frequently, until just cooked.

3 Spoon a layer of the couscous into a small greased heatproof dish, add a layer of rhubarb, and repeat until all the ingredients have been used up, finishing with couscous. Bake at 180°C/350°F (Gas Mark 4) for 20 to 30 minutes. Serve hot.

Note: For a firmer textured pudding, add an egg to the couscous. For a change, make an extra layer using custard, white sauce, or tofu and syrup blended together to make a sauce.

Yogurt Egg Custard

4 medium	free-range eggs	4 medium
55g (2 oz)	sugar	⅓ cup
285ml (½ pt)	yogurt	1⅓ cups
285ml (½ pt)	milk	1⅓ cups
½ tsp	vanilla essence	½ tsp
	freshly grated nutmeg	

1 Beat together the eggs and sugar, then add the yogurt, milk and vanilla essence. Pour into a small greased pie dish, sprinkle with the nutmeg.

2 Bake uncovered at 150°C/300°F (Gas Mark 2) for 45 minutes to 1 hour, or until a knife inserted in the centre comes out clean.

Note: You can use ready ground, but freshly grated nutmeg makes all the difference in this recipe. To speed up the cooking time, divide the mixture between four small dishes.

Traditional Christmas Pudding

115g (4 oz)	wholemeal (wholewheat) flour	1 cup
1 tsp	baking powder	1 tsp
85g (3 oz)	sugar	½ cup
115g (4 oz)	vegetarian suet, grated	½ cup
2 tbs	orange peel, grated	2 tbs
1 tbs	lemon peel, grated	1 tbs
170g (6 oz)	raisins	1 cup
170g (6 oz)	sultanas (golden seedless raisins)	1 cup
225g (8 oz)	currants	1⅓ cups
225g (8 oz)	prunes, stoned and chopped	2 cups
½ tsp	ground nutmeg	½ tsp
½ tsp	ground cinnamon	½ tsp
1 tsp	ground mixed spice	1 tsp
55g (2 oz)	wholemeal (wholewheat) breadcrumbs	1 cup
200ml (⅓ pt)	orange juice	¾ cup
	brandy 'butter' or soya custard to serve	

1 Sift together the flour and baking powder, add the sugar, suet, peel, dried fruit and spices. Soak the breadcrumbs in the juice and, when the liquid has been absorbed, add to the other ingredients and stir until thoroughly blended. The mixture should be fairly moist so if it seems too dry, add a little more juice or water.

2 Pack tightly into a greased, medium-sized basin, cover with foil and secure well. In a heavy pan with enough hot water to reach half way up the basin, steam covered for 3 hours, adding more hot water as necessary.

3 Eat at once, or cool and then freeze.

Note: This rich, fruity pudding keeps well. If freezing it, defrost completely and then cook for another 1 to 1½ hours. For vegan brandy 'butter', add sugar and brandy to a vegan block margarine.

Little Fig Puddings with Vanilla Cream

115g (4 oz)	dried figs, chopped	1 cup
1 tbs	lemon juice	1 tbs
1 tbs	lemon peel, grated	1 tbs
1 small	cooking apple, peeled, cored and finely grated	1 small
3 tbs	water	3 tbs
3 tbs	brandy	3 tbs
30g (1 oz)	block margarine	2½ tbs
115g (4 oz)	sugar	⅔ cup
4 tbs	molasses	4 tbs
2 small	free-range eggs, lightly beaten	2 small
160g (6 oz)	wholemeal (wholewheat) flour	1½ cups
1 tsp	baking powder	1 tsp
½ tsp	ground cinnamon	½ tsp
1 tsp	ground mixed spice	1 tsp
55g (2 oz)	almonds, coarsely chopped	½ cup

Vanilla cream

200ml (⅓ pt)	crème fraîche or sour cream	¾ cup
1-2 tsp	caster sugar, or to taste	1-2 tsp
1-2 tsp	vanilla essence, or to taste	1-2 tsp

1 In a small saucepan, stir together the figs, lemon juice and peel, apple and water, and cook gently, stirring continually, until soft. Beat to make a purée, then add the brandy.

2 Cream together the softened margarine and sugar, add the molasses and then the eggs. Sift the flour, baking powder and spices and fold into the first mixture with the nuts.

3 Spoon the mixture into 6 to 8 small basins, press down firmly, then cover each one with foil and secure. Stand in a heatproof tray filled with hot water to come half way up the basins. Bake at 170°C/325°F (Gas Mark 3) for 2 hours, adding to the water as necessary.

4 Combine the crème fraîche or sour cream with the sugar and vanilla essence, chill briefly and serve with the hot puddings.

Note: Old cups may be used instead of basins. Use other dried fruits, as liked, or hazelnuts instead of almonds.

9
Cheesecakes

If desserts are considered to be indulgent, cheesecakes are undoubtedly top of the list. Yet this needn't be the case. The recipes that follow include traditional, exotic, baked and chilled cheesecakes - all of which are good for you! The main differences with these recipes are that they contain low fat rather than full fat cream cheese, sugar is kept to a minimum and any cereal used is unrefined. (The cheeses are interchangeable - look out for Quark, ricotta, low and medium fat soft cheeses and crème fraîche, but remember that they will not set as firmly as full fat soft cheese.) The chilled cheesecakes are set, not with gelatine, but with agar agar, a gelling agent made from seaweed. There is also a selection of vegan cheesecakes.

Some tips to remember

Although you can use a flan dish for cheesecakes, loose-bottomed tins that will gently push your cheesecake up are best as they reduce the risk of it being damaged. Alternatively, use a flan ring placed on a baking sheet, preferably lined with silver foil. To release the cheesecake, slide it off the baking sheet and stand it on, for example, the base of a small saucepan. The ring will then slide down and you can transfer the cheesecake to a serving dish.

When your cheesecake is cooked, leave it to cool in the oven with the door ajar. This will help to prevent cracks from forming across the top.

In the recipes that combine flour with the cheese, sieve out the bran (keep for use in another recipe) as this will affect the creamy texture.

Most of the following recipes are interchangeable, in that you can use just about any filling with the base of your choice. Crushed digestive biscuits and fat produce the traditional base - Mitchelhill are vegan so are ideal - but many more suitable biscuits are available. You may need to adjust the amount of fat used if, for example, you are using a very dry biscuit, or one containing extra fat of its own such as chocolate coated biscuits. Spread the mixture evenly and press gently with the back of a wet spoon so that it binds to make a firm crust. Chill briefly before adding the filling. If the filling is particularly moist and is not going to be cooked, cook the base in a moderate oven for 10 to 20 minutes to harden it, and so prevent the filling from seeping through.

A medium-sized flan ring (approx. 8 in wide) will make a cheesecake that serves 4 to 6 people, or even more if it is one of the richer versions.

Chocolate Nut Cheesecake

Base

225g (8 oz)	wholemeal (wholewheat) chocolate biscuits	8 oz
55g (2 oz)	margarine, melted	¼ cup
30g (1 oz)	hazelnuts, roasted and finely chopped	¼ cup

Filling

55g (2 oz)	margarine	¼ cup
115g (4 oz)	sugar	⅔ cup
455g (1 lb)	crème fraîche	2 cups
2 large	free-range eggs, beaten	2 large
2 tbs	wholemeal (wholewheat) flour	2 tbs
170g (6 oz)	chocolate, chopped into pieces	6 oz
140ml (¼ pt)	sour cream	⅔ cup
30g (1 oz)	hazelnuts, roasted and chopped	¼ cup

1 Crush the biscuits and stir into the margarine with the hazelnuts, mixing well. Use the mixture to line the base and sides of your prepared flan dish (see chapter introduction).

2 Beat together the margarine and sugar until light and fluffy, then add the crème fraîche and flour. Gradually add the eggs, beating well after each addition.

3 Place the chocolate in a bowl over a pan of hot water and stir gently until it melts. Add this to the first mixture and stir in the sour cream.

4 Pile the filling into the prepared base. Sprinkle with the remaining nuts and bake at 170°C/325°F (Gas Mark 3) for 45 minutes or until firm. Allow to cool in the oven.

Note: A ring of whipped cream on top (mix it with some thick yogurt to lower the fat content) adds visual interest as well as providing a soft moist contrast to the rather heavy texture of the cake itself. Use a carob bar instead of chocolate, if liked.

Red Fruit Cheesecake

Base

170g (6 oz)	wholemeal digestive biscuits	6 oz
55g (2 oz)	margarine, melted	¼ cup
½ tsp	ground cinnamon	½ tsp

Filling

140ml (¼ pt)	yogurt	⅔ cup
225g (8 oz)	Quark	1 cup
2 medium	free-range eggs, separated	2 medium
55g (2 oz)	sugar	⅓ cup
1 tsp	vanilla essence	1 tsp
1 tsp	grated lemon peel	1 tsp
1 tbs	lemon juice	1 tbs

Topping

approx. 455g (1 lb)	mixed red fruit (e.g. redcurrants, strawberries, raspberries, plums, etc)	1 lb
3 tbs	syrup or honey	3 tbs
3 tbs	water	3 tbs
2 tsp	arrowroot	2 tsp

1 Crush the biscuits and mix with the margarine and cinnamon. Use to line the base and sides of your prepared flan dish (*see* chapter introduction).

2 In a bowl, combine the yogurt, Quark, egg yolks, sugar, vanilla essence, lemon peel and juice.

3 Whisk the egg whites until stiff and carefully fold into the cheese mixture. Spoon into the case, smooth the top and bake at 190°C/375°F (Gas Mark 5) for 30 to 35 minutes, or until the top is lightly browned. Leave to cool in the oven.

4 Clean and dry the fruit, cutting into smaller pieces as necessary. Gently heat the syrup and most of the water in a saucepan. Mix the arrowroot with the remaining water to make a paste then add this to the saucepan and continue boiling until the sauce thickens, stirring continually. Cool briefly.

5 Pile the fruit over the top of the cheesecake and pour on the arrowroot glaze. Chill before serving.

Note: A green fruit mixture makes an attractive topping too – use kiwi fruit, greengages, grapes, gooseberries.

Almond Cheesecake

Base

| 225g (8 oz) | macaroons (see page 31) | 8 oz |
| 85g (3 oz) | margarine | ⅓ cup |

Filling

55g (2 oz)	margarine	¼ cup
55g (2 oz)	sugar	⅓ cup
1 tbs	grated orange peel	1 tbs
2 medium	free-range egg yolks	2 medium
455g (1 lb)	cottage cheese	2 cups
55g (2 oz)	almonds, ground	½ cup
55g (2 oz)	fresh wholemeal breadcrumbs	1 cup
	caster sugar for topping	

1 Crush the biscuits, mix with the margarine and use to line your prepared flan dish (*see* chapter introduction).

2 Cream together the margarine and sugar and add the peel and egg yolks. Sieve the cottage cheese and stir into the mixture with the almonds and crumbs.

3 Pile the mixture into the case. Bake at 200°C/400°F (Gas Mark 6) for 40 minutes. Leave to cool in the oven. Sprinkle with extra sugar before serving.

Note: This is more like a cake in texture and has a lovely subtle flavour. If liked, add candied peel or dried fruit. Don't forget to remove the rice paper from the macarooons!

Mango and Lime Cheesecake

Base

170g (6 oz)	oat biscuits	6 oz
85g (3 oz)	melted margarine	⅓ cup

Filling

225g (8 oz)	low fat soft cheese	1 cup
140ml (¼ pt)	sour cream	⅔ cup
2 tbs	lime juice	2 tbs
2 tbs	grated lime peel	2 tbs
30g (1 oz)	wholemeal flour	¼ cup
2 medium	mangoes, ripe	2 medium

1 Crush the biscuits and mix with the melted margarine. Use to line the base of your prepared flan dish (see chapter introduction).

2 Cream together the cheese, sour cream, lime juice, peel and flour. Mix well, then pile into the flan case. Bake at 180°C/350°F (Gas Mark 4) for 40 to 50 minutes, or until just firm. Leave to cool in the oven.

3 When ready, peel and slice the mangoes and arrange in overlapping slices across the top of the cheesecake. Chill before serving.

Note: To slice the mangoes, do not try to remove the stone first. Instead, use a sharp knife to slice down one side as close to the stone as possible, cut down the other side in the same way, then pull off the skin. Then cut the slices from the stone.

Ginger Cheesecake

Base

225g (8 oz)	wholemeal digestive biscuits	8 oz
85g (3 oz)	margarine	⅓ cup

Filling

340g (12 oz)	curd cheese	1½ cups
3 medium	free-range eggs, separated	3 medium
85g (3 oz)	caster sugar	½ cup
1 tbs	wholemeal (wholewheat) flour	1 tbs
140ml (¼ pt)	yogurt	⅔ cup
1 tsp	vanilla essence	1 tsp
2 tbs	preserved ginger, finely chopped	2 tbs
	ginger preserve - optional	

1 Crush the biscuits and mix with the margarine. Use to line the base of your prepared flan dish (see chapter introduction).

2 Beat together the cheese, egg yolks, sugar, flour, yogurt and vanilla essence. Whisk the egg whites until stiff and

carefully fold into the first mixture with the chopped ginger.

3 Pour into the prepared flan case and bake at 170°C/325°F (Gas Mark 3) for 1 to 1¼ hours or until set. Leave to cool in the oven. If liked, spread the top of the cake with ginger preserve before serving.

Note: Alternatively, spread the ginger preserve onto the prepared base and then top with the cheese mixture. Crushed ginger biscuits may also be used for the base and/or topping.

Continental Style Cheesecake

Base

225g (8 oz)	wholemeal (wholewheat) flour	2 cups
115g (4 oz)	margarine	½ cup
2 tbs	sugar	2 tbs
2-4 tbs	cold water	2-4 tbs
	egg white to glaze	

Filling

455g (1 lb)	ricotta cheese	2 cups
4 medium	free-range eggs, separated	4 medium
85g (3 oz)	sugar	½ cup
1 tbs	wholemeal (wholewheat) flour	1 tbs
1 tsp	ground cinnamon	1 tsp
55g (2 oz)	raisins	⅓ cup
55g (2 oz)	candied peel	2 oz
	extra ground cinnamon	

1 First make a shortcrust pastry: put the flour into a bowl, use fingertips to rub in the fat to make a crumb–like mixture, stirring in the sugar, then add just enough cold water to make a dough. Knead briefly then wrap in foil and chill for 30 minutes.

2 Reserve a small portion of the dough, then roll out the rest to a circle and line a flan dish. Bake blind at 180°C/350°F (Gas Mark 4) for 10 minutes.

3 Meanwhile, beat together the cheese, egg yolks, sugar, flour and cinnamon. Whisk the egg whites until stiff and carefully fold into the first mixture with the raisins and peel. Spoon the mixture into the flan case, smoothing the top. Shape the remaining pastry into thin strips and use these to make a lattice pattern over the top of the cheesecake, brushing this with egg white so that it browns attractively.

4 Return the cheesecake to the oven for a further 45 minutes or until set. Cool in the oven. Serve sprinkled with extra cinnamon.

Note: If you cannot get ricotta cheese, Quark makes a good substitute.

Blueberry Cheesecake with Muesli Base

Base

85g (3 oz)	margarine, melted	⅓ cup
3 tbs	honey	3 tbs
225g (8 oz)	muesli	8 oz

Filling

225g (8 oz)	low fat soft cheese	1 cup
140ml (¼ pt)	yogurt	⅔ cup
2 medium	free-range eggs, separated	2 medium
2 tbs	wholemeal (wholewheat) flour	2 tbs
55g (2 oz)	sugar	⅓ cup

Topping

340g (12 oz)	blueberries	12 oz
4 tbs	water	4 tbs
30g (1 oz)	sugar	2 tbs
2 tsp	arrowroot	2 tsp

1 Combine the melted margarine, honey and muesli. Use to line the base and sides of your prepared flan (*see* chapter introduction). Bake at 180°C/350°F (Gas Mark 4) for 10 minutes.
2 Meanwhile, beat together the cheese, yogurt, egg yolks, flour and sugar. Whisk the egg whites until stiff then carefully fold into the cheese mixture. Pour into the flan case and bake at the same temperature for 30 to 40 minutes, or until the top just begins to colour. Leave to cool in the oven.
3 Clean the blueberries and put them into a saucepan with most of the water and sugar. Simmer gently until just beginning to soften, then use a slotted spoon to remove the fruit and set aside. Mix together the remaining water and arrowroot to make a paste, add to the saucepan and cook until the sauce thickens. Take off the heat and add the cooked blueberries.
4 Spread the slightly cooled fruit and sauce across the top of the cheesecake, and serve.

Note: Blueberries are a popular topping for cheesecakes in America, although they are harder to find in British shops. If you cannot get fresh ones, use tinned or frozen, or alternatively, blackcurrants.

Individual Apricot Cheesecakes

Base

170g (8 oz)	wholemeal (wholewheat) flour	1½ cups
85g (3 oz)	margarine cold water to mix	⅓ cup

Filling

225g (8 oz)	curd cheese	1 cup
2 tbs	single cream	2 tbs
1 large	free-range egg, beaten	1 large
2 tbs	sugar	2 tbs
¼ tsp	ground mixed spice	¼ tsp
12	apricots	12

1 Put the flour into a bowl, use your fingertips to rub in the fat to make a crumb-like mixture, then add just enough cold water to make a dough. Knead this briefly, then wrap in foil and chill for 30 minutes.
2 Meanwhile, beat the curd cheese, add the cream and then the egg. Stir in the sugar and spice.
3 Roll out the pastry, cut into small circles, and use to line 12 small patty tins. Put an apricot into the circle of each and add a few spoonfuls of the cheese mixture.
4 Bake at 200°C/400°F (Gas Mark 6) for 10 to 15 minutes, or until set.

Note: These can also be made using dried apricots or with other fruits.

Mint Carob Chip Cheesecake

Base

170g (6 oz)	wholemeal (wholewheat) flour	1½ cups
85g (3 oz)	margarine	⅓ cup
2-4 tbs	cold water	2-4 tbs

Filling

340g (12 oz)	crème fraîche	1½ cups
3 tbs	honey	3 tbs
1 tbs	wholemeal (wholewheat) flour	1 tbs
1 tbs	lemon juice	1 tbs
2 medium	free-range eggs, beaten	2 medium
85g (3 oz)	mint carob chocolate, cut into pieces	3 oz
140ml (¼ pt)	whipping cream extra carob bar for decoration	⅔ cup

1 Place the flour in a bowl and rub in the fat with fingertips to make a crumb-like mixture. Add enough water to make a dough, knead briefly, then chill for 30 minutes. Roll out and use to line a flan dish. Bake blind at 200°C/400°F (Gas Mark 6) for 10 minutes.
2 Meanwhile, blend together the crème fraîche, honey, flour and lemon juice. Gradually add the eggs, beating well after each addition. Stir in the carob chips.
3 Pour the mixture into the flan case. Lower the heat to 170°C/325°F (Gas Mark 3) and cook the cheesecake for 45 to 50 minutes or until set. Cool in the oven.

4 Whip the cream and use to decorate the top of the cake. Sprinkle with extra carob chips, and chill before serving.

Note: If liked, flavour the cream for the topping with peppermint essence – you could even colour it with natural green colouring.

Crustless Russian Cheesecake

455g (1 lb)	curd cheese	2 cups
55g (2 oz)	sugar	1/3 cup
55g (2 oz)	raisins	1/3 cup
1/2 tsp	vanilla essence	1/2 tsp
1 tsp	lemon juice	1 tsp
1 large	free-range egg, beaten	1 large
30g (1 oz)	butter	2½ tbs
	extra caster sugar for topping	
	sour cream or Hedgerow compôte (see page 87) to serve	

1 Beat together the curd cheese, sugar, raisins, vanilla, lemon juice and egg. Grease and line a small flan dish and pour in the mixture. Bake at 180°C/350°F (Gas Mark 4) for 20 to 30 minutes until cooked but not too firm.
2 Eat while still warm, topped with sour cream. If this topping is too heavy for your taste, a wild fruit compôte makes a good alternative.

Note: Instead of making this into a cheesecake, pile spoonfuls of the mixture into small ramekins, cook them, then chill and serve.

Orange Cheesecake

Base
115g (4 oz)	wholemeal digestive biscuits	4 oz
55g (2 oz)	wholemeal ginger biscuits	2 oz
55g (2 oz)	margarine, melted	¼ cup

Filling
340g (12 oz)	cottage cheese	1½ cups
140ml (¼ pt)	yogurt	⅔ cup
1 tbs	orange peel, finely chopped	1 tbs
140ml (¼ pt)	concentrated orange juice	⅔ cup
2 tsp	agar agar	2 tsp
2 medium	free-range egg whites	2 medium
2	oranges, peeled and cut across into slices	2

1 Crush the biscuits and mix with the melted margarine. Use to line your prepared flan dish (*see* chapter introduction).
2 Sieve the cottage cheese and place in a bowl with the yogurt, orange peel, and most of the orange juice. Beat well. In a small saucepan, stir together the remaining orange juice and agar agar, gently bring the mixture almost to the boil, then simmer for a few minutes. Cool briefly before adding to the cheese.
3 Pour the mixture into the prepared flan case and chill for a couple of hours, preferably longer. Top with the orange slices arranged in a circle.

Note: For an alternative topping, crush some biscuits and sprinkle over cheesecake.

Grape Cheesecake with Nut Crust

Base
55g (2 oz)	fresh wholemeal (wholewheat) breadcrumbs	1 cup
30g (1 oz)	margarine	2½ tbs
55g (2 oz)	walnuts, finely chopped	½ cup

Filling
340g (12 oz)	cottage cheese	1½ cups
200ml (⅓ pt)	sour cream	¾ cup
200ml (⅓ pt)	yogurt	¾ cup
4 tbs	cold water	4 tbs
1 tbs	agar agar	1 tbs
340g (12 oz)	black and green grapes	12 oz
1-2 tbs	warmed honey	1-2 tbs

1 Make the crumbs as fine as possible. Toast them briefly until crisp, stirring occasionally, then mix with the melted margarine and nuts. Press into the base of your prepared flan dish (*see* chapter introduction).
2 Sieve the cottage cheese and then mix with the sour cream and yogurt. In a small saucepan, stir together the water and agar agar, bring gently almost to the boil, then continue simmering for a few minutes. Cool slightly then add to the first mixture, stirring well. Pour into the prepared case and chill until set.
3 Wash and dry the grapes, halve and remove the pips. Arrange them in circles on top of the cheesecake and brush with warmed honey.

Note: This is a good cheesecake for any dieters at the table!

Ginger Banana Cheesecake

Base

170g (6 oz)	wholemeal ginger biscuits	6 oz
85g (3 oz)	margarine	⅓ cup

Filling

225g (8 oz)	low fat soft cheese	1 cup
225g (8 oz)	fromage fraîs	1 cup
55g (2 oz)	sugar	⅓ cup
3 medium	ripe bananas	3 medium
140ml (¼ pt)	pineapple juice	⅔ cup
1 tbs	agar agar	1 tbs
1 tbs	lemon juice	1 tbs
3	extra ginger biscuits - optional	3

1 Crush the biscuits, mix with the margarine and use to line the base of your prepared flan dish (*see* chapter introduction). Chill briefly.
2 Mix together the cheese, fromage fraîs and sugar. Mash two of the bananas and stir into the mixture. (A food processor will make it extra smooth.)
3 In a small pan, heat the fruit juice, sprinkle in the agar agar, and bring gently to the boil. Simmer for a few minutes, cool slightly, then add to the cheese mixture, stirring well. Pour into the flan case and chill for at least 2 hours, preferably longer.
4 Cut the remaining banana into slices, brush with lemon juice, and use to decorate the top of the cheesecake. If liked, sprinkle with some coarsely crushed ginger biscuits.

Note: For an extra luxurious version of this cheesecake, add crushed stem ginger between the biscuit base and creamy filling. You can use apple juice instead of the pineapple.

Apple Cheesecake

Base

225g (8 oz)	wholemeal digestive biscuits	8 oz
55g (2 oz)	margarine, melted	¼ cup
½ tsp	ground cinnamon	½ tsp

Filling

4	dessert apples, peeled, cored and sliced	4
140ml (¼ pt)	sweet cider	⅔ cup
1 tbs	grated lemon peel	1 tbs
1 tsp	ground mixed spice	1 tsp
55g (2 oz)	dates, chopped	⅓ cup
55g (2 oz)	walnuts, chopped	½ cup
225g (8 oz)	Quark	1 cup
140ml (¼ pt)	whipping cream	⅔ cup

1 Crush the biscuits, mix with the margarine and cinnamon, and use to line the base and sides of your prepared flan dish (*see* chapter introduction).
2 Put the apples into a saucepan with the cider, lemon peel and spice. Cook just long enough for the apples to break down. Drain well and mash, then stir in the dates and walnuts.
3 Beat the Quark until smooth. Whip the cream and stir into the Quark with the apple mixture. Pile into the prepared flan base, smooth the top and chill well before serving.

Note: This is an easy cheesecake as it requires neither a setting ingredient, nor cooking. It has a softer texture than usual.

Avocado Crunch Cheesecake

Base

55g (2 oz)	margarine	¼ cup
1 tbs	honey or syrup	1 tbs
2 tbs	sugar	2 tbs
170g (8 oz)	oats	1½ cups

Filling

1 large	ripe avocado	1 large
1 tbs	lemon juice	1 tbs
115g (4 oz)	medium fat soft cheese	½ cup
140ml (¼ pt)	sour cream	⅔ cup
2 tbs	sugar	2 tbs
2 tbs	apple juice	2 tbs
2 tsp	agar agar	2 tsp
1 medium	free-range egg white	1 medium
115g (4 oz)	granola, coarsely crushed (see page 62)	4 oz

1 Melt the margarine, stir in the sweetener, sugar and oats and use to line the sides and base of your prepared flan dish (*see* chapter introduction). Bake at 180°C/350°F (Gas Mark 4) for 20 minutes, then set aside to cool.
2 Peel and stone the avocado, then mash well with the lemon juice, cheese, cream and sugar to make a smooth mixture. In a small saucepan, heat the apple juice and agar agar. Bring almost to boiling point, then simmer gently for a few minutes. Cool briefly, then add to the avocado mixture.
3 Whisk the egg white until stiff and fold into the other ingredients. Use to fill the flan case. Chill well. Just before serving, sprinkle with the crushed granola.

Note: This flapjack-style base makes a perfect contrast to the subtly flavoured and creamy avocado filling. If you don't want to use the oven, try crumbling flapjacks and mixing with melted fat, then proceed in the usual way.

Fresh Strawberry Tofu Cheesecake

Base

225g (8 oz)	wholemeal digestive biscuits	8 oz
85g (3 oz)	margarine, melted	⅓ cup

Filling

285g (10 oz)	firm tofu, well drained	1¼ cups
2 tbs	lemon juice	2 tbs
55g (2 oz)	sugar	⅓ cup
1 tsp	vanilla essence	1 tsp
4 tbs	vegetable oil	4 tbs
4 tbs	concentrated soya milk	4 tbs

Topping

225g (8 oz)	fresh strawberries	8 oz
2 tbs	cold water	2 tbs
1 tsp	arrowroot	1 tsp
1 tbs	syrup	1 tbs

1 Crush the biscuits and stir into the margarine. Use to line the base and sides of your prepared flan dish (*see* chapter introduction).

2 Blend the tofu until creamy. Combine with all the other filling ingredients. Pour into the flan case and bake at 160°C/325°F (Gas Mark 3) for 50 minutes or until just firm. Leave to cool.

3 To make the topping, first clean and halve the strawberries. Mix the water and arrowroot to a paste, pour into a small pan and heat gently, stirring continually, until the sauce thickens. Add the syrup, then cool for a few minutes.

4 Arrange the strawberries over the top of the cheesecake and carefully spoon the syrup over the fruit. Chill until needed.

Note: Other fruits may be used in the same way. For an even more special cheesecake, lay extra strawberries in the flan beneath the filling or spread strawberry jam over the base.

Candied Peel Soya Cheesecake

Base:

225g (8 oz)	shortbread biscuits	8 oz
55g (2 oz)	margarine, melted	¼ cup

Filling:

115g (4 oz)	block margarine	½ cup
55g (2 oz)	sugar	⅓ cup
4 tbs	rice or other syrup	4 tbs
115g (4 oz)	soya flour	1 cup
140ml (¼ pt)	milk	⅔ cup
2 tbs	lemon juice	2 tbs
2 tbs	grated lemon peel	2 tbs
115g (4 oz)	candied peel	4 oz

1 Crush the biscuits and add to the margarine, mixing well. Press into the base and sides of your prepared flan dish (*see* chapter introduction) and chill briefly.

2 Melt the block margarine in a saucepan and add the sugar and syrup. Stir in the soya flour and continue cooking gently, stirring continually, until the mixture thickens.

3 Beat in the milk. Remove the pan from the heat and add the lemon juice, peel and candied peel. Turn the mixture into the prepared flan case, smooth the top, and chill before serving.

Note: You can use any syrup in this recipe, but rice syrup gives the cheesecake a special flavour.

Tropical Fruit Coconut Cheesecake

Base

225g (8 oz)	wholemeal digestive biscuits	8 oz
55g (2 oz)	margarine, melted	¼ cup
½ tsp	ground cinnamon	½ tsp

Filling

455g (1 lb)	tofu, well drained	2 cups
3 tbs	thick coconut milk	3 tbs
3 tbs	syrup	3 tbs
3 tbs	concentrated soya milk or soya 'cream'	3 tbs

Topping

	selection of fruit as available (e.g. pineapple, kiwi, strawberries, starfruit, cape gooseberries, etc.)	
2 tbs	flaked coconut, roasted	2 tbs

1 Mix the biscuits with the margarine and cinnamon, then press into the base and sides of your prepared flan dish (*see* chapter introduction). Either chill well, or bake at 180°C/350°F (Gas Mark 4) for 10 to 20 minutes.
2 Mash or blend the tofu to make a smooth purée, then stir in the coconut milk, syrup and soya milk. Pile into the flan case, smooth the top and chill.
3 Prepare the fruit: cut the pineapple into small cubes; halve the larger strawberries and slice the kiwis and starfruit. Arrange the fruit decoratively across the top of the cheesecake, sprinkle with the coconut flakes and serve at once.

Note: The coconut milk is best made from a block of creamed coconut, but powdered coconut can also be used.

Banana Tofu Cheesecake

Base

170g (6 oz)	wholemeal digestive biscuits	6 oz
55g (2 oz)	margarine, melted	¼ cup

Filling

455g (1 lb)	tofu, well drained	2 cups
2 medium	ripe bananas, mashed	2 medium
2 tbs	caster sugar	2 tbs
½ tsp	vanilla essence	½ tsp
55g (2 oz)	flaked almonds, roasted	½ cup

1 Crush the biscuits and mix well with the melted margarine. Use the mixture to line the base and sides of your prepared flan dish (*see* chapter introduction).
2 Blend together the tofu, mashed bananas, sugar and vanilla essence. Spoon into the prepared flan dish, smooth the top and sprinkle with almonds. Chill well before serving.

Note: For an extra quick dessert, just make up the filling, divide it between 4 to 6 glasses and top with nuts or a few red berries for colour.

Marbled Lemon Cheesecake

Base

180g (6 oz)	wholemeal digestive biscuits	6 oz
55g (2 oz)	margarine, melted	¼ cup
1 tbs	sugar	1 tbs

Filling

285g (10 oz)	tofu, well drained	1¼ cups
3 tbs	lemon juice	3 tbs
2 tbs	grated lemon peel	2 tbs
200ml (⅓ pt)	soya 'creem' or concentrated soya milk	¾ cup
2 tbs	cornflour	2 tbs
55g (2 oz)	sugar	⅓ cup
½ tsp	lemon essence - optional	½ tsp

Topping

approx. 3 tbs	vegan lemon curd (see page 114)	approx. 3 tbs
2 tbs	soya yogurt or soya 'cream'	2 tbs

1 Crush the biscuits, stir into the melted margarine and add the sugar. Use to line the base and sides of your prepared flan dish (*see* chapter introduction).
2 Mix together the tofu, lemon juice, lemon peel and soya 'cream'. When well blended, add the cornflour, sugar and lemon essence, if using it. Pile the mixture into the flan dish and smooth the top. Bake at 180°C/350°F (Gas Mark 4) for 20 to 30 minutes, then set aside to cool.
3 Spread the top with the lemon curd, then add the yogurt or soya 'cream', using a fork to make a marbled pattern. Serve at once.

Note: If using home-made lemon curd, you might like to add a few drops of yellow colouring so that the marbling is more effective. An alternative topping to yogurt or soya 'cream' is lemon curd, sprinkled with coarsely grated plain chocolate.

10
Fruit Based Desserts

A bowl of mixed fresh fruit is undoubtedly one of the healthiest of all desserts. But there are times when it's not quite enough. The recipes that follow show ways of turning a wide variety of fruits into more special desserts - some quick and easy, others more complicated but all designed to make the very best of the fruit.

While some of the dishes involve cooking the fruit, never be tempted to use anything but the best specimens. Fruit should always be unblemished and as fresh as possible. Although it is occasionally possible to buy organic, untreated fruit, most commercially grown fruit is treated with chemicals during the growing process and, possibly again before being exported from countries around the world to our shores. Some items even have a sheen added to make them look healthier. Since most of the vitamins lie just beneath the skin of the fruit, do not discard it. Instead, wash fruit or, better still, scrub it gently, then dry and use as described.

Lastly, do try the many new and exotic fruits now available. Be adventurous: you never know what you might find.

Prune and Apple Fool

225g (8 oz)	prunes, stoned	2 cups
285ml (½ pt)	water	1⅓ cups
3 tbs	concentrated apple juice, or to taste	3 tbs
3 medium	free-range egg whites	3 medium
30g (1 oz)	roasted hazelnuts, coarsely chopped - optional	¼ cup

1 Bring to the boil the prunes and water in a saucepan, then cover and simmer for 10 minutes or until cooked. Drain off the water, stir in the apple juice and set aside to cool.
2 Blend the prunes to make a purée.
3 Whisk the egg whites until stiff, then use a metal spoon to fold the prune purée into the egg whites. Divide between four glasses and chill well. Serve topped, if liked, with some chopped nuts.

Note: Large sweet California prunes are best for this recipe.

Fresh Fruit Flambé

30g (1 oz)	butter or margarine	2½ tbs
55g (2 oz)	sugar	⅓ cup
1 small	pineapple, peeled and diced	1 small
4	apricots, halved	4
8	strawberries, halved	8
55g (2 oz)	blanched almonds	½ cup
2 tbs	brandy	2 tbs
	thick yogurt or soya 'creem' to serve	

1 In a large pan, melt the butter, stir in the sugar, and cook briefly.
2 Add the prepared fruit and the nuts, stir well, and cook a few minutes more.
3 In a separate pan warm the brandy, then pour it over the fruit and set light to it, shaking the pan gently. Take it to the table at once. As soon as the flame dies, spoon the hot fruit into four bowls. Serve with yogurt or soya 'creem'.

Note: Any fruit can be used for this simple but impressive dessert. Try to choose colours that contrast attractively.

Coconut Stuffed Papaya Shells

2 large	papayas	2 large
55g (2 oz)	margarine	¼ cup
55g (2 oz)	sugar	⅓ cup
55g (2 oz)	desiccated coconut	⅔ cup
55g (2 oz)	coconut flakes, roasted - optional	⅔ cup

1 Halve and peel the papayas and remove the seeds. Stand the shells on a heatproof tray.
2 Mix together the margarine, sugar and coconut. Pack into the prepared shells and put them under a grill for 3 to 5 minutes, or until sizzling hot. Serve at once sprinkled – if liked – with coconut flakes.

Note: Served this way, papayas (also called pawpaws) make a quick, easy and impressive dessert. Although margarine works well, vegetarians might like to use butter which gives the dish a special flavour. If you cannot get papayas, use peaches in the same way.

Marbled Summer Fool

455g (1 lb)	red summer fruits (i.e. plums, cherries, blackcurrants etc)	1 lb
1 large	free-range egg white	1 large
55g (2 oz)	sugar - optional	⅓ cup
200ml (⅓ pt)	yogurt or fromage fraîs	¾ cup

1 Clean and trim the fruit. Cook with the minimum of water. Depending on the fruit you choose and how ripe it is, you might need to add sugar to sweeten.
2 Blend the fruit in a blender to make a thick purée. Whisk the egg white until stiff and carefully fold into the purée.
3 Divide the yogurt or fromage fraîs between four small glasses or bowls. Use a fork to swirl the purée into the yogurt or fromage fraîs to give it an attractive marble effect.
4 Chill briefly before serving.

Note: Other fruit may be used in exactly the same way, either singly or in combination.

Gooseberry Crunch

455g (1 lb)	gooseberries, topped and tailed	1 lb
140ml (¼ pt)	water	⅔ cup
85g (3 oz)	sugar	½ cup
55g (2 oz)	margarine	¼ cup
170g (6 oz)	fresh wholemeal (wholewheat) breadcrumbs	3 cups
30g (1 oz)	sunflower seeds	2 tbs
½ tsp	ground cinnamon	½ tsp
1 tbs	lemon rind, finely grated	1 tbs
55g (2 oz)	sugar	⅓ cup

1 In a saucepan, stir together the gooseberries, water and sugar. Bring to the boil, then lower the heat and simmer until just cooked.
2 In another saucepan, melt the margarine, stir in the breadcrumbs and sunflower seeds, and fry until the breadcrumbs are crisp. Sprinkle in the cinnamon and lemon rind and cook for 1 minute more, then remove from the heat and add the sugar.
3 In a glass serving bowl, layer the ingredients by putting one-third of the gooseberries across the base, topping with one-third of the breadcrumbs, and repeating until all the ingredients are used. Chill for at least an hour.

Note: Using a glass bowl for this dish shows the attractive appearance of the separate layers. Alternatively serve in individual glasses. If liked, serve with soya or dairy 'cream'. A quicker – but equally crunchy! – version can be made by replacing the breadcrumbs with granola.

Dried Fruit Compôte

115g (4 oz)	prunes, soaked overnight	1 cup
115g (4 oz)	dried apricots, soaked overnight	1 cup
115g (4 oz)	dried apple rings, soaked overnight	1 cup
115g (4 oz)	dried figs, soaked overnight	1 cup
200ml (⅓ pt)	grape juice	¾ cup
1 tsp	ground cinnamon	1 tsp
1 tbs	lemon peel, grated	1 tbs
1 tbs	lemon juice	1 tbs

1 Drain the dried fruit well, place in a saucepan and add the other ingredients. Bring to the boil, cover and lower the heat, and simmer for 10 minutes or until the fruit is tender and the liquid has been absorbed.
2 Serve hot or chilled as a dessert dish, as a pancake filling, or topped with a crumble and served with custard.

Note: Be careful that the fruit does not boil dry, adding a drop more grape juice if necessary. It is hard to judge exactly how much will be required, as it depends on the size and freshness of the dried fruit. Use other fruits as liked.

Hedgerow Compôte

1.15 kilos (2 lbs)	wild fruit, (e.g. wild apples, blackberries, damson, plums, etc.)	2 lbs
200ml (⅓ pt)	water	¾ cup
85g (3 oz)	sugar, or to taste	½ cup
2 tbs	elderflower cordial	2 tbs

1 Clean the fruit well and trim as necessary. Cut the larger fruit into small pieces.
2 Combine the fruit with the water and sugar in a saucepan. Bring to the boil, then lower the heat and simmer for a few minutes until the fruit is just cooked. Do not overcook. Add the cordial and serve hot or cold.

Note: Use any fruits you can find in the wild, preferably those that are growing well away from main roads or areas that have been sprayed with chemicals. The amount of sugar needed will depend on the kind of fruit you choose and how ripe it is. When buying elderflower cordial, try to ensure that it contains the minimum of additives.

Pineapple and Banana Fritters

115g (4 oz)	wholemeal (wholewheat) flour	1 cup
1 tsp	baking powder	1 tsp
½ tsp	ground cinnamon	½ tsp
1 small	free-range egg, beaten	1 small
approx.	milk	approx.
4 tbs		4 tbs
1 small	pineapple	1 small
2 medium	bananas	2 medium
	vegetable oil for frying	
	caster sugar	

1 Sift the flour, baking powder and cinnamon into a bowl. Gradually add the egg, then enough milk to make a batter the consistency of single cream. Cover this and leave to stand in the fridge for 30 minutes.
2 Prepare the fruit. Peel the pineapple and cut into even-sized rings. Peel the bananas and cut into thick even-sized sticks.
3 Pour enough vegetable oil into a saucepan to cover the fruit. Heat this until a cube of stale bread dropped into it browns in about 40 seconds. Dip the fruit in batter, tap the fork against the side of the bowl to remove any excess, then drop into the fat and deep fry for a few minutes or until crisp and just browning. Cook a few pieces of fruit at a time. Drain well on paper towels and keep them hot while cooking the remaining fruit. Serve sprinkled with caster sugar.

Note: It is important that the oil reaches the same temperature between batches, so that the fruit cooks evenly. If necessary test between batches.

Chinese Style Apple Fritters

170g (6 oz)	wholemeal (wholewheat) flour	1½ cups
1 tsp	baking powder	1 tsp
¼ tsp	bicarbonate of soda	¼ tsp
2 tbs	sesame seeds	2 tbs
140ml (¼ pt)	water	⅔ cup
4 medium	apples, peeled and thickly sliced	4 medium
	vegetable oil for frying	

1 Sift two-thirds of the flour together with the baking powder, bicarbonate of soda and sesame seeds. Gradually add the water, whisking as you do so to make a thick smooth batter. Cover and chill for 30 minutes if possible.
2 Coat the apple slices with the remaining flour.
3 Heat the oil (*see* previous recipe). Using a fork, dip the apple slices into the batter mixture, tap against the side of the bowl to remove any excess batter, and drop them into the oil. Cook for 5 minutes, or until lightly browned. Drain well. Prepare a small batch at a time, keeping them warm as you cook the rest. Serve hot.

Note: Each of these recipes for fruit fritters can be used with a variety of other fruits, for example, apricots, peaches, pears and strawberries.

Banana Maple Cream

4 large	ripe bananas	4 large
200ml (⅓ pt)	crème fraîche	¾ cup
1 tbs	lemon juice	1 tbs
2 tbs	maple syrup	2 tbs
	small bar of plain chocolate or *granola*	

1 Peel and either mash the bananas and mix them with the crème fraîche, lemon juice and syrup, or combine all these ingredients in a blender.
2 Divide between four small bowls or glasses and chill briefly. Serve topped with grated chocolate, or a sprinkling of granola.

Note: Sour cream or thick yogurt may be used instead of crème fraîche. Vegans can also use concentrated soya milk or silken tofu for a similar effect.

Avocado Citrus Fruit Salad

1 large	avocado, peeled, stoned, and cubed	1 large
115g (4 oz)	fresh dates, stoned	1 cup
1 large	orange, peeled and cut into segments	1 large
1 medium	grapefruit, peeled and cut into segments	1 medium
30g (1 oz)	desiccated coconut	2 tbs

Syrup

30g (1 oz)	sugar	2 tbs
1-2 tsp	orange flower water	1-2 tsp
4 tbs	water	4 tbs
55g (2 oz)	pistachio nuts	½ cup

1 In a large bowl stir together the avocado, dates, orange and grapefruit segments, and sprinkle with coconut.
2 In a small saucepan, combine the sugar, orange flower water and water, and heat gently, stirring continually, until the sugar dissolves. Heat for 2 more minutes, until it begins to thicken, then remove from the heat and cool briefly before trickling over the fresh fruit. Chill the fruit salad before serving topped with the pistachio nuts.

Note: Use raw, unsalted pistachio nuts. Alternatively, use coconut flakes, which taste best when lightly roasted.

Fruit Salad Deluxe

4	kiwi fruits, peeled and sliced	4
1 large	mango, peeled and cubed	1 large
12	lychees, peeled and stoned	12
½ small	pineapple, peeled and cubed	½ small
4	fresh figs, quartered	4
approx. 140ml (¼ pt)	mango juice	⅔ cup
1 tsp	ground mixed spice soya 'cream', thick set yogurt or nut cream to serve	1 tsp

1 Mix together all the fruits, cover with fruit juice mixed with the spice, and chill for at least 1 hour.
2 Serve in individual bowls with the topping of your choice.

Note: For an even more exotic taste, add a spoonful or two of the pulp of passion fruit to the juice, scooped out with a sharp scoop. Use fresh or tinned lychees.

Hot Fruit Salad with Coconut Custard

Fruit Salad

680g (1½ lbs)	fresh fruit (e.g. blackcurrants, greengages, redcurrants, apricots, etc.)	1½ lbs
200ml (⅓ pt)	water	⅔ cup
1 tbs	lemon juice	1 tbs
½ tsp	ground coriander	½ tsp
30g (1 oz)	sugar	2 tbs
1 tsp	arrowroot	1 tsp

Custard

3 tbs	coconut powder	3 tbs
30g (1 oz)	sugar	2 tbs
140ml (¼ pt)	hot water	⅔ cup
2 tbs	soya 'cream'	2 tbs
2 tsp	cold water	2 tsp
2 tsp	arrowroot	2 tsp

1 Prepare all the fruit by trimming and cutting into halves as necessary. Bring to the boil in a saucepan with the water, lemon juice, spices and sugar and simmer for just 3 to 5 minutes. (The idea is to heat the fruit through, not to cook it.)
2 Use a slotted spoon to remove the fruit from the juice and set aside. Mix a little of the juice with the arrowroot, then return this to the saucepan and mix with the remaining liquid. Heat gently until the sauce thickens, then stir the fruit back.
3 At the same time prepare the custard. In a saucepan, combine the coconut powder, sugar and hot water, stir or whisk until well blended, and heat gently. Add the soya 'creem'. Stir together the remaining cold water and arrowroot and add this to the saucepan. Heat very gently, stirring continuously until the sauce thickens, and remove from the heat the moment this happens. Stir in the soya 'cream'.
4 Serve the hot fruit topped with custard.

Note: Try to use fruits of various colours to give the fruit salad an attractive appearance.

Fresh Berry Baskets

1 portion	brandy snap recipe (see page 15)	1 portion
225g (8 oz)	strawberries, cleaned	8 oz
225g (8 oz)	raspberries, cleaned	8 oz
225g (8 oz)	crème fraîche	8 oz

1 Make up the brandy snap mixture. Drop spoonfuls onto well-greased baking sheets to make four or six large circles. Bake at 190°C/375°F (Gas Mark 5) for 8 to 10 minutes or until beginning to harden. Cool for 1 to 2 minutes only, then use to line four to six small pie dishes, preferably fluted. Leave to cool.

2 Carefully remove the crisp baskets from the tin, and stand on plates. These should be hard now. Put one or two spoonfuls of cream in the bottom of each of the baskets and top with some strawberries and raspberries. Serve at once.

Note: Any fruits may be used in this recipe. Vegans can use puréed tofu mixed with sugar instead of the cream as a base for the fruit.

Pear Strudel Bundles

455g (1 lb)	sweet pears, peeled, cored and grated	1 lb
1 tbs	lemon juice	1 tbs
85g (3 oz)	walnuts, coarsely chopped	¾ cup
1 tsp	ground cinnamon	1 tsp
½ tsp	ground nutmeg	½ tsp
8 sheets	filo pastry	8 sheets
55g (2 oz)	melted margarine	¼ cup

1 Stir together the grated pears, lemon juice, nuts and spices.

2 Unfold the pastry and peel off the top sheet. (Cover the remainder with a dampened cloth). Lay this on a lightly floured board and use a brush to cover the surface with melted fat, going right to the edges.

3 Lay a second sheet on top, brush with more fat, then fold them together in half, so that you have a square of four thicknesses. Brush the top with more butter or oil.

4 Spoon some of the pear mixture into the middle and gather the corners up to make a bundle. Either pinch the pastry together to make a neck or tie carefully with a piece of string. Use the remaining ingredients to make three more bundles.

5 Stand these on a lightly greased baking sheet. Bake at 180°C/350°F (Gas Mark 4) for 20 to 30 minutes or until crisp and golden. If using string, don't forget to cut and remove it before serving.

Note: This is an unusual version of the better known apple strudel.

Apricot Hazelnut Triangles

225g (8 oz)	frozen puff pastry, defrosted	8 oz
170g (6 oz)	dried apricots, chopped	1¼ cups
1 tbs	orange juice	1 tbs
2 tbs	concentrated juice	2 tbs
30g (1 oz)	ground hazelnuts caster sugar	2 tbs

1 Roll out the pastry and cut into four squares, approximately 13cm (5 in) in size. Set aside.

2 Place the apricots and orange juice in a saucepan. Add a drop of water and simmer gently for 10 minutes, adding more water if necessary. The fruit should be as dry as possible, so keep this to the minimum. Cool briefly, then use a fork to stir in the ground nuts.

3 Drain any excess liquid from the apricot mixture before dividing it between the squares. Dampen the edges of the pastry with water, fold into a triangle, and press the edges together to seal. Cut three small slits across the top of each triangle, brush with water and sprinkle with sugar.

4 Transfer carefully to a baking sheet. Bake at 200°C/400°F (Gas Mark 6) for 20 minutes. Eat warm with a dairy or soya cream topping, or leave to cool completely and serve at teatime.

Note: Jam, marmalade or honey fillings may be used for these delicious triangles, perhaps with a few cake crumbs or chopped nuts added.

Banana Filo Rolls

4 sheets approx.	filo pastry	4 sheets approx.
4 tbs	vegetable oil	4 tbs
4 large	ripe bananas	4 large
30g (1 oz)	sultanas (golden seedless raisins)	2 tbs
½ tsp	ground cinnamon	½ tsp
30g (1 oz)	sugar	2 tbs
	butterscotch sauce (see page 111)	

1 On a floured board, fold each of the sheets of pastry into squares and brush well with vegetable oil.

2 Place a peeled banana in the centre of each, sprinkle with some of the sultanas, cinnamon and sugar, then fold the pastry to make a neat roll. Brush well with extra oil.

3 Place the rolls on a baking tray and bake at 200°C/400°F (Gas Mark 6) for 20 minutes or until crisp.

4 Meanwhile make the butterscotch sauce. Serve the hot rolls with a little butterscotch sauce poured over the top of each.

Note: A fruit sauce may be used instead of the butterscotch sauce, for example apricot purée (*see page 110*) or redberry purée (*see page 109*).

Winter Pudding with Tofu Cream

Pudding

455g (1 lb)	apples, peeled, cored and sliced	1 lb
225g (8 oz)	pears, peeled, cored and sliced	8 oz
225g (8 oz)	blackberries, cleaned and trimmed	8 oz
85g (3 oz)	sugar	½ cup
approx. 8 slices	wholemeal (wholewheat) bread	approx. 8 slices

Tofu cream

285g (10 oz)	silken tofu	1¼ cups
1 tbs	vegetable oil	1 tbs
½ tsp	vanilla essence	½ tsp
55g (2 oz)	sugar	⅓ cup
1 tsp	lemon peel, grated, or to taste soya milk	1 tsp

1 Combine all the fruit in a saucepan, then add the sugar, and some cold water. Cover and simmer until the fruit is just tender. Drain well, reserving the juice in a jug.
2 Trim the crusts from the bread. Line a bowl with the slices, making sure that they are closely packed together. Spoon in the fruit and top with more bread. Press down, top with a plate weighted down so that the mixture is firmly pressed together and chill well, preferably overnight.
3 For the tofu cream, simply combine the well-drained tofu, vegetable oil, vanilla essence, sugar and lemon peel in a blender to make a thick purée, then add just enough soya milk to achieve the consistency of cream. Chill before serving.
4 Carefully invert the pudding over a plate. Serve cut into thick slices and accompanied by the tofu cream.

Note: Lining the bowl with silver foil makes it easier to remove the pudding without it falling apart. For the more traditional summer version, use a selection of berries instead of winter fruits.

Strawberry Almond Galettes

170g (6 oz)	wholemeal (wholewheat) flour	1½ cups
115g (4 oz)	butter or margarine	½ cup
85g (3 oz)	almonds, ground	¾ cup
285ml (½ pt)	whipping cream	1⅓ cups
455g (1 lb)	strawberries, cleaned and trimmed	1 lb
55g (2 oz)	flaked almonds, lightly roasted	½ cup

1 Use your fingertips to rub the fat into the flour to make a crumb-like mixture. Stir in the almonds, then continue kneading the mixture until you make a dough. Wrap this in silver foil and chill for 30 minutes. Use the heel of your hand or a rolling pin to shape into three circles of equal size about 23cm (9 in). Place these on a greased baking sheet, marking one into eight triangles.
2 Bake at 170°C/325°F (Gas Mark 3) for 15 to 20 minutes or until golden – do not overcook. Cool briefly, then use a sharp knife to trim the edges before transferring the circles to a wire rack and leaving them to cool completely.
3 Whip the cream until stiff. Put one piece of shortbread onto a serving dish, spread with some of the cream and dot with the strawberries. Repeat this. Top with the marked piece of shortbread and decorate with more cream and strawberries and a sprinkling of flaked almonds. Serve cut into thick wedges.

Note: This shortbread tastes better if made with butter, but you can use margarine if you prefer.

Kiwi and Raspberry Pavlova

Meringue

3 medium	free-range egg whites	3 medium
115g (4 oz)	caster sugar	⅔ cup
1 tsp	lemon juice	1 tsp
1 tsp	cornflour	1 tsp

Filling

140ml (¼ pt)	whipping cream	⅔ cup
285ml (½ pt)	thick yogurt	1⅓ cups
225g (8 oz)	raspberries	8 oz
2	kiwis, peeled and sliced	2

1 Whisk the egg whites until stiff, then gradually add the sugar, still whisking after each addition, and continue whisking until the mixture forms soft glossy peaks. Carefully fold in the lemon juice and cornflour.
2 On a sheet of non-stick baking parchment, draw a circle 23cm (9 in) across and place on a baking sheet. Spoon or pipe the meringue mix to fill the circle, make a dip in the centre. Bake at 150°C/300°F (Gas Mark 2) for about one hour or until set. When cool, peel away the paper and put the meringue onto a plate.
3 When ready to serve, beat the cream until it is just beginning to form stiff peaks, then fold in the yogurt. Pile this into the centre of the meringue circle and top with the mixed raspberries and kiwi slices. Serve immediately.

Note: An unusual topping - not exactly healthy, but delicious - can be made by sprinkling flakes of dark and white chocolate over the fruit.

Grapefruit with Spiced Yogurt

450ml (¾ pt)	thick yogurt	2 cups
55g (2 oz)	caster sugar	⅓ cup
¼ tsp	ground nutmeg	¼ tsp
½ tsp	ground cinnamon	½ tsp
¼ tsp	ground cardamom	¼ tsp
2 large	ripe pink grapefruit	2 large
35g (2 oz)	flaked coconut, lightly roasted	½ cup

1 Combine the yogurt, sugar and spices and chill for at least one hour, preferably longer.
2 Carefully peel the grapefruit and use a sharp knife to cut off slices of flesh. Put these into four small bowls and serve topped with the spiced yogurt. Sprinkle with coconut if liked.

Note: This is a simple, but exotic tasting dessert. You can also use orange flower or rosewater to flavour the yogurt, but not too much or you will lose the creaminess of the yogurt. Other nuts can be used instead of coconut.

Melon Baskets

1 small	honeydew melon	1 small
1 small	cantaloupe melon	1 small
½ small	water melon	½ small
approx. 4 tbs	orange juice	approx. 4 tbs
2 tbs	liqueur - optional	2 tbs
30g (1 oz)	hazelnuts, roasted and coarsely chopped	¼ cup

1 Cut all the melons in half, then use a melon baller to scoop up balls of flesh, putting them into a bowl.
2 Pour the orange juice over the fruit and stir well. Add the liqueur if using it. Chill in the fridge for at least 30 minutes, preferably longer.
3 Choose four of the best shaped melon shells, cut them so that they are as evenly sized as possible, and trim the tops. Pile the balls back into them, sprinkle with nuts and serve at once.

Note: This simple dessert dish, wonderful on summer evenings, can also be used as a starter. An unusual version can be made by adding chopped avocado flesh to the melon and, perhaps, a sprinkling of mint.

Grape and Cheese Dessert

340g (12 oz)	green seedless grapes	12 oz
2 tbs	honey	2 tbs
1 tbs	lemon juice	1 tbs
225g (8 oz)	cottage cheese	1 cup
1-2 tbs	sugar	1-2 tbs

1 Wash the grapes and mix them with the honey and lemon. Either sieve or purée the cheese in a blender until thick and smooth.
2 Put the grapes into serving dishes with the juice, spoon the cheese over them, sprinkle with brown sugar and serve at once.

Note: Although it sounds like an unusual combination, cottage cheese goes well with fresh fruit. Try it with other fruit and fruit combinations too.

Quinoa Rhubarb Crumble

Fruit		
680g (1½ lbs)	rhubarb, washed and chopped	1½ lbs
140ml (¼ pt)	orange juice	⅔ cup
140ml (¼ pt)	water	⅔ cup
2-4 tbs	syrup	2-4 tbs

Crumble		
170g (3 oz)	margarine	⅓ cup
170g (6 oz)	quinoa flour	1½ cups
55g (2 oz)	sugar	⅓ cup
1 tsp	ground mixed spice	1 tsp
30g (1 oz)	sunflower seeds	2 tbs
30g (1 oz)	pumpkin seeds	2 tbs
	custard or soya milk - optional	

1 Combine the rhubarb, orange juice, water and syrup in a saucepan. Bring slowly to the boil then cover the pan and simmer for 10 minutes or until just tender.
2 Meanwhile, rub the fat into the quinoa flour to make a crumb-like mixture, then stir in the sugar, spice and seeds.
3 Transfer the rhubarb to an ovenproof dish, draining off any excess liquid. Sprinkle with the crumble. Bake at 200°C/400°F (Gas Mark 6) for 30 minutes, or until the topping begins to brown. Serve with hot custard.

Note: Quinoa is a highly nutritious grain that originated in South America but is now grown in the UK. To make flour, wash and dry the grains, then grind them. You could also use the grains whole for a crunchier topping.

Sunshine Crumbles

Fruit

455g (1 lb)	golden fruit (e.g. yellow plums, oranges, leveller gooseberries, apricots, yellow apples)	1 lb
55g (2 oz)	sugar	⅓ cup

Topping

115g (4 oz)	margarine	½ cup
85g (3 oz)	oats	¾ cup
85g (3 oz)	wholemeal (wholewheat) flour	¾ cup
55g (2 oz)	sugar	⅓ cup
1 tsp	ground coriander soya 'cream' to serve	1 tsp

1 Prepare the fruit as necessary, cut into even-sized pieces. In a saucepan, combine the fruit, a drop of water and the sugar and cook for about 10 minutes, adding more sugar if necessary.
2 Meanwhile, make the crumble. Rub the margarine into the oats and flour to make a crumb-like mixture, then stir in the sugar and coriander. Divide the fruit between four small ovenproof dishes or ramekins, sprinkling each one with some of the crumble.
3 Bake at 180°C/350°F (Gas Mark 4) for about 20 minutes or until the crumble is crisp and brown. Serve at once with crème fraîche or soya 'cream' topping.

Note: Instead of the lovely sunny golden combination of colours given here, you can also use a fiery red selection of fruits or the cool greens of greengages, gooseberries, apples and so on. Try ground ginger instead of coriander. Vegetarians could use crème fraîche as a topping.

Fruit Crumble-in-a-Hurry

Fruit

455g (1 lb)	ripe plums, stoned and halved	1 lb
225g (8 oz)	greengages, stoned and halved	8 oz
140ml (¼ pt)	water	⅔ cup
115g (4 oz)	sugar	⅔ cup
1 tsp	ground mixed spice	1 tsp
6	Semolina Shortbread (see page 36)	6
30g (1 oz)	margarine, melted	2½ tbsp

Yogurt cream

285ml (½ pt)	yogurt	1⅓ cups
¼ tsp	vanilla essence or to taste	¼ tsp
1 tbs	honey or syrup	1 tbs

1 Stir together the plums and greengages, water, sugar and spice in a saucepan. Bring to the boil, then lower the heat, cover the pan and simmer for 5 to 10 minutes or until just tender.
2 Meanwhile crumble the shortbreads and mix with the margarine.
3 Prepare the yogurt cream by whisking together the yogurt, vanilla essence and sweetener. Pour into a jug.
4 Pile the fruit into a heatproof dish, smooth the top, spread with the biscuit crumbs and heat under a hot grill for a few minutes. Serve at once with the yogurt cream.

Note: Try this quick recipe using different biscuits, either home-made or shop bought. Ginger biscuits with an apple or rhubarb base are a particularly good combination.

Tropical Trifle

approx.	wholemeal (wholewheat)	approx.
225g (8 oz)	cake	8 oz
140ml (¼ pt)	pineapple juice	⅔ cup
2 medium	bananas, peeled and sliced	2 medium
1 tbs	lemon juice	1 tbs
1	papaya, peeled and seeded	1
2	kiwis, peeled and cubed	2
1 serving	Coconut Custard (see page 88)	1 serving
1 tbs	rosewater - optional	1 tbs
3 tbs	desiccated coconut	3 tbs

1 Crumble the cake and sprinkle across the base of a large glass serving dish. Pour on the pineapple juice, distributing it evenly.
2 Toss the bananas in the lemon juice, mix with the papayas and kiwis, and distribute this mixture over the crumbs.
3 Make up the custard according to instructions, adding the rosewater if using it. Spoon the custard over the fruit, smooth the top of the trifle and sprinkle with desiccated coconut. Chill before serving.

Note: Trifles can be as simple or as complicated as you choose. This vegan version has an unusual flavour yet takes little time to prepare. It may also be topped with a custard made from soya milk, and include a layer of fruit jelly made with agar agar. Vegetarians can make an even quicker trifle by replacing the custard with whipped cream. As an alternative to stale cake, use crumbled biscuits; instead of fresh fruit, a purée and instead of the coconut topping, sprinkle with chopped nuts, candied peel, glacé cherries, or fresh fruit dipped in sherry . . . The combinations are endless.

Pears with Chestnut Chocolate Sauce

425g (15 oz) can	chestnut purée	15 oz can
55g (2 oz)	margarine	¼ cup
55g (2 oz)	plain chocolate	2 oz
4 medium	commice pears	4 medium
140ml (¼ pt)	water	⅔ cup
1 tbs	lemon juice	1 tbs
½ tsp	ground mixed spice	½ tsp
¼ tsp	ground cloves	¼ tsp

1 In a small saucepan, stir together the chestnut purée and margarine, and heat gently until melted. Crumble the chocolate and add this to the mixture, stirring until you have a smooth sauce. Set aside to cool.
2 Peel the pears but leave them whole, put them into a pan and cover with the water, lemon juice and spices. Simmer gently for 30 minutes, turning occasionally, and basting with the syrup. Cool the pears before spooning into four small bowls, topping each one with some of the sauce.

Note: This is a delicious alternative to the better known pears with chocolate sauce. Use white wine instead of the lemon juice when cooking the pears if liked.

Baked Stuffed Pears

4 large	firm pears	4 large
2 tbs	lemon juice	2 tbs
85g (3 oz)	wholemeal (wholewheat) cake crumbs	1½ cups
2 tbs	syrup	2 tbs
2 tbs	tahini	2 tbs
30g (1 oz)	almonds, coarsely chopped	¼ cup
	cream - optional	

1 Peel, halve and core the pears. Brush them with lemon juice, then pack closely in a shallow baking dish. Pour just a little water over them.
2 Mix together the cake crumbs, syrup, tahini and nuts, and use the mixture to fill the pear halves. Cover the dish with a lid or greased foil.
3 Bake at 190°C/375°F (Gas Mark 3) for 20 minutes or until the pears are cooked. Drain them well and divide between four dishes. Serve hot or chilled with cream.

Note: Breadcrumbs may be used instead of cake crumbs and for extra sweetening, add another spoonful of syrup, or some raisins. Candied peel also works well in this recipe.

Fruit Kebabs

2	kiwi fruit, peeled and sliced	2
½ small	pineapple, peeled and diced	½ small
2 large	peaches, peeled and quartered	2 large
2	bananas, cut into chunks	2
2 tbs	lemon juice	2 tbs
2 tbs	honey or syrup	2 tbs
1 tsp	ground mixed spice	1 tsp

1 Arrange the prepared fruit on four small skewers, alternating the colours.
2 Lightly beat together the lemon juice, sweetener and spice, then brush the syrup over the fruit, or carefully pour it, turning the fruit so that everything is evenly coated.
3 Grill the kebabs gently, turning frequently until all the fruit is hot, but not overcooked. Serve at once.

Note: These are perfect for barbecues. Use other fruits as available.

Fresh Figs with Yogurt Cream

8	fresh figs, washed and quartered	8
6 tbs	whipping cream	6 tbs
140ml (¼ pt)	yogurt	⅔ cup
1 tsp	vanilla essence	1 tsp
¼ tsp	ground cinnamon	¼ tsp
1-2 tbs	honey	1-2 tbs

1 Divide the prepared figs between four small bowls.
2 Blend together the cream and yogurt and continue beating until thick and smooth. Add the vanilla, cinnamon, and honey to taste. Drop a spoonful or two on top of the figs and serve at once.

Note: Simple to prepare, this perfect combination is not only low in fats, but tastes wonderful. Use crème fraîche instead of yogurt, either straight from the tub, or flavoured with cinnamon and honey. Choose figs that are just ripe but not over-ripe, and free from blemishes.

11

Traditional Sweets

Because they need a high sugar content to make them set, most traditional sweets cannot be called healthy. The ones that follow are no exception. However, they do contain some nutrients. Most of the ingredients are natural and unadulterated, the sugar content has been reduced as much as possible without spoiling the finished effect and colourings and additives have been kept to a minimum.

When making syrups, always use heavy-based saucepans and make sure the sugar has dissolved completely before bringing it to the boil. Make sure your wooden spoons and spatulas have long handles to avoid splashing yourself with boiling syrup. If you intend to make sweets often, a sugar thermometer is a good buy. However, you can judge the various stages your syrup has reached by dropping a teaspoon of it into a cup of cold water and noting its reaction. (Always remove the saucepan from the heat while testing so the syrup does not go past setting point.) Syrup will go through the following stages:

Smooth	105°C/220°F	Sugar clings to fingers in a sticky film
Soft ball	114°C/237°F	Syrup can be rolled into a soft ball between fingers
Firm ball	119°C/247°F	Forms a firm but pliable ball
Soft crack	137°F/280°F	Separates into threads which break quite easily
Hard crack	154°C/310°F	Separates into hard, brittle threads
Caramel	171°C/340°F	Sugar goes much harder

Remember that all the recipes in this section are made without preservatives, and therefore will not keep as well as commercially produced sweets. If intending to keep them for some time, wrap items individually and store in a cool, dry place.

Chocolate Hazelnuts

115g (4 oz)	whole hazelnuts, lightly roasted	1 cup
approx. 115g (4 oz)	plain chocolate	4 oz

1 The nuts should be free of any skin – if this is hard to remove, roast them briefly in the oven so that the skins flake.
2 Break the chocolate into small pieces and place it in the top of a double boiler, or a bowl over a pan of hot water (making sure it does not touch the water). Cover and leave to melt, stirring occasionally.
3 Check the consistency of the melted chocolate: if it is too thin, cool briefly; or too thick, heat gently for a few more minutes.
4 Drop the nuts, a few at a time, into the chocolate. Turn so that they are completely coated, then use a fork to lift them out, tapping gently to remove any excess chocolate.
5 Space small clusters of two or three coated nuts well apart on a tray lined with greaseproof paper or silver foil, and allow to set until hard.

Note: Try also using Brazil nuts or almonds. Although eating chocolate can be used for this recipe, a more professional finish will be achieved with cooking chocolate. It is likely that this will be made with refined white sugar.

Orange Brazils

225g (8 oz)	sugar	1⅓ cups
140ml (¼ pt)	concentrated orange juice	⅔ cup
340g (12 oz)	whole Brazil nuts	3 cups

1 Stir together the sugar and orange juice in a saucepan and bring to the boil gently, stirring continually. Continue boiling until the mixture reaches soft ball stage (*see page 94*), then remove from the heat.
2 Check that the nuts are free from any skins (see note above). Add them to the orange syrup and continue stirring as this cools. When the mixture thickens, use a teaspoon to drop the coated nuts onto greaseproof paper. Leave to get cool completely.

Note: Other fruit juices may be used in the same way.

Raisin and Nut Carob Clusters

115g (4 oz)	plain carob bar	4 oz
55g (2 oz)	raisins	⅓ cup
55g (2 oz)	hazelnuts, roasted and coarsely chopped	½ cup

1 Break the carob bar into small pieces and melt it gently in the top of a double boiler, or a bowl over a pan of hot water (taking care it does not touch the water). Cover and stir occasionally.
2 Remove from the heat, then drop the raisins and chopped nuts into the carob and stir well.
3 Use a small metal spoon to lift out a cluster of the mixture, and drop it either onto silver foil or greaseproof paper, or into individual paper cases. Leave until firm.

Note: You can also use chocolate or white chocolate in the same way. Add stem ginger for a change.

Honey Toffee Apples

4 medium	apples	4 medium
225g (8 oz)	sugar	1⅓ cups
4 tbs	thick honey	4 tbs
55g (2 oz)	butter or margarine	¼ cup
1 tsp	vinegar	1 tsp

1 Wipe the apples and, if the skin is extra shiny, score with a grater or sharp knife. Remove the stalks.
2 Combine the sugar, honey, fat and vinegar and, over a medium heat, bring the mixture to the boil, stirring continually until the sugar dissolves. Continue boiling for 20 minutes or until it reaches hard crack stage (*see page 94*). Remove from the heat at once.

3 Spear each apple with a stick. Dip them, one at a time, into the toffee, turning them so that they are evenly coated. Leave to cool on a greased tray, or standing in a jam jar.

Note: If the toffee starts to get too thick before all the apples have been dipped, heat it again briefly.

Sesame Crunch

225g (8 oz)	sesame seeds	1¾ cups
55g (2 oz)	sugar	⅓ cup
225g (8 oz)	honey	⅔ cup

1 Lightly cook the sesame seeds in a frying pan over a medium heat for 5 minutes, or until they are just beginning to colour. Stir them as you do so, taking care not to let them over cook.
2 In a heavy-based pan, combine the seeds, sugar and honey. Bring to the boil and then continue boiling slowly for about 15 minutes, until the mixture reaches hard crack stage (*see page 94* - chapter introduction).
3 Pour into a medium-sized greased tin (a Swiss roll tin is ideal). Smooth the top, mark into squares, and leave to cool. Break into squares before storing or eating.

Note: In this unusual crunch sweet, a mixture of coarsely chopped nuts may be substituted for half of the seeds.

Marzipan Mice

225g (8 oz)	almonds, ground	2 cups
115g (4 oz)	caster sugar	⅔ cup
1	free-range egg white	1
few drops	almond essence	few drops
	vegetable colouring - optional	
	angelica, string, silver balls etc.	

1 Mix the almonds and sugar, then lightly beat the egg white and use to bind the nuts and sugar. Add the almond essence, then knead well. Add colouring if using.
2 Divide the dough into even-sized pieces, shaping each into a mouse. Use pieces of angelica to make the ears, silver balls for the eyes and string for the tail. Leave to dry.

Note: Other marzipan animals or even fruits may be made in the same way. Most health food shops sell natural colourings for sweets, but otherwise, use spinach or beetroot juice, etc, which have very little flavour. A vegan marzipan can be made using ground almonds and syrup, although this will not mould as well.

Mixed Nut Brittle

225g (8 oz)	sugar	1⅓ cups
285ml (½ pt)	water	1⅓ cups
1 tsp	lemon juice	1 tsp
115g (4 oz)	almonds, lightly roasted	1 cup
115g (4 oz)	Brazil nuts	1 cup
115g (4 oz)	cashew nuts	1 cup
115g (4 oz)	peanuts, lightly roasted	1 cup

1 In a heavy-based saucepan, stir together the sugar and water and cook over a medium heat, still stirring, until the sugar dissolves. Bring to the boil and continue boiling steadily, without stirring, for 15 minutes, or until the sugar begins to darken and reaches light caramel stage (*see page 94*).
2 Meanwhile, coarsely chop the almonds and Brazil nuts and mix with the cashews and peanuts.
3 As soon as the syrup is ready, remove from the heat and stir in the lemon juice and then the nuts, making sure they are evenly distributed. Working quickly, turn the mixture onto a greased tray and spread as thinly as possible. Leave to cool completely, then break into uneven pieces.

Note: This is a deliciously chunky brittle. For a traditional praline, use unskinned almonds only, chopping them coarsely and preparing in the same way.

Honeycomb

3 tbs	runny honey	3 tbs
15g (½ oz)	margarine	1 good tbs
55g (2 oz)	sugar	⅓ cup
4 tbs	water	4 tbs
½ tsp	cider vinegar	½ tsp
½ tsp	bicarbonate of soda	½ tsp

1 In a large saucepan, stir together the honey, margarine, sugar, water and cider vinegar. Heat gently, stirring continually, until boiling. Boil briefly then turn the heat even higher and continue cooking until the mixture reaches hard crack stage (*see page 94*).
2 Remove from the heat and add the bicarbonate of soda, which will make the mixture froth up instantly. Pour it into a greased shallow tin and leave to get cold.
3 Break into small pieces and eat.

Note: Unlike commercially made honeycomb, this does not keep well, so eat it within one or two days.

Creamy Carob Fudge

200ml (⅓ pt)	milk	⅔ cup
55g (2 oz)	butter or margarine	¼ cup
30g (1 oz)	carob powder	¼ cup
225g (8 oz)	sugar	1⅓ cups
5 tbs	skimmed milk powder	5 tbs
4 tbs	water	4 tbs
1 tsp	vanilla essence	1 tsp
1 tsp	lemon juice	1 tsp

1 Combine the milk, fat and carob powder in a saucepan and heat gently, stirring continually. Add the sugar, heating until it dissolves.
2 Bring the mixture to the boil and boil gently, stirring occasionally, until it reaches firm ball stage (*see page 94*). Set aside to cool briefly.
3 Stir the skimmed milk powder into the water, add the essence and lemon juice. Pour into a shallow greased tin, smooth the top and leave until firm. Cut into squares to serve.

Note: As an alternative to carob, cocoa powder may be used. A vegan version can be made with soya milk (fresh or powdered).

Nougat

115g (4 oz)	almonds, lightly roasted	1 cup
55g (2 oz)	angelica	2 oz
55g (2 oz)	glacé cherries	2 oz
115g (4 oz)	sugar	⅔ cup
4 tbs	honey	4 tbs
2 tbs	water	2 tbs
2 medium	free-range egg whites	2 medium
	rice paper	

1 Coarsely chop the nuts, angelica and cherries, and set aside.
2 Gently heat the sugar, honey and water in a saucepan, stirring until the sugar dissolves. Continue cooking gently until the mixture reaches firm ball stage (*see page 94*). Beat the egg whites until stiff, then add to the syrup, beating continually.
3 Add the nuts, angelica and cherries, mixing well.
4 Line a small tin with rice paper, pour in the mixture and top with more rice paper. Press down evenly with a weight and leave to set before cutting into squares.

Note: Look out for natural angelica and cherries or, for a healthier version, replace them altogether with other dried fruit such as raisins, sultanas or chopped apricots.

Coconut Ice

340g (12 oz)	sugar	2 cups
140ml (¼ pt)	milk	⅔ cup
115g (4 oz)	desiccated coconut	1⅓ cups

1 In a saucepan, stir together the sugar and milk and bring slowly to the boil, stirring continually. When the sugar has dissolved and the mixture starts to boil, lower the heat and continue boiling – without stirring – for 10 minutes, or until it reaches soft ball stage (see page 94).
2 Remove from the heat immediately and stir in the coconut, making sure it is well mixed.
3 Pour into a greased, shallow tin, using a knife to smooth the top. Leave to cool completely before cutting into squares.

Note: To make peppermint coconut ice add 1 teaspoon of peppermint essence to the cooked syrup just before pouring into the tin and leaving to set.

Candied Orange Peel

4	oranges	4
170g (6 oz)	sugar	1 cup
4-6 tbs	water	4-6 tbs
55g (2 oz)	caster sugar	⅓ cup

1 Carefully pare away the thin outer peel of each orange, cut into strips, place in a pan with water and boil for 10 minutes. If any white pith remains on the peel it should now be easy to remove.
2 In a clean saucepan, combine the sugar and water, stir, and heat to make a syrup. Add the peel and simmer gently until it becomes transparent. (This can take up to an hour.)
3 Drain the peel well, roll in the caster sugar, and leave on a wire rack to dry. Keep in an airtight container until needed. Eat as a candy, add to cakes or sprinkle over ice creams.

Note: Lemon, lime or grapefruit peel can be candied in the same way.

Turkish Delight

½ tsp	tartaric acid	½ tsp
2 tsp	rosewater	2 tsp
55g (2 oz)	cornflour	½ cup
455g (1 lb)	sugar	2⅔ cups
285ml (½ pt)	water	1⅓ cups
30g (1 oz)	pistachio nuts, chopped	¼ cup
	caster sugar for coating	

1 Stir together the tartaric acid, rosewater, and a tablespoon of cold water, then set aside.

2 Combine the cornflour, sugar and water in a saucepan and bring gently to the boil, stirring continually. Continue boiling, without stirring, until the mixture reaches the smooth stage (see page 94).
3 Add the rosewater, stir well, then add the nuts and distribute evenly. Pour the mixture into a shallow, lightly-greased tin and leave to cool completely.
4 When set, cut into squares and roll in the remaining sugar.

Note: For a prettier effect, colour half of the mixture with pink natural colouring, leaving the rest white.

Molasses Toffee

55g (2 oz)	margarine	¼ cup
55g (2 oz)	butter	¼ cup
225g (8 oz)	sugar	1⅓ cups
170g (6 oz)	molasses	6 oz

1 Melt the margarine and butter in a saucepan, then add the sugar and continue heating and stirring until it dissolves. Add the molasses, blend well and boil the syrup gently – without stirring again – until it reaches hard crack stage (see page 94).
2 Pour immediately into a greased, medium-sized shallow tin and leave to set hard. Break into rough portions.

Note: For a milder flavoured (but less nutritious!) version, use treacle instead of molasses.

Marrons Glacés

455g (1 lb)	fresh chestnuts, equal sized	1 lb
455g (1 lb)	sugar	2½ cups
140ml (¼ pt)	water	⅔ cup
few drops	vanilla essence	few drops

1 To prepare the chestnuts, make a cross in the top of each one then add to boiling water and boil for 10 minutes. Carefully remove the peel and inner skins using a sharp knife.
2 Make a thick syrup by stirring the sugar into the water and heating gently until it dissolves. Bring to the boil, drop the chestnuts into the syrup, and boil for 10 minutes. Leave in the syrup overnight, preferably in a warm place.
3 The following day, bring the syrup and chestnuts to the boil again, then leave overnight once more.
4 On the third day, add the vanilla to the syrup, bring it back to the boil once more and simmer the chestnuts gently for a few minutes. Transfer to warm, clean jars, making sure that the chestnuts are completely covered with syrup. Seal well.

Note: Although these are not the same as real French marrons glacés, they are very tasty. Dried chestnuts can be used instead of fresh ones, in which case you should reconstitute them before adding to the syrup.

Pine Nut Clusters

140g (5 oz)	pine nuts	1 cup
340g (12 oz)	sugar	2 cups
140ml (¼ pt)	water	⅔ cup
2 tbs	lemon peel, finely grated	2 tbs

1 Gently roast the pine nuts in a frying pan for just a few minutes, taking care that they do not colour. Set aside.
2 Combine the sugar and water in a saucepan and bring to the boil slowly, stirring so that the sugar dissolves completely. Continue boiling until the syrup reaches hard crack stage (*see page 94*), then remove from the heat immediately.
3 Stir in the nuts and lemon peel. Drop teaspoons of the mixture onto a baking sheet covered with greased foil and leave to cool completely.

Note: These Italian-style sweets can be lightly crushed to make a delicious topping for ice cream sundaes.

Carrot and Almond Balls

225g (8 oz)	sugar	1⅓ cups
4 tbs	water	4 tbs
455g (1 lb)	carrots, peeled and finely grated	1 lb
1 tbs	lemon juice	1 tbs
30g (1 oz)	almonds, coarsely chopped	¼ cup
30g (1 oz)	almonds, ground	¼ cup

1 In a saucepan, and over a low heat, dissolve the sugar in two tablespoons of the water, stirring continually. Add the grated carrot and continue cooking, without stirring, until the carrots are soft.
2 Add the remaining water and lemon juice and stir. Cook gently until the mixture thickens to a paste. Stir in the chopped almonds.
3 Pour the mixture into a lightly-greased tray and leave to cool. Then divide the paste into even-sized pieces, roll into balls and coat with the ground almonds. Set aside to cool before serving.

Note: If the dough is sticky to handle, wet your hands.

Crème de Menthe Jellies

30g (1 oz)	agar agar	2 tbs
285ml (½ pt)	water	1⅓ cups
4 tbs	crème de menthe	4 tbs
340g (12 oz)	sugar	2 cups
2 tbs	lemon juice	2 tbs
½ tsp	tartaric acid	½ tsp
	few drops natural green colouring - optional	
	extra caster sugar	

1 Add the agar agar to the water and heat gently, stirring continually, until the agar agar dissolves. Stir in the sugar and continue heating gently, stirring continually, until the sugar dissolves. Bring to the boil and continue boiling for 5 minutes, stirring continually.
2 Stir in the crème de menthe, lemon juice and tartaric acid, mixing well. If using colouring, add it now. Wet a large shallow tin, pour off any excess water and spoon in the mixture, spreading it evenly. Leave until cold and firm.
3 Cut the jelly into small squares and roll them in extra sugar.

Note: Use peppermint essence instead of crème de menthe if you prefer.

Sunflower Seed Toffee

115g (4 oz)	margarine or butter	½ cup
225g (8 oz)	sugar	1⅓ cups
55g (2 oz)	sunflower seeds	½ cup

1 Melt the margarine in a heavy-based saucepan, add the sugar, and continue heating gently and stirring continually until the sugar has dissolved. Continue heating - without stirring - until the mixture reaches hard crack stage (*see page 94*).
2 Remove from the heat at once and pour a thin layer into a greased shallow tray. Sprinkle half the seeds over the top, carefully pour on the remaining syrup and top with the rest of the seeds. Cool briefly then mark into squares. Leave to cool before breaking into pieces.

Note: If giving this toffee as a gift, wrap pieces individually as it tends to become sticky if not eaten quite soon.

Carob Easter Egg

225g (8 oz)   *carob bar, broken into*   *8 oz*
            pieces
            filling of your choice

1 You will need two small egg moulds for this. Make sure they are clean and dry before using.
2 Melt the carob in a bowl over a pan of hot water, stirring continually until you have a smooth paste.
3 Divide most of the paste between the moulds, tipping them so that the surfaces are completely and evenly covered. Then place them open side down on a plate and leave in the fridge until the carob is firm.
4 Carefully remove them from the moulds, and fill with sweets of your choice. Heat the remaining carob paste and use this to stick the two pieces together. When set, wrap in silver foil or other decorative foil and add bows or trimmings.

Note: Fill your Easter egg with any of the sweets described above, preferably individually wrapped. Use shredded tissue to hold them in place. Alternatively, make small individual eggs and fill them with marzipan.

12

Flans

Flans, pies, tarts – whatever you like to call them – all consist of a pastry base and a filling, and can be served hot or cold, with coffee or as a dessert. Occasionally flan bases are made of biscuit or other crumbs mixed with fat, but most of the ones that follow are pastry based, some of them rich, others sweet, a number of them suitable for vegans.

When making pastry keep the following in mind:

Always keep your hands and utensils as cold as possible, and work quickly so that the pastry itself doesn't get too warm.

Chilling the dough before using it gives time for the bran to soften, or, for a lighter pastry, sift out the bran and save it for another recipe. Alternatively use 81% flour which has already had the bran removed.

Use the minimum amount of flour on the board when rolling out the dough and roll only in one direction.

The finished sheet of dough should never be thicker than 5mm (¼ in).

Wholemeal pastry can be crumblier than that made with white flour. As you use it you'll soon get the knack of making pastry that holds together, but in the early stages you might like to roll it out between two sheets of cling-film, then peel off the top sheet and use the bottom one to help lift the pastry when transferring it to the flan dish.

Baking pastry 'blind' means without a filling. When baking blind pastry made with white flour, hold in place with foil and cooking beans as it tends to buckle. Heavier wholemeal pastry is less likely to do this, but it is a good idea to prick the base with a fork to allow hot air to escape.

As with cheesecakes, using a flan dish looks more attractive, but using a flan ring standing on a baking sheet makes it easier to remove.

When making pastry, try to make extra quantities to roll out into cases and freeze for future use.

Papaya Flan

Pastry

140g (5 oz) approx.	margarine	⅔ cup approx.
2 tbs	cold water	2 tbs
225g	wholemeal (wholewheat) flour	2 cups

Filling

1 medium	ripe papaya, peeled and stoned	1 medium
115g (4 oz)	margarine	½ cup
170g (6 oz)	sugar	1 cup
1 tbs	concentrated orange juice	1 tbs
2 medium	free-range eggs, beaten	2 medium

1 In a bowl, use a fork to mix together the margarine, water, and some of the flour. Gradually add the rest of the flour to make a firm dough. Turn onto a lightly floured board and knead until the dough is smooth and elastic. Wrap in silver foil and chill for 30 minutes.

2 Meanwhile, mash or blend the papaya flesh to make a thick purée. Cream together the margarine and sugar, add the orange juice and then the eggs. Carefully stir in the papaya purée.

3 Roll out the pastry and use to line a flan dish or ring standing on a baking sheet. Pour in the purée and smooth the top. Bake at 190°C/375°F (Gas Mark 5) for 20 to 30 minutes or until set. Serve warm or cold.

Note: This all-in-one pastry is quicker to make than the more usual method where the fat has to be rubbed into the flour. Use it for other recipes too. In the above recipe you can use lemon juice instead of the concentrated orange juice if preferred.

Coconut Tart

Pastry

170g (6 oz)	wholemeal (wholewheat) flour	1½ cups
85g (3 oz)	margarine	⅓ cup
2-3 tbs	cold water	2-3 tbs

Filling

3 tbs	jam	3 tbs
55g (2 oz)	margarine	¼ cup
55g (2 oz)	sugar	⅓ cup
1 large	free-range egg, beaten	1 large
85g (3 oz)	desiccated coconut	1 cup
55g (2 oz)	wholemeal (wholewheat) flour	½ cup
½ tsp	baking powder	½ tsp
	cold water as required	

1 Put the flour into a bowl and use fingertips to rub in the margarine to make a crumb-like mixture. Add just enough cold water to make a fairly firm dough. Knead this briefly then wrap in silver foil and chill for 30 minutes. When ready, roll out the pastry and use to line a flan dish or flan ring standing on a baking sheet.

2 Spread the jam across the base of the prepared pastry. Cream together the margarine and sugar, then gradually add the egg, stirring well. Add most of the coconut. Sift together the flour and baking powder and add this to the mixture with just enough cold water to give a soft dropping consistency.

3 Spoon the mixture into the prepared flan case and sprinkle with the remaining desiccated coconut. Bake at 190°C/375°F (Gas Mark 5) for 30 to 40 minutes or until the filling is firm. Leave for a few minutes before either serving immediately or transferring to a wire rack to cool completely.

Note: Apricot is the traditional jam for this tart but blackcurrant, plum and even lemon curd taste very good. Alternatively, try a thick fruit purée.

Sour Cream Pie with Hazelnut Pastry

Pastry

140g (5 oz)	wholemeal (wholewheat) flour	1¼ cups
85g (3 oz)	hazelnuts, ground to a powder	¾ cup
85g (3 oz)	margarine	⅓ cup
30g (1 oz)	sugar	2 tbs
2-3 tbs	cold water	2-3 tbs

Filling

2 tsp	wholemeal (wholewheat) flour	2 tsp
½ tsp	ground mixed spices	½ tsp
200ml (¾ pt)	sour cream	¾ cup
2 medium	free-range eggs, well beaten	2 medium
115g (4 oz)	sugar	⅔ cup
1 tsp	vanilla extract	1 tsp
55g (2 oz)	candied peel	2 oz

1 Mix together the flour and nuts, then use fingertips to rub in the margarine so that the mixture resembles fine breadcrumbs. Stir in the sugar and enough water to make a dough. Transfer to a lightly floured board and knead briefly before wrapping in silver foil to chill for 30 minutes.

2 Sift the flour (reserve the bran for use in another recipe), add the spices and a little of the sour cream, then gradually add the remaining cream. Stir in the eggs, sugar and candied peel.

3 Roll out the pastry and use to line a flan dish or ring standing on a baking sheet. Heat the oven to 200°C/400°F (Gas Mark 6), place the pie in the oven, and immediately lower the heat to 170°C/325°F (Gas Mark 3). Bake for about 40 minutes or until the filling is firm. Serve warm or cold, either alone or with a topping of fruit purée or fresh fruit such as berries or banana.

Note: If you cannot get sour cream, thick yogurt may be used instead to make a yogurt pie.

Tofu Pumpkin Pie

Pastry

140g (5 oz)	wholemeal (wholewheat) flour	1¼ cups
30g (1 oz)	rolled oats	¼ cup
85g (3 oz)	margarine	¾ cup
2-3 tbs	cold water	2-3 tbs

Filling

455g (1 lb)	pumpkin, peeled and seeded	1 lb
2 tbs	cornflour	2 tbs
4 tbs	syrup	4 tbs
1 tsp	ground mixed spice	1 tsp
1 tsp	ground cinnamon	1 tsp
½ tsp	ground nutmeg	½ tsp
285g (10 oz)	tofu, drained	1¼ cups
1 medium	apple, peeled, cored and sliced - optional	1 medium
1 tbs	lemon juice - optional	1 tbs

1 Stir together the flour and oats, then use fingertips to rub the margarine into the ingredients to make a crumb-like mixture. Add enough water to make a dough, knead this briefly, then wrap in silver foil and chill for 30 minutes.

2 Meanwhile, prepare the filling. Chop the pumpkin into small pieces and steam until very soft, then drain well. Combine the pumpkin, cornflour, syrup, spices and tofu, either mashing them well to make a thick smooth mixture or using a blender.

3 Roll out the pastry and use to line a flan dish or flan ring standing on a baking sheet. Pour in the pumpkin mixture. If liked, top the pie with a ring of apple slices brushed with lemon juice. Bake at 200°C/400°F (Gas Mark 6) for 40 to 50 minutes or until firm.

Note: Any syrup can be used in this recipe but maple syrup gives it a delicious flavour.

Crunch Nut Topped Pumpkin Pie

Pastry

170g (6 oz)	wholemeal (wholewheat) flour	1½ cups
85g (3 oz)	margarine	⅓ cup
1 tbs	caster sugar	1 tbs
2-3 tbs	cold water	2-3 tbs

Filling

455g (1 lb)	pumpkin, peeled and seeded	1 lb
2 medium	free-range eggs, lightly beaten	2 medium
140ml (¼ pt)	yogurt	⅔ cup
3 tbs	honey	3 tbs
1 tsp	ground cinnamon	1 tsp
1 tsp	ground ginger	1 tsp
½ tsp	vanilla essence	½ tsp

Topping

85g (3 oz)	margarine, melted	¾ cup
85g (3 oz)	sugar	½ cup
2 tsp	ground cinnamon	2 tsp
15g (½ oz)	wholemeal (wholewheat) flour	2 tsp
30g (1 oz)	walnuts, chopped	¼ cup

1 Make the pastry by using fingertips to rub together the margarine and flour so that the mixture resembles fine breadcrumbs. Stir in the sugar, then add enough water to make a medium firm dough. Knead this briefly, then wrap in silver foil and chill for 30 minutes. When ready, roll out the pastry and use to line a flan dish or a flan ring standing on a baking sheet.

2 Cut the pumpkin into cubes and steam them until just tender. Drain well and mash to a thick purée. Add the eggs, yogurt, honey, spices and vanilla essence, beating all the ingredients together so that they are well mixed. Pour the filling into the flan case and smooth the top.

3 Melt the margarine, then stir in the sugar, spices, flour

and chopped nuts and sprinkle over the pie. Bake at 190°C/375°F (Gas Mark 5) for 30 to 40 minutes or until firm.

Note: This subtly flavoured pumpkin pie with its sweet and crunchy topping is delicious warm or cold. If you prefer, just use nuts and avoid the extra sugar.

Lime Chiffon Pie

Pastry

170g (6 oz)	muesli base	6 oz
1 tbs	sesame seeds	1 tbs
3 tbs	vegetable oil	3 tbs
3 tbs	honey or syrup	3 tbs

Filling

3 tsp	agar agar	3 tsp
3 tbs	lime juice	3 tbs
2 medium	free-range eggs	2 medium
4 tbs	honey syrup	4 tbs
140ml (¼ pt)	whipping cream	⅔ cup
	lime slices - optional	

1 Mix together the muesli base, seeds, oil and honey and use to line the base and sides of a flan ring standing on a baking tray, pressing it down evenly with your fingers. Bake at 200°C/400°F (Gas Mark 6) for 20 minutes. Cool before removing the case very carefully and transferring it to a serving dish.

2 Combine the lime juice and agar agar in a small saucepan and heat gently until almost boiling, then simmer for 3 minutes. Set aside.

3 In a bowl over a pan of hot water, stir together the egg yolk and honey until thick and creamy, then add the agar agar mixture and cook for a few more minutes. Cool slightly. Whip the whipping cream until foamy, fold in the whisked egg whites, and add this to the other ingredients.

4 Pour the mixture into the prepared case, smooth the top, and chill well. Decorate with lime slices, if liked.

Note: Use lemon juice instead of the lime if limes are difficult to find. You can also use low fat white cheese or crème fraîche instead of whipping cream.

Three Fruit Marmalade Flan

Pastry

170g (6 oz)	wholemeal (wholewheat) flour	1½ cups
85g (3 oz)	margarine	⅓ cup
30g (1 oz)	sugar	2 tbs
1 medium	free-range egg, lightly beaten	1 medium

Filling

4 tbs	Three Fruit Marmalade (see page 114)	4 tbs
2 tbs	margarine	2 tbs
6 tbs	wholemeal cake crumbs	6 tbs
1 large	free-range egg, lightly beaten	1 large
55g (2 oz)	whole blanched almonds	½ cup
	crème fraîche or thick yogurt to serve - optional	

1 Put the flour into a bowl and use fingertips to rub in the margarine to make a crumb-like mixture. Stir in the sugar and add the egg to make a dough. Knead this briefly and then wrap in silver foil and chill for 30 minutes.
2 Mix together the marmalade, margarine, breadcrumbs and egg, stirring well.
3 Roll out the pastry and use to line a flan dish or flan ring standing on a baking sheet. Spoon the filling into the case and smooth the top. Bake at 190°C/375°F (Gas Mark 5) for 20 minutes, then arrange the blanched almonds on the top of the flan and continue cooking for another ten minutes or until set. Serve warm or cold.

Note: Any marmalade can be used with this recipe. For those who like oranges, add a tablespoon or two of coarsely chopped orange peel.

Banana Custard Pie

Pastry

115g (4 oz)	margarine	½ cup
55g (2 oz)	caster sugar	⅓ cup
170g (6 oz)	wholemeal (wholewheat) flour	1½ cups
1 tsp	baking powder	1 tsp

Filling

2 large	bananas, peeled and sliced	2 large
425ml (¾ pt)	soya milk	2 cups
85g (3 oz)	sugar	½ cup
3 tbs	arrowroot	3 tbs
1 tsp	vanilla essence	1 tsp
3 tbs	granola (see page 62)	3 tbs

1 Cream together the margarine and sugar until light and fluffy. Sift the flour and baking powder and add to the first mixture, stirring until you have a dough. Knead this briefly before wrapping in silver foil and chilling for 30 minutes. When ready, roll out the pastry and use to line a flan dish or ring standing on a baking sheet. Prick with a fork, then bake at 200°C/400°F (Gas Mark 6) for 20 minutes or until cooked. Leave to cool.
2 Arrange the sliced bananas across the base of the pie. In a small saucepan, combine most of the milk and the sugar and heat gently. Stir the arrowroot into the remaining milk, then add this to the saucepan and continue heating and stirring until the custard is thick and smooth. Add the vanilla essence and cool slightly before pouring over the bananas and smoothing the top.
3 Chill before serving, sprinkled with the granola.

Note: As an alternative use apple purée instead of banana.

Chilled Rhubarb Flan

Pastry

200g (7 oz)	wholemeal (wholewheat) flour	1¾ cups
1 tsp	ground ginger	1 tsp
100g (3½ oz)	margarine	a good ⅓ cup
1 tbs	caster sugar	1 tbs
1 medium	free-range egg yolk	1 medium
1-2 tbs	cold water	1-2 tbs

Filling

approx. 170g (6 oz)	sugar	approx. 1 cup
200ml (⅓ pt)	water	¾ cup
455g (1 lb)	rhubarb, cleaned and cut into small pieces	1 lb
4 tsp	agar agar	4 tsp
3 tbs	cold water	3 tbs

Topping

200ml (⅓ pt)	whipping cream	¾ cup
½ tsp	ground ginger - optional	½ tsp
1-2 tbs	syrup from stem ginger - optional	1-2 tbs

1 Sift together the flour and ginger, then use fingertips to rub in the margarine to make a mixture resembling fine breadcrumbs. Stir in the sugar, then add the egg yolk and enough water to make a dough. Wrap in silver foil and chill for half an hour. Roll out and use to line a flan dish or ring standing on a baking sheet. Prick the base with a fork and bake blind at 190°C/375°F (Gas Mark 5) for 20 minutes or until cooked.

2 Combine the sugar and water in a saucepan and cook gently, stirring continually, to make a syrup. Add the rhubarb, stir well and cover the pan. Cook for ten minutes or until the rhubarb is soft, then blend to make a thick purée.

3 In a small saucepan, combine the agar agar and water and bring gently to the boil stirring continually, then simmer for 3 more minutes. Combine this with the sweetened rhubarb purée. Pour the mixture into the flan case, smooth the top, and chill until set.

4 Whip the cream together with the ginger and, when stiff, stir in the syrup. Use to decorate the top of the flan.

Note: The exact amount of sugar and water needed will depend on the rhubarb, so taste it as you go along, but take care not to add too much liquid or the jelly will not set. Vegans can use nut cream instead of whipped cream as a topping.

Tumbled Fruit Flan

Pastry

170g (6 oz)	wholemeal (wholewheat) flour	1½ cups
85g (3 oz)	margarine	⅓ cup
1 tbs	orange peel, finely grated	1 tbs
3 tbs	orange juice	3 tbs

Filling

170g (6 oz)	tofu, well drained	¾ cup
1 tsp	ground cinnamon	1 tsp
3 tbs	maple syrup, or to taste	3 tbs
455g (1 lb)	mixed fruit (e.g. peaches, kiwis, pineapples, grapes etc.)	1 lb
approx. 2 tbs	lemon juice	approx. 2 tbs

1 Put the flour into a bowl and use fingertips to rub in the margarine to make a mixture resembling fine breadcrumbs. Stir in the orange peel, then add the juice to bind. Knead briefly, wrap in silver foil, and chill for 30 minutes. When ready, roll out the pastry and use to line a flan dish or flan ring standing on a baking sheet. Prick the dough and bake at 200°C/400°F (Gas Mark 6) for 20 minutes. Set aside to cool.

2 Blend together the tofu, cinnamon and maple syrup to make a thick, creamy mixture. Spread this over the base of the flan.

3 Clean and chop the fruit as necessary – this will depend on the fruits you have chosen to use, but try to have pieces as even in size as possible. Add lemon juice so that the fruit retains its colour, but drain off any excess liquid.

4 Tumble the fruit into the flan base and serve at once.

Note: This is ideal for dinner parties. Prepare the flan and the tofu in advance and put the whole mixture together just before serving. Use whatever fruits are in season. You may also use a cream cheese such as ricotta or quark instead of the tofu.

Honey Pecan Pie

Pastry

170g (6 oz)	wholemeal (wholewheat) flour	1½ cups
1 tsp	baking powder	1 tsp
85g (3 oz)	margarine	⅓ cup
2-3 tbs	cold water	2-3 tbs

Filling

55g (2 oz)	sugar	⅓ cup
2 large	free-range eggs, lightly beaten	2 large
55g (2 oz)	margarine	¼ cup
140ml (¼ pt)	honey	⅔ cup
1 tsp	vanilla essence	1 tsp
170g (6 oz)	pecan nut halves	1¼ cups
	crème fraîche or ice cream to serve	

1 Blend together the flour and baking powder, then use fingertips to rub in the margarine to make a crumb-like mixture. Add enough water to make a medium firm dough, knead this briefly, wrap in silver foil and chill for 30 minutes.

2 Meanwhile, mix together the sugar and beaten eggs. In a small saucepan combine the margarine and honey and heat gently until melted. Add the vanilla essence and mix with the sugar and eggs. Stir in most of the nuts, making sure they are evenly distributed.

3 Roll out the dough and use to line a flan case or flan ring standing on a baking sheet. Prick the base with a fork and bake at 200°C/400°F (Gas Mark 6) for 15 minutes or until just beginning to become firm.

4 Carefully add the filling and decorate the top with the remaining nuts. Return to the oven, lower the heat to 180°C/350°F (Gas Mark 4), and continue cooking for 40 to 50 minutes or until the filling is set. Serve warm with crème fraîche or ice cream as a topping. Alternatively, serve cold.

Note: This is probably one of the most calorific flans there is! However, this version is slightly less fattening and has a few more nutrients.

Cinnamon Lemon Yogurt Pie

Pastry

170g (6 oz)	wholemeal (wholewheat) flour	1½ cups
2 tsp	cinnamon	2 tsp
85g (3 oz)	margarine	⅓ cup
2-3 tbs	cold water	2-3 tbs

Filling

45ml (¾ pt)	thick yogurt	2 cups
225g (8 oz)	ricotta cheese	1 cup
3 tbs	lemon juice	3 tbs
2-3 tbs	lemon peel, finely grated	2-3 tbs
3 tbs	syrup or honey or to taste	3 tbs

Topping

1-2 tbs	sugar	1-2 tbs
1-2 tsp	ground cinnamon	1-2 tsp

1 Sift together the flour and cinnamon, then use fingertips to rub in the margarine so that the mixture resembles fine breadcrumbs. Add just enough cold water to bind the ingredients together, making a medium firm dough. Knead this briefly then wrap in silver foil and chill for 30 minutes. Roll out the dough and use to line a flan dish or ring standing on a baking sheet. Prick the base with a fork, and bake at 200°C/400°F (Gas Mark 6) for 20 minutes or until just cooked. Set aside to cool.

2 Blend together the yogurt, ricotta cheese, lemon juice, lemon peel and sweetener and pour into the prepared flan case. Smooth the top and chill well, preferably overnight.

3 Just before serving, stir together the sugar and cinnamon and sprinkle generously over the pie.

Note: Freshly ground cinnamon makes all the difference to this recipe.

Cherry Bakewell Tart

Pastry

170g (6 oz)	wholemeal (wholewheat) flour	1½ cups
85g (3 oz)	margarine	⅓ cup
55g (2 oz)	caster sugar	⅓ cup
2-3 tbs	milk	2-3 tbs

Filling

85g (3 oz)	glacé cherries, halved	½ cup
85g (3 oz)	margarine	⅓ cup
85g (3 oz)	sugar	½ cup
1 large	free-range egg, beaten	1 large
¼ tsp	almond essence	¼ tsp

55g (2 oz)	wholemeal (wholewheat) flour	½ cup
1 tsp	baking powder	1 tsp
115g (4 oz)	ground almonds	1 cup
30g (1 oz)	flaked almonds	¼ cup

1 Put the flour into a bowl and use fingertips to rub in the margarine to make a crumb-like mixture, then stir in the sugar. Add just enough milk to make a soft dough, kneading this briefly before wrapping it in silver foil and chilling for at least 30 minutes.

2 Roll out the pastry and use to line a flan dish or flan ring standing on a baking sheet. Cover the base evenly with the cherries, putting them cut side down.

3 Cream together the margarine and sugar. Add the egg and almond essence. Sift together the flour and baking powder, then add this to the first mixture. Finally, stir in the ground almonds making sure they are well mixed. Spread this mixture evenly over the cherries, and top with the flaked almonds.

4 Bake at 190°C/375°F (Gas Mark 5) for 35 to 45 minutes or until firm. Serve warm or cold.

Note: Buy glacé cherries at the health shop where they will be as close to natural as possible i.e. free from artificial colouring and perhaps preserved in raw cane sugar. Alternatively, use jam or marmalade underneath the almond topping.

Pear Crumble Flan

85g (3 oz)	desiccated coconut	1 cup
2 tbs	sugar	2 tbs
115g (4 oz)	wholemeal (wholewheat) flour	1 cup
115g (4 oz)	margarine	½ cup
445g (1 lb)	pears	1 lb
1 tbs	lemon juice	1 tbs
30g (1 oz)	hazelnuts, roasted and coarsely chopped	¼ cup

1 Combine the coconut and sugar in a bowl, then stir in the flour. Use fingertips to rub in the margarine to make a crumb-like mixture. Lightly grease a flan ring standing on a baking sheet and press most of the mixture into the bottom, using your fingertips to smooth it.

2 Peel, core and slice the pears and spread them over the base. Sprinkle with the remaining crumble, mixed with the hazelnuts.

3 Bake at 200°C/400°F (Gas Mark 6) for 20 minutes or until the top is nicely browned. Serve warm or cold.

Note: This quick and easy flan is meant to be crumbly! Other fruits may be used instead of the pears, but avoid those that are too moist or the base will disintegrate.

Oaty Lemon Meringue Pie

Base

170g (6 oz)	oat crunch cereal or granola (see page 62)	6 oz
85g (3 oz)	margarine, melted	⅓ cup

Filling

2 tbs	cornflour	2 tbs
285ml (½ pt)	water	1⅓ cups
55g (2 oz)	sugar	⅓ cup
3 medium	free-range eggs, separated	3 medium
4 tbs	lemon juice	4 tbs
2 tbs	lemon peel, grated	2 tbs

Topping

85g (3 oz)	caster sugar	½ cup
¼ tsp	cream of tartar	¼ tsp

1 Mix the oat crunch cereal with the margarine, making sure they are well blended, then press the mixture against the base of a flan ring standing on a baking sheet.
2 Combine the cornflour with a drop of the water. Heat the rest of the water, then stir the cornflour paste into it and return it to the pan. Bring gently to the boil, stirring continually and cook for two minutes. Add the sugar and cool briefly before adding the egg yolks, lemon juice and peel. Pour this mixture into the prepared case.
3 Beat the egg whites until frothy, add the sugar and cream of tartar and pile the mixture over the pie. Bake at once at 180°C/350°F (Gas Mark 4) for 8 minutes or until the top begins to brown. Best served warm.

Note: For a citrus meringue pie, use half lemon juice, half orange juice and combine some orange peel with the lemon peel.

Chocolate Orange Flan

Pastry

225g (8 oz)	wholemeal (wholewheat) flour	2 cups
140ml (¼ pt)	vegetable oil	⅔ cup
2-3 tbs	cold water	2-3 tbs

Filling

3 tbs	cocoa	3 tbs
3 tbs	cornflour	3 tbs
115g (4 oz)	sugar	⅔ cup
700ml (1¼ pts)	soya milk	3 cups
1 tsp	ground cinnamon	1 tsp
1 tbs	concentrated orange juice	1 tbs
1 tbs	orange peel, finely grated	1 tbs

Topping

2 small	oranges, peeled	2 small
2 tbs	apricot jam, warmed	2 tbs

1 Put the flour into a bowl, add the oil, and use fingertips to blend it well with the flour. Add just enough water to bind the ingredients to a dough and knead this briefly. Wrap in silver foil and chill for at least 30 minutes. Press the dough across the base and sides of a flan ring standing on a baking sheet and bake at 230°C/450°F (Gas Mark 8) for 10 minutes. Set aside to cool.
2 To make the filling, sift together the cocoa and cornflour, then add the sugar and soya milk. Transfer to a small saucepan and cook gently, stirring continually, until the custard thickens. Add the cinnamon, orange juice and peel and cook for 2 more minutes. Cool briefly before pouring into the prepared case, smoothing the top and chilling well.
3 Either break the orange into segments or cut it into rings with a sharp knife. Use these to decorate the top of the flan, brushing the fruit with some of the jam for a shiny effect.

Note: If fresh oranges are unavailable, use canned mandarin oranges instead. You can also use carob powder instead of cocoa.

French Apple Flan

Pastry

85g (3 oz)	margarine	⅓ cup
55g (2 oz)	sugar	⅓ cup
140g (5 oz)	wholemeal (wholewheat) flour	1¼ cups
1 medium	free-range egg, lightly beaten	1 medium

Filling

115g (4 oz)	marzipan (see page 95)	4 oz
455g (1 lb)	tart apples, cored and thinly sliced	1 lb
2 tbs	warmed honey	2 tbs

1 Cream together the margarine and sugar. Gradually sprinkle in the flour, using a wooden spoon to mix it with the fat, then add the egg and enough water to make a firm dough. Knead this briefly before wrapping in silver foil and chilling for 30 minutes. Roll out and use to line a flan dish or flan ring standing on a baking sheet. Prick the bottom with a fork, and bake blind at 200°C/400°F (Gas Mark 6) for 10 minutes. Cool slightly.
2 Roll out the marzipan, cut it into a circle to fit the flan

dish, and place over the base. Arrange the slices of apples overlapping in circles across the top of the flan. .

3 Bake at 200°C/400°F (Gas Mark 6) for 10 minutes, then lower the heat to 180°C/350°F (Gas Mark 4) and continue cooking for a further 20 to 30 minutes or until the pastry is crisp. Brush the apples with the warmed honey before serving.

Note: Fleur pastry is light and crisp and ideal for this flan, though you can use any pastry you like. Apples may be replaced by other fruits, for example pears.

Butterscotch and Walnut Pie

Pastry

225g (8 oz)	wholemeal (wholewheat) flour	2 cups
115g (4 oz)	margarine	½ cup
3-4 tbs	cold water	3-4 tbs

Filling

55g (2 oz)	margarine, melted	¼ cup
115g (4 oz)	dark sugar	⅔ cup
85g (3 oz)	fine semolina	¾ cup
570ml (1 pt)	soya milk	2½ cups
55g (2 oz)	walnut halves	½ cup
	soya 'cream', to serve	

1 Put the flour into a bowl and use fingertips to rub in the margarine to make a crumb-like mixture. Stir in just enough cold water to bind to a dough, knead this briefly, then wrap in silver foil and chill for 30 minutes. When ready, roll out the pastry and use to line a flan dish or flan ring standing on a baking sheet and prick the base with a fork. Bake blind at 200°C/400°F (Gas Mark 6) for 20 to 30 minutes or until cooked. Set aside to cool.

2 Add the sugar to the melted margarine and heat – stirring continually – until it foams. Allow to continue foaming for 2 more minutes, then stir in the semolina and cook briefly. Stir in the soya milk and continue cooking, stirring continually until the sauce thickens. Simmer for a further 2 minutes before pouring into the prepared case.

3 Leave to cool briefly, then top with the walnut halves arranged decoratively. Chill the pie before serving with soya 'cream'.

Note: This delicious pie is far less calorific than it tastes. Instead of the soya 'creem' vegetarians could use crème fraîche or whipped cream.

Dried Fruit Flan

Pastry

170g (6 oz)	maize flour	1½ cups
85g (3 oz)	firm margarine	⅓ cup
55g (2 oz)	sugar	⅓ cup
approx. 2 tbs	cold water	approx. 2 tbs

Filling

115g (4 oz)	dried prunes, soaked overnight	1 cup
115g (4 oz)	dried apricots, soaked overnight	1 cup
115g (4 oz)	dried pears, soaked overnight	1 cup
115g (4 oz)	raisins	⅔ cup
2 tbs	lemon peel, grated	2 tbs
1 tsp	vanilla essence	1 tsp
55g (2 oz)	sugar - optional	⅓ cup
55g (2 oz)	walnut pieces, coarsely chopped	½ cup
55g (2 oz)	margarine, melted	¼ cup

1 Put the flour into a bowl and use fingertips to rub in the margarine to make a crumb-like mixture. Stir in the sugar and enough cold water to bind to a dough. Knead this briefly before wrapping in silver foil and chilling for 30 minutes.

2 If the dried fruit is tender, simply drain it. If still firm, you may like to cook it briefly in the minimum of water for 5 to 10 minutes, then drain well. Chop the larger fruit into small pieces and mix well with the raisins, peel, vanilla essence and sugar, if using it. Stir in the nuts and melted margarine, blending well.

3 Roll out the pastry and use to line a flan case standing on a baking sheet. Add the fruit and nut mixture, spreading it evenly. Bake the flan at 190°C/375°F (Gas Mark 5) for 30 minutes or until the pastry is crisp. Serve hot, warm or cold.

Note: This unusual pastry is gluten-free, and can be used with a variety of other fillings.

Wild Blackberry Tart

Pastry

115g (4 oz)	wholemeal (wholewheat) flour	1 cup
55g (2 oz)	rolled oats	½ cup
1 tbs	sugar	1 tbs
1 tbs	sesame seeds	1 tbs
2 tbs	sunflower seeds, chopped	2 tbs
½ tsp	ground mixed spice	½ tsp
85g (3 oz)	margarine	⅓ cup
3-4 tbs	cold water	3-4 tbs

Filling

455g (1 lb)	wild blackberries	1 lb
2-3 tbs	blackcurrant or apple juice	2-3 tbs
30-55g	sugar, or to taste (1-2 oz)	2-4 tbsp
	soya 'cream' or dairy cream to serve	

1 Stir together the flour and oats, then add the sugar, seeds and spice. Use fingertips to rub in the margarine to make a crumb-like mixture, then add enough cold water to bind. Wrap the dough in silver foil and chill for at least 30 minutes. When ready, press the dough into a flan ring standing on a baking sheet, using your fingers or the back of a spoon to make it as even as possible.

2 Prick it with a fork, then bake at 220°C/425°F (Gas Mark 7) for 10 minutes. Cool, then remove very carefully and transfer to a serving plate.

3 Clean the blackberries removing any stalks and mix them with the juice, draining off any excess. Pile the fruit into the prepared case, sprinkle it with sugar, and serve at once with cream.

Note: This very simple dessert is surprisingly good, especially when the blackberries used are big and sweet. Other fruits can be used in the same way.

13
Sauces, Spreads and Jams

While this might sound like an odd combination, sauces, spreads and jams have one thing in common: they can all be used as ingredients when making desserts, either added as flavourings, poured over ice creams or puddings, or used as fillings. Spreads and jams can also be used just as they are on toast, biscuits or muffins.

So what is the difference? Spread can be almost pure fruit, fresh or dried, with one or two other ingredients added. They are rarely cooked and so need to be kept in a cool place, and consumed within a relatively short time. Jams, on the other hand, are a combination of fruit and sugar boiled to reach setting point. This means that they contain more calories – but that they keep considerably longer.

Some basic rules for making jams:

Always use a heavy-based saucepan – and one large enough to prevent the jam from boiling over.
Cook the fruit slowly, both to soften the skins and release the pectin (a natural setting substance).

It is important to stop cooking jam the moment setting point is reached, which can take 3 to 5 minutes or longer. Check frequently and take the pan off the heat while doing so. The easiest way to check is to pour a spoonful of the jam into a very cold saucer and leave for a minute. If, when touched, it wrinkles, the jam is ready. Any jam that contains no whole fruit can be poured at once into clean, warm jars. If it contains fruit pieces it should be left to stiffen a little first, then stirred. Fill the jars right to the top, cover at once with waxed discs, then add a cellophane cover and seal. Store in a cool, dark, dry place.

Nut Cream

170g (6 oz) approx.	nut pieces	1½ cups approx.
140ml (¼ pt)	fruit juice	⅔ cup
	syrup or honey - optional	
	ground spices - optional	

1 In a grinder combine the nuts with enough fruit juice to make a cream of the desired consistency.
2 If necessary, sweeten to taste. Add spices if liked. Pour the cream into a jug and serve at once, or chill briefly. Delicious in place of dairy cream as a topping for fruit salad or other desserts.

Note: You can use any nuts and any fruit juices to make nut cream. Cashews are especially good, but you could also use almonds, Brazil nuts or peanuts. Hazelnuts taste best if roasted and then combined with concentrated soya milk.

Red Berry Purée

1.15kg	mixed red fruits (i.e. raspberries, blackberries, strawberries, loganberries etc.)	2 lbs
55g (2 oz) approx.	caster sugar	⅓ cup approx.
4 tbs	cold water	4 tbs
½ tsp	vanilla essence	½ tsp
½ tsp	ground cardamom	½ tsp

1 Prepare the fruit by washing and trimming as appropriate. Set aside.

2 In a small saucepan, stir together the sugar, cold water, vanilla essence and cardamom. Heat gently, stirring, until the sugar dissolves, then continue cooking for a few more minutes to thicken.

3 Add the prepared fruit, stir well, cover and cook for 5 minutes, or until the fruit softens. You may need to add a little more water, but do not make the mixture too wet.

4 This purée can be served mashed or blended, or with the fruit left intact, hot or cold, with cream, yogurt, nut creams, whatever you like.

Note: Make a green fruit purée in the same way using greengages, gooseberries, kiwi fruit, or a golden purée, using apricots, peaches and yellow plums. These purées are ideal for fruit fools – make extra and freeze in advance for instant desserts.

Tofu Chocolate Sauce

170g (6 oz)	plain chocolate broken into pieces	6 oz
340g (12 oz) approx.	silken tofu, well drained soya milk	1½ cups approx.
4 tbs		4 tbs

1 Place the chocolate in the top of a double boiler, or a bowl over a saucepan of hot water, and stir continually until melted.

2 Blend the tofu to make a thick smooth cream and gradually add this to the melted chocolate, stirring well. Add the soya milk. Serve hot or cold.

Note: This is particularly good with ice cream or cooked pears. You can use a carob bar instead of the chocolate.

Kumquat Sauce

455g (1 lb)	kumquats	1 lb
285ml (½ pt)	water	1⅓ cups
115g (4 oz)	sugar	⅔ cup
1 tsp	ground cinnamon	1 tsp

1 Carefully wash the kumquats, wipe dry, then cut in half lengthways. Put them into a pan with the other ingredients, bring to the boil, then cover and simmer for 30 minutes.

2 Serve hot.

Note: These tiny oranges have a wonderful flavour much of which comes from the peel which should be left on. For special occasions, add a few spoonfuls of brandy to the sauce.

Apple Purée

1.15kg (2 lbs)	apples, peeled, cored and quartered	2 lbs
285ml (½ pt)	water	1⅓ cups
2 tbs	concentrated apple juice, or to taste	2 tbs
1 tbs	lemon juice	1 tbs

1 Blend the apples with most of the water to make a purée, put this into a pan, add the remainder of the water, the apple and the lemon juice. Cook gently for 15 minutes or until thick and smooth. Serve hot or cold.

Note: The amount of concentrated apple juice you will need to sweeten your purée will depend on the type of apples you use. This basic purée can be adapted in a wide variety of ways, for example, by adding spices, raisins or nuts. For a creamier purée, stir in some cream, yogurt, tofu or tahini.

Apricot Sauce

225g (8 oz)	dried apricots, washed	2 cups
200ml (⅓ pt)	water	¾ cup
2 tbs	orange juice	2 tbs
2 tbs	orange peel, finely grated	2 tbs
½ tsp	ground cinnamon	½ tsp
4 tsp	arrowroot	4 tsp
1 tbs	water	1 tbs

1 Soak the apricots in the water for at least an hour, preferably longer. Bring them to the boil in the same water, lower the heat and cook gently for 10 minutes or until soft (the time this takes will depend on how fresh the apricots are). Stir in the orange juice and peel and cinnamon, then set aside to cool before blending to make a thick purée.

2 In a small bowl, stir together the arrowroot and water. Add this to the apricot purée and bring back to the boil gently before lowering the heat and simmering for a few minutes, or until the sauce thickens.

3 Serve hot or cold over ice cream, puddings, fruit salad etc.

Note: Use apple juice instead of orange juice for a sweeter sauce. Raspberry, strawberry, and other fruit purées can be made in exactly the same way – allow approximately 225g/8oz fresh fruit to replace the apricots.

Spiced Cream Sauce

1 tbs	cornflour	1 tbs
285ml (½ pt)	milk	1⅓ cups
30g (1 oz)	sugar	2 tbs
140ml (¼ pt)	whipping cream	⅔ cup
½ tsp	ground ginger	½ tsp
½ tsp	ground mixed spice	½ tsp
¼ tsp	ground nutmeg	¼ tsp

1 In a small bowl, stir the cornflour into a few spoonfuls of the milk. Put the rest of the milk into a saucepan, heat gently, then gradually whisk in the cornflour mixture. Continue heating until the sauce thickens. Stir in the sugar and continue stirring until melted.
2 Whip the whipping cream until thick and smooth, then fold this into the white sauce with the spices and serve at once.

Note: This pale creamy sauce is particularly delicious with dark spicy sponges or heavier puddings such as Christmas pudding. Without the cream it can be flavoured in a variety of ways to make other sweet sauces, for example, melted chocolate, or fruit purée.

Hot Lemon Sauce

2 medium	lemons	2 medium
	cold water	
55g (2 oz)	sugar	⅓ cup
1 tbs	arrowroot	1 tbs
¼ tsp	ground nutmeg	¼ tsp

1 Thinly peel the lemons, reserving the peel. Squeeze as much juice as possible from the lemons, add enough water to make up to 285ml/½ pint and set aside two tablespoons of this. Pour the rest into a small saucepan, add the sugar, and bring gently to the boil, stirring continually.
2 Mix the remaining liquid with the arrowroot to make a smooth paste, then slowly pour on the hot syrup, mixing well. Return this to the pan, add the nutmeg, and continue simmering until the sauce becomes thick and clear. Stir in some of the finely chopped peel, if liked.

Note: Use this sauce with puddings, over pancakes or waffles, or as a delicious alternative to custard when served with such dishes as apple crumble.

Quickest Ever Lemon Sauce

225g (8 oz)	lemon curd (see page 114)	8 oz
3 tbs	lemon juice	3 tbs
	water	

1 Tip the lemon curd into a saucepan, add the lemon juice and enough water to give the mixture a pouring consistency. Heat gently then transfer to a jug.
2 This sauce can also be used cold as a topping for sundaes, lemon meringue pie, etc.

Note: Other curds can be used in the same way to make instant sauces.

Marmalade Sauce

30g (1 oz)	margarine	2½ tbs
15g (½ oz)	cornflour	2 tbs
3 tbs	marmalade	3 tbs
3-6 tbs	orange juice	3-6 tbs

1 Melt the margarine in a small pan, stir in the flour and cook briefly, stirring continually to make a smooth paste.
2 Add the marmalade, mix well, then thin down with enough orange juice to make a sauce - the consistency is up to you. Serve at once.

Note: Apart from being delicious with puddings, especially sponges, try this sauce with ice cream and a sprinkling of chopped roasted hazelnuts.

Butterscotch Sauce

2 tbs	syrup	2 tbs
115g (4 oz)	sugar	⅔ cup
30g (1 oz)	margarine	2½ tbs
2 tbs	hot water	2 tbs
few drops	vanilla essence	few drops
4 tbs	concentrated soya milk or cream	4 tbs

1 Combine the syrup, sugar and margarine in a small saucepan and heat gently, stirring, until the sugar dissolves. Boil for a few minutes, then remove from the heat.
2 Stir in the hot water and add the vanilla essence and milk, mixing well. Serve at once or leave to cool.

Note: This sauce is delicious served over fresh fruit salads, or with puddings.

Honey Butterscotch Sauce

1 tbs	butter	1 tbs
4 tbs	thick honey	4 tbs
4 tbs	crème fraîche	4 tbs

1 Stir all the ingredients together in a small pan, bring gently to the boil and continue boiling and stirring for 2 minutes. Cool slightly before serving.

Note: This very rich sauce only needs to be used in tiny amounts for effect. Try it with home–made vanilla ice cream.

Mango Lassi

2 large	ripe mangoes	2 large
570ml (1 pt) approx.	natural yogurt	2½ cups approx.
55g (2 oz)	caster sugar	⅓ cup

1 Peel and remove the stones from the mangoes. Mash or purée the flesh in a blender.
2 Combine with the yogurt and sugar, adjusting the sweetness as necessary. Serve as a drink in four glasses.

Note: This traditional Indian drink is also delicious as a sauce with fruit salad or poured over a sorbet. You may need to adjust the consistency depending on how you intend to serve it. Tinned mango purée is ideal in this recipe – usually it is ready sweetened so you won't need to add sugar. Vegans can make lassi with vegan yogurt or soya milk.

Carob Sauce

85g (3 oz)	carob powder	¾ cup
200ml (⅓ pt)	water	¾ cup
3 tbs	syrup or honey, or to taste	3 tbs
1 tsp	vanilla essence	1 tsp

1 Whisk together the carob powder and water, transfer to a small saucepan, and cook over a low heat for 5 minutes or until the mixture begins to thicken. Use extra carob powder for a thicker sauce, or extra water for a thinner sauce.
2 Stir in the syrup or honey to taste, add vanilla essence, and serve either hot or cold.

Note: This is a very simple and basic carob sauce that can be adapted in a wide variety of ways. For example, add butter, ground nuts, yogurt or soured cream. A chocolate sauce can be made in the same way using cocoa instead of the carob powder.

Sweet Peanut Spread

170g (6 oz)	peanut butter	⅔ cup
4 tbs	syrup	4 tbs
1 tsp	vanilla essence	1 tsp

1 Simply combine all the ingredients and store in a screw top jar in the fridge.

Note: Use better quality peanut butter for this spread which has not been sweetened and has a minimum of additives. Instead of the syrup, sweeten it with honey or stir in some jam for an American-style spread.

Malted Sesame Sunflower Spread

115g (4 oz)	sesame seeds, ground	¾ cup
115g (4 oz)	sunflower seeds, ground	¾ cup
2 tbs	vegetable oil	2 tbs
2 tbs	barley malt syrup	2 tbs

1 Put the seeds into a bowl, stir in the oil, then add the barley malt syrup and mix thoroughly, until everything is well blended.
2 You should have a thick smooth paste – if not, add extra oil or syrup as required. Store in a screw–top jar in the fridge where it should keep for a few weeks.

Note: It is the barley malt syrup that gives this spread its distinctive flavour, plus of course lots of valuable nutrients. Other syrups or honey may be used instead, and carob powder may be added for a chocolate flavoured spread.

Cinnamon Apple Butter

1.15 kilos (2 lbs)	apples	2 lbs
6 tbs	water	6 tbs
2 tbs	syrup or honey	2 tbs
1 tsp	ground cinnamon, or to taste	1 tsp
¼ tsp	ground mixed spice	¼ tsp
¼ tsp	ground cloves	¼ tsp

1 Wash and chop the apples coarsely. Remove the cores but leave the skin, if liked. Cook the apples in the water for about 1 hour or until the mixture becomes thick. Make sure it does not boil dry but do not add more water than is absolutely necessary.
2 In a blender, make a smooth purée of the apples, adding the sweetener and spices, then return the mixture to the pan and continue heating gently until thick and dry.
3 Transfer to hot clean jars, cool, then cover carefully and store in the fridge. This butter should keep for several weeks.

Note: The cinnamon needs to be the strongest flavour here although any other spices may be used.

Carob and Coconut Spread

115g (4 oz) approx.	creamed coconut	½ cup approx.
6 tbs	hot water	6 tbs
2 tbs	sugar, or to taste	2 tbs
4 tbs	Carob Spread	4 tbs
	concentrated soya milk - optional	

1 Grate the coconut into a bowl, stir in the boiling water to make a thick cream, add sugar and the Carob Spread immediately, so that it will also dissolve. Mix well.
2 For a creamier spread, add a few spoonfuls of concentrated soya milk.
3 Store the cream in a screw top jar in a cool place, preferably the fridge.

Note: You can buy Carob Spread in wholefood shops. It is usually available either sweetened or unsweetened, so if you buy the sweetened version you may not need to add any extra sugar to this particular spread. Alternatively, use the recipe for Carob Sauce (*see page 112*) in this spread but make it with less water. Coconut cream sets quite firm, so you will find this is a fairly stiff spread – ideal to use on hot toast or muffins, or as a filling for cakes or biscuits. To make it into a sauce use more water or soya milk, preferably serving it hot or warm as, even with extra liquid, it will become very thick when cold.

Cashew Spread with Raisins

115g (4 oz)	cashew nuts, ground	1 cup
4 tbs	water or fruit juice	4 tbs
55g (2 oz)	raisins	⅓ cup

1 Blend all the ingredients in a blender, adjusting the liquid as necessary. Transfer to a jar, seal well and store in the fridge for one to two weeks.

Note: You can use dried dates, figs or apricots instead of the raisins.

Maple Soya Spread

4 tbs	vegetable oil	4 tbs
4 tbs	soya flour	4 tbs
2 tbs	maple syrup, or to taste	2 tbs

1 Stir together the oil and soya flour and when well blended and free from lumps, add maple syrup to taste. Store in a screw-top jar in the fridge.
2 Use in small amounts with toast or warm-from-the-oven cakes, or sandwiched between biscuits.

Note: To make a maple tahini spread, combine equal amount of tahini and maple syrup. This is delicious trickled over pancakes.

Pineapple Spread

395g (14 oz) can	pineapple pieces in natural juice	14 oz
3 tbs	arrowroot	3 tbs
2 tbs	syrup - optional	2 tbs

1 Drain the pineapple well, reserving the juice. Mince or crush the fruit as finely as possible.
2 In a small dish stir the arrowroot into 3 tbs of the reserved juice, then transfer this paste to a small saucepan and heat gently, stirring continually until thick.
3 Add the pineapple and sweetener, if using it, and continue cooking for 20 to 30 minutes or until the spread is dry and smooth, stirring frequently. Check that it does not get too dry, adding a little more pineapple juice if necessary.
4 Transfer to a small, clean jar and seal well. Store in the fridge and use to fill cakes, or spread on bran muffins.

Note: You may like to add ginger to the spread - either ground or chopped preserved - but do not use too much or you will spoil the flavour of the pineapple. To make this into a pouring sauce, simply add extra juice as needed - orange juice makes an unusual change from pineapple juice.

Wild Apricot Spread

455g (1 lb)	dried wild apricots	1 lb
2 tsp	orange flower water	2 tsp
1-2 tbs	caster sugar - optional	1-2 tbs

1 Cover the apricots with water, bring to the boil, turn off the heat and leave for 1 hour. Pour off the water, then add fresh water and bring to the boil before simmering for 10 minutes or until the apricots are soft.
2 Drain off the liquid. Remove the stones and mash the apricot flesh or purée in a blender. Add the orange flower water and sugar as necessary. Blend again before spooning the spread into sterilized jars and leaving to cool. Cover and store in the fridge.

Note: Wild apricots - also called Hunza apricots - give this spread its distinctive taste. To make a sauce simply add water and orange juice.

Creamy Date and Ricotta Spread

225g (8 oz)	dates, chopped	2¼ cups
1 tbs	lemon juice	1 tbs
approx.	water	approx.
4 tbs		4 tbs
55g (2 oz)	ricotta cheese	¼ cup

1 Place the dates in a saucepan with the lemon juice and water, and cook gently, stirring frequently with a wooden spoon, until the mixture is thick and creamy. Beat well to make sure there are no lumps. Cool.
2 Add the cream cheese and blend thoroughly. Store in the fridge and eat within a few days. Serve on toast or muffins, or use as a filling for a sponge cake.

Note: This sugar-free spread is surprisingly sweet – add more cheese if you like or use thick yogurt or Quark instead of ricotta. For a vegan version, mix tahini or blended tofu with the dates.

Banana and Pineapple Curd

115g (4 oz)	butter, melted	½ cup
115g (4 oz)	sugar	⅔ cup
1 large	lemon	1 large
3 large	ripe bananas, peeled and mashed	3 large
2 tsp	ground mixed spice	2 tsp
3 medium	free-range eggs, beaten	3 medium
3 slices	pineapple, fresh or tinned in natural juice	3 slices

1 In a saucepan, stir together the melted butter, sugar, juice and grated rind of the lemon, bananas and spice. Simmer gently for 10 minutes, stirring frequently.
2 Stir a couple of spoonfuls of the mixture into the beaten eggs. Then add the eggs to the mixture in the pan and continue to simmer, stirring continually, until the mixture is thick enough to coat the back of a wooden spoon.
3 Drain and crush the pineapple and stir into the banana mixture. Transfer to hot clean jars and seal well. Store in the fridge until needed. Serve spread on bread or muffins, as a filling for cakes, mixed with yogurt to make a mousse-like dessert, or as a topping for puddings.

Note: This curd can be made using other fruit instead of the pineapple, or you can simply omit the pineapple for a Banana Curd. To make Lemon Curd the traditional way, follow the same method, combining the juice and rind of two large lemons with the butter and sugar, then add the eggs.

Lemon Curd

55g (2 oz)	margarine	¼ cup
170g (6 oz)	sugar	1 cup
2 large	lemons	2 large
85g (3 oz)	arrowroot	¾ cup

1 Melt the margarine in a saucepan, then stir in the sugar and juice from the lemons. Heat gently for a few minutes, add the arrowroot, and stir well so that there are no lumps. Continue simmering until the mixture thickens.
2 Stir in 1 or 2 tablespoons of finely grated peel if liked. Allow the mixture to cool before storing in airtight jars in a cool place.

Note: Lower in fat and calories than the better known lemon curd which is made with eggs, this version is just as tasty and is easier to make too! As with the more traditional lemon curd, this recipe can be used with other citrus fruits. It can also be flavoured with spices.

Three-Fruit Marmalade

455g (1 lb)	citrus fruit (e.g. lemons, grapefruit and sweet oranges)	1 lb
1.7l (3 pt)	water	7½ cups
1.4kl (3 lb)	sugar	8 cups

1 Wash and halve the fruit, squeeze out the juice and set aside. Chop the peel. Put the seeds into a muslin bag and tie firmly.
2 Pour the water into a large saucepan and add the peel and seeds. Bring to the boil, then lower the heat and simmer for 1 hour or until reduced by about one-third.
3 Remove the bag containing the seeds and carefully squeeze out any excess liquid before discarding it. Use a wooden spoon to stir in the juice from the fruit and the sugar, then continue heating gently, stirring all the time, until it dissolves.
4 Bring back to the boil and cook without stirring for 10 minutes or until setting point is reached (see chapter introduction). When ready, cool the marmalade for a few minutes, stir well and transfer to warmed jars. Cover with waxed discs and seal.

Note: It is important to start testing early and keep testing when making this marmalade or it may not set easily. You can make marmalade using a single fruit in the same way.

Rhubarb and Fig Jam

1.15 kilos (2 lbs)	rhubarb, cleaned and trimmed	2 lbs
225g (8 oz)	dried figs, cleaned and dried	1¾ cups
1.15 kilos (2 lbs)	sugar	2 lbs
3 tbs	orange juice	3 tbs
2 tbs	lemon juice	2 tbs

1 Chop the rhubarb and figs as finely as possible. Put them into a heavy-based pan, add the sugar and fruit juice, stir well and leave to stand, preferably overnight.
2 Bring the mixture to the boil, stirring so that the sugar dissolves, then continue boiling rapidly until the mixture reaches setting point (see chapter introduction).
3 Leave to cool slightly before stirring again to distribute the fruit evenly. Transfer to warm jars, seal well and store in the fridge.

Note: This unusual fruit jam can also be made by combining rhubarb with other dried fruits.

Exotic Fruit Jelly

1.15 kilos (2 lbs)	fruits (e.g. mangoes, peaches, papayas, melons)	2 lbs
5 tbs	orange juice	5 tbs
2 tbs	orange peel, finely grated	2 tbs
2 sticks	cinnamon	2 sticks
285ml (½ pt)	water	1⅓ cups
1 tbs	agar agar extra water	1 tbs

1 Peel and stone the fruit as necessary, then chop the flesh into small pieces. Put it into a heavy-based saucepan with the orange juice and peel, and the cinnamon sticks, add the water, and bring to the boil. Lower the heat and simmer the fruit for 10 minutes.
2 Remove the cinnamon sticks.
3 In a small bowl, stir the agar agar with a few spoonfuls of cold water to make a paste, add this to the pan, then bring back to the boil gently. Simmer for a few minutes, then cool slightly and transfer to warm jars and seal. Store in the fridge.

Note: Use the same method to make other fruit jellies, either combining different varieties or using just one. For a firmer jelly, increase the amount of agar agar slightly. As no sugar has been added, this will not keep for very long.

Pumpkin Jam

680g (1½ lbs)	pumpkin, peeled, seeded and diced	1½ lbs
170g (6 oz)	sugar	1 cup
1 tbs	ground ginger	1 tbs
½ tsp	ground nutmeg	½ tsp
3 tbs	lemon juice	3 tbs

1 Steam the diced pumpkin until tender, drain well and purée or press through a sieve.
2 Place this mixture in a heavy-based pan with the sugar, spices and lemon juice. Stir well, then cook over a low heat for 50 minutes or until thick and smooth. Stir the mixture occasionally to make sure it does not burn.
3 Transfer to hot clean jars, then seal and store in the fridge for up to two weeks.

Note: For a more subtly flavoured jam use honey instead of sugar. Another interesting variation can be made by replacing the spices with ½-1 tsp of almond essence.

Vegetarian Mincemeat

225g (8 oz)	raisins, minced	1⅓ cups
225g (8 oz)	sultanas (golden seedless raisins), minced	1⅓ cups
455g (1 lb)	currants	1⅓ cups
115g (4 oz)	Brazil nuts, coarsely grated	1 cup
115g (4 oz)	almonds, coarsely grated	1 cup
225g (8 oz)	cooking apples, peeled, cored and grated	8 oz
1 tsp	ground nutmeg	1 tsp
2 tsp	ground cinnamon	2 tsp
2 tsp	ground mixed spice	2 tsp
2 tbs	lemon juice	2 tbs
2 tbs	lemon peel, finely grated	2 tbs
2 tbs	orange juice	2 tbs
2 tbs	orange peel, finely grated	2 tbs
2 tbs	brandy	2 tbs
115g (4 oz)	vegetarian suet, grated	½ cup

1 Simply combine all the ingredients, mixing well. Store in well sealed jars in the fridge until needed.

Note: You may omit the brandy although alcohol does help preserve mincemeat as well as adding to its flavour. Add some chopped stem ginger to the basic recipe to make a vegetarian ginger mincemeat if liked.

Marrow Jam with Ginger

1.15 kilos (2 lbs)	marrow, peeled, seeded and diced	2 lbs
565g (1¼ lbs)	sugar	1¼ lbs
1 tbs	lemon juice	1 tbs
55g (2 oz)	preserved ginger, finely chopped	2 tbs

1 Steam the marrow until tender, drain well and transfer to a bowl. Sprinkle with the sugar, cover and leave overnight.
2 Tip the mixture into a heavy-based saucepan, add lemon juice and bring to the boil. Lower the heat and cook for about 1 hour, stirring occasionally.
3 Test to see if jam has reached setting point (see chapter introduction). When ready, use a spoon to remove any froth from the top of the jam, then stir in the ginger, making sure it is well mixed. Pour the jam into hot jars and cool before covering. Seal and store in the fridge.

Note: Marrows for use in this recipe should be ripe but not too soft or they will be watery which will affect the quality of the jam.

Carrot Jam

approx. 1.4 kilos (3 lbs)	carrots, peeled and chopped	3 lbs
455g (1 lb)	sugar	2½ cups
4 tbs	lemon juice	4 tbs
2 tbs	lemon peel, finely grated	2 tbs

1 Add the carrots to a pint of boiling water, bring back to the boil, then simmer for 10 minutes or until soft. Drain well and mash or push through a sieve to make a purée. You should have about 455g/1 lb pulp – weigh this to be sure as too much will affect the quality of the jam.
2 In a heavy-based saucepan, stir together the carrot purée, sugar, lemon juice and peel. Heat gently, stirring continually until the sugar dissolves. Bring to the boil, and continue boiling gently, stirring and skimming occasionally, until the mixture begins to set. This can take from 10 to 20 minutes, so keep testing (*see* chapter introduction).
3 Transfer to clean jars, seal and store.

Note: This unusual jam can be adapted in a variety of ways. For a crunchier texture, add chopped cashew nuts.

No-sugar Strawberry Jam

680g	fresh strawberries, (1½ lbs)	1½ lbs cleaned and hulled
2 tbs	Pear and Apple Spread	2 tbs
1 tbs	lemon juice cold water as needed	1 tbs

1 Chop the strawberries and place them in a heavy-based pan with the spread and water, stirring so that they are thoroughly mixed.
2 Cook gently, mashing them frequently with a wooden spoon, until the mixture is thick and smooth. Take care that the mixture does not burn, but if you need to add extra water, keep this to the minimum.
3 Transfer to warmed jars and seal in the usual way. Store in the fridge for up to two weeks.

Note: This is a perfect recipe for less-than-perfect strawberries! Use other berries in the same way. As an alternative to Pear and Apple Spread, use concentrated apple juice.

14
Sweets from other Cultures

This is your chance to try out some of the sweets and sweet foods that are popular in other parts of the world. Some you may already know, others may be new to you but none are too difficult to make. While the recipes are as close as possible to the originals, some small changes have been made to allow for certain ingredients and tools being unavailable in your local shops.

Note that many of these sweets may have different names in different countries.

Amaretti

2 medium	free-range egg whites	2 medium
140g (5 oz)	sugar	¾ cup
½ tsp	almond essence	½ tsp
85g (3 oz)	almonds, ground	¾ cup
	rice paper	

1 Whisk the egg whites until frothy, then gradually add the sugar, a few spoonfuls at a time, and continue beating until the mixture is firm enough to hold peaks.
2 Fold in the almond essence and almonds. Place sheets of rice paper on baking sheets and drop teaspoons of the mixture onto the paper, leaving a little space between each mound.
3 Bake at 180°C/350°F (Gas Mark 4) for 20 minutes or until just beginning to colour. Cool, then tear or cut around the paper. Store in an airtight container.

Note: Serve these popular Italian macaroons at tea time, with creamy desserts such as chocolate mousse or with ice creams. Alternatively, crumble and use as a base for trifle, mix into cream to top fruit salad or soak in liqueur and spoon over sorbets.

Granita di Café (Coffee Water-Ice)

425ml (¾ pt)	water	2 cups
170g (6 oz)	sugar	1 cup
425ml (¾ pt)	strong coffee	2 cups

1 Boil the water and add the sugar, stirring gently until it has completely dissolved. Set aside to cool briefly then add the coffee.
2 Pour the mixture into a freezing tray and leave until it begins to turn mushy. Whisk well and freeze again. Repeat this until the mixture has a soft, fluffy texture rather like snow.
3 Serve in chilled glasses. If serving as a dessert, top with whipped cream.

Note: Coffee Water-Ice is especially popular with Italians, but you can make other versions using fruit juice or purées. Granita di melone, made with crushed melon, is delicious.

Zabaglione (Egg Creams)

4 medium	free-range egg yolks	4 medium
30g (1 oz)	sugar	2 tbs
3 tbs	Marsala wine	3 tbs
	biscuits to serve - optional	
	whipped cream and grated chocolate - optional	

1 Whisk together the egg yolks and sugar in a bowl over a pan of hot water until the mixture is creamy.
2 Add the Marsala, mix well, and continue heating until the sauce thickens to the consistency of custard.

3 Serve warm in tall glasses, accompanied by macaroons or other delicately flavoured biscuits. Alternatively, chill the zabaglione before serving and top with whipped cream and grated chocolate.

Note: You can replace the sugar with honey, or, to avoid alcohol, use grape juice instead of Marsala. However, Marsala is a vital ingredient of the truly Italian zabaglione!

Cenci (Fried Pastry Knots)

115g (4 oz)	81% wholemeal (wholewheat) flour	1 cup
1 small	free-range egg, beaten	1 small
1 small	free-range egg yolk	1 small
30g (1 oz)	sugar	2 tbs
1 tbs	brandy - optional vegetable oil for frying caster sugar	1 tbs

1 Mix the flour with the egg and egg yolk, add the sugar and brandy. Knead until smooth and elastic, then cover the dough with a damp cloth and leave to rest for 30 minutes.
2 Divide into 2 pieces, rolling each one out as thinly as possible. Use a sharp knife to cut the pastry into strips approximately 10cm (4 in) × 1cm (½ in) in size. Gently tie each strip to make a simple knot.
3 Heat enough oil for deep frying. Drop in the knots, a few at a time, and cook for 2 to 3 minutes, or until they start to crisp. Remove with a slotted spoon and leave to drain on paper towels while cooking the rest of the knots in the same way.
4 Sprinkle with sugar and serve with drinks.

Note: If not using brandy you might need to use large eggs. 81% flour is better than 100% wholewheat for this recipe as the rolled out pastry should be almost paper thin (the bran in 100% flour will make it coarser).

Pine Nut Sweets

140g (5 oz)	pine nuts	1¼ cups
340g (12 oz)	sugar	2 cups
140ml (¼ pt)	water	⅔ cup
2 tbs	lemon peel, finely grated	2 tbs

1 Place the pine nuts in a heavy-based pan and cook them over a medium heat for a few minutes, taking care not to let them colour.
2 In another pan, combine the sugar and water and heat gently, stirring continually, until the sugar dissolves. Bring to the boil and continue boiling, without stirring again, until the syrup reaches hard crack stage (*see page 94*). Remove from the heat at once.
3 Stir in the nuts and peel, mixing well. Drop small spoonfuls onto a baking sheet lined with foil. Leave to cool and set, then store in an airtight container.

Note: The pine nuts give this nut brittle a special taste. Try crushing a few pieces and sprinkling over a sundae.

Crème Caramel

140ml (¼ pt)	water	⅔ cup
115g (4 oz) + 2 tbs	sugar	⅔ cup + 2 tbs
4 medium	free-range eggs	4 medium
570ml (1 pt)	milk	2½ cups
½ tsp	vanilla essence fromage frais to serve	½ tsp

1 Gently heat the water and 115g/4 oz of the sugar in a saucepan, stirring continually until the sugar dissolves. Bring the mixture to the boil and continue boiling until the syrup thickens and darkens.
2 Pour the caramel into a 15cm (6 in) soufflé dish, tipping it so that the caramel spreads. Set aside to cool.
3 Lightly beat the eggs. Warm the milk with the vanilla essence and remaining sugar, add to the eggs, then strain the mixture into the soufflé dish.
4 Stand the dish in a larger pan and pour in hot water until it is half way up the side of the dish. Bake at 170°C/325°F (Gas Mark 3) for 1 hour, or until set. Cool, then transfer to the fridge to chill. When ready to serve, place a plate over the top and invert the dish, shaking it gently to loosen. As you remove it, the caramel will spill down the sides. Divide between four bowls and top with fromage frais.

Note: You can also make crème caramel in individual portions but reduce the cooking time by about 20 minutes, or until set.

Beignet de Pruneaux (Prunes in Batter)

225g (8 oz)	large prunes	1¾ cups
225ml (½ pt)	weak tea	1⅓ cups
2 tbs	rum	2 tbs
115g (4 oz)	wholemeal (wholewheat) flour	1 cup
3 tbs	vegetable oil	3 tbs
200ml (⅓ pt)	warm water	¾ cup
1 medium	free-range egg white	1 medium
1 tbs	rum	1 tbs
	vegetable oil for frying	
2 tbs	cocoa	2 tbs
2 tbs	vanilla sugar	2 tbs

1 Soak the prunes in the tea for a few hours, then drain, sprinkle with the rum, and set aside briefly.
2 Meanwhile, make the batter. Stir together the flour, oil, and enough warm water to make a thick smooth mixture. Leave in the fridge for 30 minutes. Beat the egg white and add to the batter with 1 tbs rum.
3 Remove the stones from the prunes. Dip each one into the batter and then deep fry for a few minutes, or until the batter is golden and crisp. Drain well and leave to cool.
4 Stir together the cocoa powder and vanilla sugar, and roll the battered prunes in the mixture. Arrange on a plate and serve.

Note: Omit the rum if you prefer.

Côeur à la Crème

225g (8 oz)	low fat soft white cheese	1 cup
140ml (¼ pt)	thick natural yogurt red berry purée (see page 109)	⅔ cup

1 Blend together the cheese and yogurt in a bowl. When well mixed, spoon into one large or 4 small heart-shaped moulds. Chill for at least 2 hours, preferably longer.
2 Carefully release the hearts, then tip each one onto a small plate. Top each heart with a generous serving of red berry purée, fresh wild strawberries or mulberries and serve at once.

Note: You can use a combination of different ingredients for these traditional French creams, for example, sieved cottage cheese, curd cheese, crème fraîche or double cream. The higher the fat content of the cheese, the better the hearts will hold their shape. You can also add whisked egg whites. Make sure the moulds are perforated to allow excess liquid to drain away (or line with muslin).

Crêpes Suzette

Crêpes

85g (3 oz)	wholemeal (wholewheat) flour	¾ cup
85g (3 oz)	plain white flour	¾ cup
2 medium	free-range eggs	2 medium
425ml (¾ pt)	milk	2 cups
1 tsp	vegetable oil	1 tsp
	vegetable oil for frying	

Sauce

55g (2 oz)	margarine	¼ cup
1 large	orange	1 large
55g (2 oz)	sugar	⅓ cup
2 tbs	Cointreau, or other liqueur	2 tbs
1 tbs	brandy	1 tbs

1 Sift together the two flours, make a well in the centre and add the eggs, milk and oil. Gently use a wooden spoon to combine the ingredients, then beat well to ensure the batter is lump-free and light. Set aside to cool for 30 minutes.
2 Meanwhile, in a small saucepan, combine the margarine, juice and grated peel of the orange, and the sugar. Stir over a medium heat until the sugar dissolves. Bring to the boil, then lower the heat again, add the Cointreau, and keep the sauce warm.
3 Beat the batter before using. The consistency should be like single cream so, if necessary, add a little more liquid. Heat a little oil in a small heavy-based pan, pour in a couple of spoonfuls of batter and tip the pan so that it spreads evenly. Cook gently until it starts to brown underneath, then flip or turn the crêpe with a spatula and cook the other side. Keep warm while using the rest of the batter in the same way.
4 Fold each crêpe into quarters and lay them in the sauce for a minute or two to heat up and absorb some of the syrup. Transfer to a heated serving dish.
5 Stir the brandy into the pan to blend it with any remaining sauce and heat gently. Then carefully set light to it, pour it over the crêpes, and take them to the table at once.

Note: You can use honey instead of sugar and lemon instead of orange. If you prefer omit the Cointreau and brandy, but these are what make these simple crêpes the world famous luxury dessert.

Kadaifi (Spiced Nut Pastry)

Pastry

340g (12 oz)	kadaifi dough (see below)	12 oz
55g (2 oz)	margarine, melted	¼ cup
115g (4 oz)	almonds, chopped	1 cup
115g (4 oz)	walnuts, chopped	½ cup
2 tsp	ground cinnamon	2 tsp
½ tsp	ground nutmeg	½ tsp

Rosewater Syrup

170g (6 oz)	sugar	1 cup
200ml (⅓ pt)	water	¾ cup
1 tbs	lemon juice	1 tbs
1-2 tsp	rosewater	1-2 tsp

1 Halve the pastry, leaving half of it covered with a damp tea towel. Spread the first portion across the base of a greased, medium-sized square shallow tin, spreading it to fit the tray. Brush well with melted margarine.
2 Mix together the chopped nuts and spices and spread the mixture over the dough. Top with the remaining dough and brush well with margarine.
3 Bake at 180°C/350°F (Gas Mark 4) for 30 minutes, then raise the heat to 200°C/400°F (Gas Mark 6) and cook for 10 more minutes.
4 Meanwhile, combine the sugar and water in a small saucepan and heat gently, stirring frequently, until the sugar dissolves. Cook for 10 minutes to make a thick syrup, then add the lemon juice and rosewater.
5 Pour the syrup evenly over the hot pastry. Cover with a clean tea-towel and leave for a few hours, or overnight, to give the syrup time to sink in. Serve cut into squares.

Note: Kadaifi pastry is available from Greek Cypriot and other speciality shops. Made from flour and water, it is similar to Shredded Wheat – which you can use in this recipe if you prefer (soak it in water first, squeeze out any excess moisture, then follow instructions as above). Pistachio nuts can be used instead of walnuts and honey can be added to the sauce.

Baklava (Nut and Honey Slices)

115g (4 oz)	almonds, coarsely chopped	1 cup
140ml (¼ pt)	orange juice	⅔ cup
4 tbs	runny honey	4 tbs
1 tsp	ground cinnamon	1 tsp
55g (2 oz)	fine wholemeal (wholewheat) breadcrumbs	1 cup
6 sheets	frozen filo pastry, defrosted vegetable oil	6 sheets

1 Stir together the almonds, orange juice, honey and cinnamon. Add the breadcrumbs, mixing thoroughly.
2 Peel off one sheet of filo pastry (covering the rest with a damp cloth to keep it from drying out). Lay it on a lightly floured board and brush with oil. Transfer to a shallow oblong tin and trim to fit. Repeat using another sheet of pastry, covering it generously with oil.
3 Spread half the nut and honey mixture evenly across the top. Repeat this using two more sheets of pastry and the rest of the mixture, then cover with the remaining pastry and brush the top with oil.
4 Use a sharp knife to mark the top into slices, making 6 or 8 portions. Bake at 180°C/350°F (Gas Mark 4) for 20 to 30 minutes or until lightly browned. Cool briefly then cut into individual pieces. Serve warm or cold.

Note: This adapted version of Greek baklava is surprisingly easy to make. For vegans, use syrup instead of honey. A rosewater syrup (*see below*) is sometimes poured over the slices, making an even richer sweet! For a special occasion dessert, serve with fresh figs and thick Greek yogurt.

Yogurt Cake with Rosewater Syrup

Cake

115g (4 oz)	margarine or butter	½ cup
170g (6 oz)	sugar	1 cup
3 medium	free-range eggs, lightly beaten	3 medium
285ml (½ pt)	natural yogurt	1⅓ cups
285g (10 oz)	wholemeal (wholewheat) flour	2½ cups
1 tsp	baking powder	1 tsp

Syrup

115g (4 oz)	sugar	⅔ cup
4 tbs	honey	4 tbs
285ml (½ pt)	water	1⅓ cups
2 tbs	lemon juice	2 tbs
2 tbs	rosewater, or to taste	2 tbs

1 In a bowl beat together the fat and sugar. When light and fluffy, gradually add the eggs and then the yogurt. Sift together the flour and baking powder and add to the first mixture.
2 Lightly grease a medium-sized square cake tin, pour in the mixture and smooth the top. Bake at 200°C/400°F (Gas Mark 6) for 30 to 40 minutes, or until a sharp knife inserted into the centre comes out clean. Transfer to a wire rack and pierce all over with a skewer.

3 In a small saucepan, combine all the ingredients for the syrup except the rosewater, and bring to the boil, stirring continually. Lower the heat and simmer gently for 10 minutes – do not cover. Add the rosewater, cook for a few more minutes, then set aside to cool briefly.

4 Trickle the syrup evenly over the cake. Leave to cool at room temperature before cutting into squares and serving.

Note: Very sweet syrups such as this feature frequently in Middle Eastern cookery. If you have a less sweet tooth, reduce the sugar.

Hashmerim (Cottage Cheese Dessert)

455g (1 lb)	cottage cheese	2 cups
1 tbs	81% wholemeal (wholewheat) flour	1 tbs
4 tbs	honey	4 tbs
1 tbs	orange flower water	1 tbs
30g (1 oz)	unsalted pistachio nuts, coarsely chopped	¼ cup
1 tbs	lemon peel, finely grated	1 tbs

1 Gently heat the cottage cheese in a small saucepan for a few minutes, stirring continually. Add the flour and continue heating and stirring until the mix thickens.

2 Stir in the honey, orange flower water, nuts and peel. Cook just long enough to heat through. Divide between four small bowls and serve at once.

Note: This is a middle eastern version of a dish that is also popular in India, where saffron is added. Chopped almonds can be used instead of the pistachios – roast them lightly first to give them a fuller flavour. If you have no 81% flour, sift out the bran from 100% wholemeal flour.

Linzer Torte

170g (6 oz)	margarine	¾ cup
115g (4 oz)	sugar	⅔ cup
2 small	free-range egg yolks, beaten	2 small
1 tbs	lemon peel, grated	1 tbs
2 tsp	ground cinnamon	2 tsp
½ tsp	ground cloves	½ tsp
115g (4 oz)	almonds, coarsely ground	1 cup
170g (6 oz)	wholemeal (wholewheat) flour	1½ cups
4 tbs	cherry or raspberry spread	4 tbs

1 Cream together the margarine and sugar and, when light and fluffy, gradually add the egg yolks, mixing well. Stir in the peel and spices. Gradually add the nuts and flour and knead briefly to make a dough. Wrap in foil and chill briefly.

2 Use most of the dough to line a small shallow round tin – the dough should be quite thick. Spread with the jam.

3 Roll out the remaining dough, cut into 8 thin strips, and use to make a lattice pattern across the top of the pie. Bake at 180°C/350°F (Gas Mark 4) for 30 minutes. Cool slightly, transfer to a wire rack and leave to cool completely. Serve cut in slices.

Note: Small tarts can be made in the same way, each topped with a few flaked nuts. These will need slightly less cooking time.

Stollen

225g (8 oz)	wholemeal (wholewheat) flour	2 cups
1 dsspn	Easy-blend yeast	1 dsspn
1 tsp	ground mixed spice	1 tsp
55g (2 oz)	margarine, melted	¼ cup
55g (2 oz)	mixed candied peel	⅓ cup
55g (2 oz)	glacé cherries, chopped	⅓ cup
3-4 tbs	milk, slightly warmed	3-4 tbs
3 tbs	jam	3 tbs
115g (4 oz)	marzipan	4 oz
	caster sugar for topping	

1 Stir together the flour, yeast and spice. Add the melted margarine, the peel and cherries, and enough warm milk to make a soft dough. Knead briefly, then leave in the bowl, covered with a damp towel and leave in a warm place. After 30 minutes the dough should have risen.

2 On a lightly–floured board, knead the dough again, then roll out to make a large square. Spread this with the jam. Roll out the marzipan to make a narrow oblong and lay this in the centre of the square. Fold the sides of the dough together so that they meet to cover the marzipan. Gently press the dough together where it meets, then transfer to a greased baking sheet, turning it over so that the join is underneath.

3 Cover and leave in a warm place for 30 minutes before baking at 180°C/350°F (Gas Mark 4) for 30 minutes. Leave to cool, dust with sugar, and serve cut in slices.

Note: Stollen can also be topped with icing, or brushed with egg and sprinkled with glacé cherries and almonds, both coarsely chopped.

Apple Strudel

2 large	dessert apples, peeled, cored and chopped	2 large
140ml (¼ pt)	sweet cider	⅔ cup
55g (2 oz)	sultanas (golden seedless raisins)	⅓ cup
55g (2 oz)	margarine	¼ cup
55g (2 oz)	fresh wholemeal (wholewheat) breadcrumbs	1 cup
55g (2 oz)	caster sugar	⅓ cup
55g (2 oz)	walnuts, coarsely chopped	½ cup
1 tsp	ground cinnamon	1 tsp
¼ tsp	ground cloves	¼ tsp
4 sheets	frozen filo pastry, defrosted	4 sheets
	vegetable oil	

1 Cook the apples in the cider for 5 minutes, or until just tender. Drain off any excess liquid and stir in the sultanas.
2 In another pan, melt the margarine, add the breadcrumbs, and fry for a few minutes. Remove from the heat and add half the sugar, nuts and spices.
3 Lay the four sheets of filo pastry together, brushing each one lightly with oil first. Spread with the breadcrumb mixture and top with the apple purée. Carefully roll up the pastry from the long side, turning in the sides to keep the filling in place. Place on a lightly greased baking sheet and brush the top with more oil.
4 Bake at 180°C/350°F (Gas Mark 4) for 20 minutes, or until golden. Dust with the remaining sugar and serve warm or cold.

Note: If you use cooking apples instead, add extra sugar to the purée. Strudel may be made with other fruit purées. Puff pastry can also be used instead of filo.

Choc Nut Ice Box Cookies

225g (8 oz)	wholemeal (wholewheat) flour	2 cups
1 tsp	baking powder	1 tsp
115g (4 oz)	margarine	½ cup
115g (4 oz)	sugar	⅔ cup
1 tsp	vanilla essence	1 tsp
1 medium	free-range egg, lightly beaten	1 medium
1 medium	free-range egg, lightly beaten	1 medium
55g (2 oz)	pecan nuts, coarsely chopped	½ cup
85g (3 oz)	chocolate bar, coarsely chopped	3 oz

1 Sift together the flour and baking powder. In a bowl, cream together the margarine and sugar until light and fluffy, then stir in the vanilla essence and egg. Add the nuts and chocolate pieces.
2 Divide the dough into 3 to 4 even sized pieces and shape into rolls about 15cm (6 in) long by 3cm (1½ in) diameter. Wrap each one in foil and chill for at least 6 hours, or overnight, by which time the dough will have firmed up.
3 Use a sharp knife to cut into slices. Arrange on ungreased baking sheets and bake at 190°C/375°F (Gas Mark 5) for 7 to 10 minutes, or until golden. Carefully remove from the tray and leave on a wire rack to cool.

Note: The big plus of ice box cookies is that you can make up a large amount of the dough, leave it in the fridge ready to use when needed, and then use just as much as you want. The basic dough (as above minus nuts and chocolate) can be flavoured in a variety of ways, for example, with chopped nuts, dried fruit, lemon or orange peel, spices, coconut, etc. Add the flavouring before chilling.

Cranberry Mousse

2 medium	free-range eggs, separated	2 medium
140ml (¼ pt)	cranberry juice	⅔ cup
455g (1 lb)	cranberries, drained	1 lb
55g (2 oz)	sugar	⅓ cup
140ml (¼ pt)	whipping cream	⅔ cup

1 Beat the egg yolks together with the juice. (Use the syrup drained from the cranberries, but do not add water or it will dilute the flavour of the mousse.) Place in a bowl over a pan of hot water and heat gently, stirring continually with a wooden spoon, until the mixture is thick enough to coat the back of the spoon.
2 Add the cranberries, chill briefly.
3 Whip the cream and add to the cranberries. Whisk the egg whites until stiff and fold them into the first mixture. Divide between four small bowls and chill well before serving.

Note: If you can get fresh cranberries, cook them yourself, sweetening as necessary, then use fresh juice rather than bottled. Cranberry mousse can also be frozen and served in scoops, like ice cream.

Cashew and Pistachio Barfi (Fudge)

570ml (1 pt)	*milk*	*2½ cups*
170g (6 oz)	*cashew pieces, coarsely ground*	*1½ cups*
85g (3 oz)	*sugar*	*½ cup*
2 tsp	*rosewater,* or *to taste*	*2 tsp*
30g (1 oz)	*pistachio nuts, chopped*	*¼ cup*

1 Bring the milk to a boil in a saucepan, then lower the heat and simmer for an hour, stirring ocasionally.
2 Stir in the nuts, sugar and rosewater and continue cooking until the mixture is thick and dry.
3 Turn into a shallow, lightly-greased tin or dish, smooth the top, then sprinkle with the pistachios and press down gently. Leave to cool before cutting into small squares.

Note: Indian fudges are made with khoya, a thick creamy substance made by boiling milk in the way described above. If you can find it in local shops, use that instead and save both time and fuss. Other ingredients can be added for different flavoured fudges, for example, desiccated coconut, ground almonds and ginger.

Jalebi (Fried Indian Sweets)

Sweets

170g (6 oz)	*wholemeal (wholewheat) flour*	*1½ cups*
2 tbs	*yogurt*	*2 tbs*
7g (¼ oz)	*fresh yeast, crumbled*	*small piece*
approx. 200ml (⅓ pt)	*cold water*	*approx. ¾ cup*
1 tsp	*saffron* or *yellow colouring - optional*	*1 tsp*

Syrup

225g (8 oz)	*sugar*	*1⅓ cups*
295ml (½ pt)	*water*	*1⅓ cups*
½ tsp	*ground cardamom,* or *to taste*	*½ tsp*
	rosewater - optional	
	vegetable oil or *ghee*	

1 Beat together the flour, yogurt and yeast, adding enough water to make a thick batter. Add colouring if using it. Cover the bowl and leave in a warm place for several hours.
2 When almost ready, make the syrup. Heat the sugar and water gently in a saucepan, stirring continually, until the sugar dissolves. Then bring to the boil and continue boiling gently for 10 minutes or until the syrup thickens. Add cardamom, and rosewater if using it. Keep the syrup warm.
3 Heat enough vegetable oil or ghee for deep frying. Fill a small funnel with batter and, when the oil is hot, release a stream of batter into it, turning the funnel to make a small coil. Stop the flow, move to another position and make another one. Cook a few at a time, turning them so that they are evenly cooked. When crisp and golden remove from the fat, drain on paper towels and drop into the syrup. Leave to soak for a few minutes before removing and piling onto a plate. Cook the rest of the batter in the same way. Serve warm or cold.

Note: These vary slightly from one part of India to another - in some areas a small amount of the wheat flour is replaced with gram flour, which increases the protein content. Do not overcook.

Papaya Ice Cream

2 tbs	*arrowroot*	*2 tbs*
570ml (1 pt)	*milk*	*2½ cups*
140ml (¼ pt)	*evaporated milk*	*⅔ cup*
115g (4 oz)	*sugar*	*⅔ cup*
3 ripe	*papayas*	*3 ripe*

1 Mix the arrowroot to a paste with a few spoonfuls of the milk. Put the rest of the milk into a saucepan and heat gently, then add the paste, stir well and continue cooking for a few more minutes, or until the sauce thickens.
2 Add the evaporated milk and sugar, stirring until the sugar dissolves. Leave to cool.
3 Peel and halve the papayas, remove the seeds, chop and then either mash or blend the flesh. You should have about 285ml/½ pint. Stir this into the sauce.
4 Pour into a freezing tray and freeze until mushy. Beat the mixture, return to a clean tray and freeze again. If possible, repeat this a few more times to get air into the mixture.

Note: The evaporated milk gives this Caribbean-style ice cream its rich and creamy texture. If you prefer, use single cream, or milk with dried skimmed milk added.

Chinese Glazed Bananas

Bananas

4 medium	bananas	4 medium
2 tbs	cornflour	2 tbs
1 medium	free-range egg, lightly beaten	1 medium
	vegetable oil	

Glaze

170g (6 oz)	sugar	1 cup
6 tbs	water	6 tbs
3 tbs	corn syrup	3 tbs
3 tbs	vegetable oil	3 tbs

1 Peel the bananas and cut into even-sized chunks. Dip them in the cornflour followed by the egg.

2 Heat some oil, add the banana pieces, and deep fry until lightly browned. Drain on paper towels.

3 Gently heat the sugar, water, syrup and oil in a small saucepan, stirring continually, for 10 minutes or until the glaze darkens.

4 Using a fork, dip the cooked banana chunks into the syrup, making sure each one is evenly coated before dropping into a bowl of iced water to make the glaze harden. Drain and serve at once.

Note: This is delicious topped with sorbet or ice cream. You can use honey instead of the syrup.

Sweet Potato Pudding

455g (1 lb)	sweet potatoes, peeled and grated	1 lb
small piece	fresh root ginger, grated	small piece
30g (1 oz)	margarine, melted	2½ tbs
170g (6 oz)	sugar	1 cup
½ tsp	vanilla essence	½ tsp
285ml (½ pt)	coconut milk	1⅓ cups
½ tsp	ground cinnamon	½ tsp
¼ tsp	ground nutmeg	¼ tsp
	wholemeal (wholewheat) flour	

1 Stir together the potato, ginger, margarine, sugar, vanilla essence, coconut milk and spices.

2 Add enough wholemeal flour to bind the mixture to a stiff paste.

3 Grease a shallow ovenproof dish, pour in the mixture and smooth the top. Bake at 180°C/350°F (Gas Mark 4) for 1 hour or until cooked. Serve hot.

Note: This subtly flavoured and filling pudding can be varied by adding dried fruit and/or nuts.

Red Fruit Creams

680g (1½ lbs)	mixed soft fruit (e.g. raspberries, red currants, strawberries, blackcurrants, etc)	1½ lbs
	cold water	
	arrowroot	
170g (6 oz)	sugar, or to taste	1 cup
30g (1 oz)	almonds, flaked	¼ cup

1 Clean the fruit, then, in a heavy-based saucepan, cover with water. Bring to the boil and simmer for 5 minutes.

2 Sieve the fruit, retaining the juice. Measure this and allow 2 tbs arrowroot for every 570ml/1 pint juice. Whisk the arrowroot together with a drop of cold water. Gently heat the juice and stir in the sugar until it dissolves. Add the arrowroot paste, bring to the boil and simmer for a few minutes or until clear.

3 Pour at once into 4 to 6 small bowls. Sprinkle with nuts, and serve.

Note: This Danish dessert is sometimes served with cream.

Directory of Recipes

Vegan Recipes

All the following are either completely free from both animal and dairy ingredients, or could very easily be adapted to be vegan. Do look at other recipes too as many of them – with just a little more effort – could also be made suitable for vegans.

Peanut Butter Muffins
Fruity Marmalade Muffins
Jam Crowns
Lemon Cream Tarts
Strawberry and Kiwi Tarts
Star Mince Pies
Spiced Apple Scones
Date Scones
Spiced Banana Cakes
Fig Crumble Slices
Date and Apple Slices
Orange Carob Oat Munchies
Gingerbread
Grapefruit Cake
Pear and Ginger Loaf
Tahini Cake
Christmas Fruit Cake
No–bake Fruit Cake
Lemon Date Sponge
Coconut Cake with Apple Cream Filling
Carrot Cake
Fruit and Bran Loaf
Pear and Apple Sandwich Cake
Coconut and Carob Gateau
Cherry Almond Cookies
Pear and Peanut Bars
Millet Flake Flapjacks
Three Seed Flapjacks
Granola Lemon Bars

Florentines
Old–Fashioned Ginger Nuts
Cashew Date Drops
Tofu Apple Slices
Fig Rolls
Coconut Vanilla Crisps
Carob Digestive Biscuits
Candied Peel and Currant Cookies
Sticky Fingers
Semolina Shortbread
Peanut Butter Cookies
No–bake Carob Oatmeal Bars
Mango Water-Ice with Chocolate Curls
Creamy Lemon Lollipops
Coconut Ice Cream
Raisin Almond Ice Cream
Fruit Salad Ice Cream, with Tofu
Coffee Ice Cream
Strawberry Ice Cream
Lemon Spiced Pancakes with Bananas
Cherry Crêpes
Pineapple and Ginger Crêpes
Dried Fruit Syllabub
Apple Pumpkin Mousse
Spiced Apple Whip with Tofu
Rainbow Jellies
Coconut Tofu Dessert
Prune Whip
Ginger Marmalade Creams
Maple Halvah
Spicy Granola
Mocha Popcorn
Dried Fruit Truffles
Chocolate Banana Chips
Candied Peel and Coconut Cakes
Walnut Bites
Almond Apricot Slices

Tahini Treats
Brazilian Mix
Granola Balls
Pear 'Fudge'
Pineapple Jelly Cubes
Banana Popsicles
Exotic Rice Pudding
Creamed Rice with Wild Apricot Sauce
Fruit and Nut Bread Pudding
Spotted Dick
Sussex Pond Pudding
Aduki and Apple Pie
Apple Dumplings
Coconut Brown Betty
Blueberry Cobbler with Soya Custard
Semolina and Date Pudding
Steamed Chocolate Sponge Pudding
Coconutty Baked Bananas
Quinoa with Pineapple and Mint
Marmalade Roll
Pear Pie with Puff Pastry
Couscous Layer Pudding
Traditional Christmas Pudding
Fresh Strawberry Tofu Cheesecake
Candied Peel Soya Cheesecake
Tropical Fruit Coconut Cheesecake
Banana Tofu Cheesecake
Marbled Lemon Cheesecake
Coconut Stuffed Papaya Shells
Gooseberry Crunch
Dried Fruit Compote
Hedgerow Compote
Chinese Style Apple Fritters
Avocado Citrus Fruit Salad
Fruit Salad Deluxe
Hot Fruit Salad with Coconut Custard
Pear Strudel Bundles
Apricot Hazelnut Triangles
Banana Filo Rolls
Winter Pudding with Tofu Cream
Grapefruit with Spiced Yogurt
Melon Baskets
Quinoa Rhubarb Crumble
Sunshine Crumbles
Tropical Trifle
Pears with Chestnut Chocolate Sauce
Baked Stuffed Pears
Fruit Kebabs
Chocolate Brazil Nuts
Orange Brazils
Raisin and Nut Carob Clusters
Mixed Nut Brittle
Coconut Ice
Candied Orange Peel

Turkish Delight
Marrons Glacés
Pine Nut Clusters
Carrot and Almond Balls
Sunflower Seed Toffee
Carob Easter Egg
Tofu Pumpkin Pie
Banana Custard Pie
Tumbled Fruit Flan
Pear Crumble Flan
Chocolate Orange Flan
Butterscotch and Walnut Pie
Dried Fruit Flan
Wild Blackberry Tart
Red Berry Purée
Tofu Chocolate Sauce
Kumquat Sauce
Apple Purée
Apricot Sauce
Spiced Cream Sauce
Hot Lemon Sauce
Quickest Ever Lemon Sauce
Nut Cream
Marmalade Sauce
Butterscotch Sauce
Carob Sauce
Mango Lassi
Sweet Peanut Spread
Malted Sesame Sunflower Spread
Cinnamon Apple Butter
Carob and Coconut Spread
Cashew Spread with Raisins
Maple Soya Spread
Pineapple Spread
Wild Apricot Spread
Lemon Curd
Three-Fruit Marmalade
Rhubarb and Fig Jam
Exotic Fruit Jelly
Pumpkin Jam
Apple and Kiwi Jelly
Vegetarian Mincemeat
Marrow Jam with Ginger
Carrot Jam
No-Sugar Strawberry Jam
Grantia di Cafe
Pine Nut Sweets
Beignet de Pruneaux
Kadaifi
Stollen
Apple Strudel
Sweet Potato Pudding
Red Fruit Creams

Children's Parties

The following traditional ideas – plus some more unusual fare – are ideal for youngsters at party time. Don't forget the importance of making the food look as good as it tastes.

Apricot Doughnuts
Maple Sesame Scones
Spiced Banana Cakes
Date and Apple Slices
Orange Carob Oat Munchies
Battenberg
Pineapple Swiss Roll
Double Chocolate Cookies
Sticky Fingers
Peanut Butter Cookies
Orange and Lemon Ice Cream
Creamy Lemon Lollipops
Frozen Yogurt
Carob Nut Sundae
American Style Pancakes with Maple Cream
Apricot and Banana Crunch
Rainbow Jellies
Honey Sesame Popcorn
Tahini Treats
Peanut Sugar Puffs
Fruit and Nut Chocolate Fingers
Banana Popsicles
Sunshine Crumbles
Pineapple and Banana Fritters
Tropical Trifle
Honey Toffee Apples
Butterscotch and Walnut Pie
Sunflower Seed Toffee
Creamy Date and Ricotta Spread

Dinner Party Desserts

When you've made a special effort with the main course, don't let the last dish let you down! Here are some suggestions for a variety of desserts – some heavy, others light – which you can choose to balance the rest of the meal. Also listed are some ideas for sweet treats to serve with coffee after dinner.

Strawberry and Kiwi Tarts
Yogurt and Honey Eclairs
Brandy Snaps with Crème Fraîche
Chocolate and Almond Roulade
Frosted Almond Carrot Cake
Papaya Layer Cake
Summer Fruit Gateau with Cinnamon Cream
Florentines
Nut-Topped Caramel Cookies

Maple Pecan Ice Cream
Vanilla Yogurt Ice Cream with Hot Blueberry Sauce
Avocado Ice Cream
Mango Water Ice with Chocolate Curls
Passion Fruit Sorbets in Meringue Shells
Coffee Ice Cream
Cassata Dessert
Christmas Ice Pudding
Chestnut Purée Pancakes
Cherry Crêpes
Souffléd Oranges
Almond Soufflé
Chocolate Mint Swirls
Quick Crème Brulée with Ginger
Dried Fruit Truffles
Almond Apricot Slices
Sussex Pond Pudding
Ginger Biscuit Log
Coconutty Baked Bananas
Red Fruit Cheesecake
Ginger Cheesecake
Coconut Stuffed Papaya Shells
Chinese Style Apple Fritters
Fresh Berry Baskets
Kiwi and Raspberry Pavlova
Pears with Chestnut Chocolate Sauce
Fresh Figs with Yogurt Cream
Creme de Menthe Jellies
Sour Cream Pie with Hazelnut Pastry
Crunch Nut Topped Pumpkin Pie
Tumbled Fruit Flan
Amaretti
Zabaglione
Jalebi
Crêpes Suzette

Sweets on the Move

Whether you're picnicking, packing a lunch box or back packing, it's good to have something sweet to tuck into. Choose items that won't crumble easily, nor melt, wrapping them individually in foil. For occasions when you want something a little more special, use polythene boxes to protect your goodies.

Blueberry Buttermilk Muffins
White Chocolate Brownies
Wholemeal Rock Cakes
Malt Loaf
Marmalade and Molasses Cake
Banana Wheatgerm Biscuits
Pear and Peanut Bars
Sesame Oat Bars
Millet Flake Flapjacks
Granola Lemon Bars

Chocolate Banana Chips
Brazilian Mix
Almond Cheesecake
Sesame Crunch
Choc Nut Icebox Cookies
Cashew and Pistachio Barfi
Cherry Bakewell Tart

Sweet Gifts

Most people appreciate home-made gifts, especially the edible kind. Pack them in colourful boxes, decorate with ribbons and bows - and don't forget to warn the lucky recipients that these are natural foods, made without preservatives, so they won't keep for long.

Star Mince Pies
Christmas Fruit Cake
Honey Dundee Cake
Simnel Cake
Honey Flapjacks
Jumbo Pineapple Cookies
Candied Peel and Coconut Cakes

Peppermint Cream Carob Truffles
Pear 'Fudge'
Pineapple Jelly Cubes
Chocolate Brazil Nuts
Orange Brazils
Marzipan Mice
Honeycomb
Nougat
Turkish Delight
Marrons Glacés
Carob Easter Egg
Cinnamon Apple Butter
Wild Apricot Spread
Banana and Pineapple Curd
Rhubarb and Fig Jam
Exotic Fruit Jelly
Pumpkin Jam
Vegetarian Mincemeat
Carrot Jam
No-Sugar Strawberry Jam
Amaretti
Pine Nut Sweets
Stollen
Jalebi

Index

* refers to vegan recipes

*Aduki and apple pie 69
Almond:
  *apricot slices 64
  cheesecake 78
  soufflé 56
Amaretti 117
American style pancakes with maple
  syrup 51-2
Apple(s):
  and blackberry sorbet 41
  cheesecake 82
  *Chinese style fritters 87
  *cinnamon butter 112
  cream cake filling 25
  crêpes, chilled, with coconut nut
    cream 49
  *and date slices 17
  *dumplings 70
  flan, French 106-7
  honey toffee 95
  *pumpkin mousse 57-8
  *purée 110
  *scones, spiced 14
  *strudel 122
  *whips, spiced, with tofu 58
Apricot(s):
  and banana crunch 58
  cheesecakes, individual 80
  Danish pastries 15
  doughnuts 10
  frangipane 22
  *hazelnut triangles 89
  and nectarine sundae 44
  *sauce 110
  soufflé, chilled 55
  *spread 113
Avocado:
  *citrus fruit salad 88
  crunch cheesecake 82

ice cream 40

*Baked stuffed pears 93
Baklava 120
Banana(s):
  *baked, coconutty 73
  *cakes, spiced 16
  Chinese glazed 123-4
  cottage cheese ice cream 39
  crêpes, Christmas 52
  *custard pie 103
  *filo rolls 89-90
  *with lemon spiced pancakes 47
  maple syrup 87-8
  mousse 60
  and pineapple curd 114
  and pineapple fritters 87
  *popsicles 66
  *tofu cheesecake 84
  wheatgerm biscuits 30
  yogurt tea bread 26
Battenburg 24
*Beignet de pruneaux 119
Blackberry:
  and apple sorbet 41
  *tart 107-8
Blueberry:
  buttermilk muffins 9
  cheesecake, with muesli base 80
  *cobbler with soya custard 71-2
Brandy snaps:
  with crème fraîche 15-16
  fresh berry baskets 89
Brazil nuts:
  *chocolate 94
  *orange Brazils 95
  *Brazilian mix 64
Brownies:
  carob and walnut 12

ginger 12
  white chocolate 12
Buckwheat pancakes with kumquat
  sauce 50
Buttermilk:
  cake 21-2
  pancakes 48
Butterscotch:
  *sauce 111
  *and walnut pie 107

Cakes:
  almond carrot, frosted 26
  Battenburg 24
  buttermilk 21-2
  caraway 24
  *carrot 26
  *coconut with apple cream
    filling 27
  *coconut and carob gateau 28-9
  Dundee, honey 23
  *fruit:
    Christmas 22-3
    no-bake 23-4
  *grapefruit 21
  lemon crumble 20
  marmalade and molasses 25
  mincemeat with marzipan cream
    filling 23
  papaya layer 27
  *pear and apple sandwich 28
  Simnel 28
  summer fruit gateau with
    cinnamon cream 29
  *tahini 22
  yogurt:
    with rosewater syrup 120-1
    upside-down 27
*Candied orange peel 97

Candied peel:
*and coconut cakes 63
*and currant cookies 35
ice cream 38
*soya cheesecake 83
Caraway cake 24
Carob:
*and coconut spread 113
*digestive biscuits 35
*Easter egg 99
fudge, creamy 96
nut sundae 46
*oatmeal bars, no-bake 37
*orange carob oat munchies 18
orange pots 60
*sauce 112
sponge with hazelnut filling 19
and walnut brownies 12
Carrot:
*and almond balls 98
and almond pudding 72
*cakes 26
*jam 116
muffins 9
Cashew:
*date drops 33
and pistachio barfi (fudge) 123
*spread with raisins 113
Cassata dessert 45
Cenci 118
Cheesecakes:
almond 78
apple 82
apricot, individual 80
avocado crunch 82
*banana tofu 84
blueberry, with muesli base 80
*candied peel soya 83
chocolate nut 77–8
continental style 79
*fresh strawberry tofu 83
ginger 79
grape, with nut crust 81
*lemon, marbled 84
mango and lime 79
mint carob chip 80–1
orange 81
red fruit 78
Russian, crustless 81
*tropical fruit coconut 83
Cherry:
*almond cookies 30
Bakewell tart 105
and Brazil nut sponge 19–20
*crêpes 49–50
Chestnut:
*chocolate sauce 93
crunch maple mousse 59
ice cream 40
purée pancakes 48
chilled apple crêpes with coconut
nut cream 49
Chilled apricot soufflé 55

Chilled rhubarb flan 103–4
Chinese glazed bananas 123–4
*Chinese style apple fritters 87
Choc nut ice box cookies 122
Chocolate:
and almond roulade 21
*banana chips 63
*Brazil nuts 94
cookies 34
hazelnuts 94
ice milk 42
mint swirls 58
nut cheesecake 77–8
*orange flan 106
*sauce, tofu 110
soufflé, with macaroons 56
Christmas:
banana crêpes 52
*fruit cake 22–3
ice pudding 45
*pudding, traditional 75
Cinnamon:
*apple butter 112
brown bread ice cream 39
lemon yogurt pie 105
yogurt ramekins 61
Coconut:
*brown Betty 71
*cake with apple cream filling 25
*and carob gateau 28–9
*custard 88
*ice 97
*ice cream 43
macaroons 31
*stuffed papaya shells 86
tart 101
*tofu dessert 59
*vanilla crisps 35
vanilla soufflé 55–6
*Coconutty baked bananas 73
Côeur à la crème 119
Coffee:
*ice cream 43
*water-ice 117
Continental style cheesecake 79
Cottage cheese:
dessert 121
puddings 59
*Couscous layer pudding 75
Cranberry:
mousse 122
sorbet 41–2
*Creamed rice with wild apricot
sauce 68
Creamy carob fudge 96
Creamy custard puffs 10–11
Creamy date and ricotta spread 114
*Creamy lemon lollipops 41
Creamy yogurt ring 57
Crème brulée with ginger, quick 60
Crème caramel 118
Crème de Menthe jellies 98
Crêpes:

Belle Hélène 51
*cherry 49–50
chilled apple, with coconut
cream 49
Christmas banana 52
ice cream, with Melba sauce 52
*pineapple and ginger 53
Suzette 119
tropical fruit 51
Crunch nut topped pumpkin
pie 102
Crustless Russian cheesecake 81
Custard puffs, creamy 10–11

Danish pastries, apricot 15
Date(s):
*and apple slices 17
*cashew drops 33
and ricotta spread, creamy 114
*scones 14
stuffed 65
Double chocolate cookies 34
Double chocolate ice milk 42
Doughnuts, apricot 10
Dried fruit:
*compôte 86–7
*flan 107
*syllabub 57
*truffles 63
Dundee cake, honey 23

Easter biscuits 33–4
*Easter egg, carob 99
Eccles cakes 18
Eclairs, yogurt and honey 15
Egg creams 117–18
*Exotic fruit jelly 115
*Exotic rice pudding 67

Fig(s):
*crumble slices 17
fresh, with yogurt cream 93
puddings, with vanilla
cream 75–6
*rolls 34
Flans:
apple, French 106–7
*chocolate orange 106
*dried fruit 107
papaya 100
*pear crumble 105
rhubarb, chilled 103–4
three fruit marmalade 103
*tumbled fruit 104
Flapjacks:
honey 32
*millet flake 32
*three seed 32
*Florentines 32–3
French apple flan 106–7
Fresh berry baskets 89
Fresh figs with yogurt cream 93
Fresh fruit flambé 85

*Fresh strawberry tofu
   cheesecake 83
Fried pastry knots 118
Frosted almond carrot cake 26
Frozen yogurt 44
Fruit:
   *and bran loaf 27
   crumble-in-a-hurry 92
   *kebabs 93
   *and nut bread pudding 68
   and nut chocolate fingers 65
Fruit salad:
   *avocado citrus 88
   *deluxe 88
   *hot, with coconut custard 88
   *ice cream, with tofu 43
*Fruity marmalade muffins 10

Ginger:
   banana cheesecake 82
   biscuit log 70
   brownies 12
   cheesecake 79
   cream shortbread fingers 36
   *marmalade creams 61
*Gingerbread 20
*Gingernuts, old-fashioned 33
Gooseberry:
   almond sponge 74
   *crunch 86
   and elderflower soufflé 55
*Granita di café 117
Granola:
   *balls 65
   *lemon bars 32
   *spicy 62
Grape:
   and cheese dessert 91
   cheesecake, with nut crust 81
Grapefruit:
   *cake 21
   with spiced yogurt 91
*Halvah, maple 62
Hashmerim 121
*Hedgerow compôte 87
Honey:
   butterscotch sauce 111–12
   Dundee cake 23
   flapjacks 32
   pecan pie 104
   sesame popcorn 63
   squares 11–12
   syllabub 57
   toffee apples 95
Honeycomb 96
Hot cross buns, wholemeal 11
*Hot lemon sauce 111

Ice cream:
   avocado 40
   banana cottage cheese 39
   candied peel 38
   chestnut 40

Christmas ice pudding 45
cinnamon brown bread 39
*coconut 43
*coffee 43
crêpes, with Melba sauce 52
*fruit salad, with tofu 43
maple pecan 38
orange and lemon 39
papaya 123
praline 39
*raisin almond 43
raspberry buttermilk ice 43
rosewater and pistachio 40
*strawberry 44
vanilla yogurt, with hot blueberry
   sauce 40
Icebox banana swirl cake 45
Inca cookies 31
Indian sweets, fried 123
Individual apricot cheesecake 80

Jalebi 123
*Jam crowns 11
Jumbo pineapple cookies 33

*Kadaifi 120
Kiwi and raspberry pavlova 90
*Kumquat sauce 110

Lemon:
   cheesecake, marbled 84
   *cream tarts 13
   creams 60
   crumble cake 20
   *curd 114
   *date sponge 24
   meringue pie, oaty 106
   *sauces 111
   soufflés, with nut brittle
      topping 55
   *spiced pancakes, with
      bananas 47
   suet puddings 70
Lime:
   chiffon pie 102
   and mango mousse 56
Linger torte 121
Little fig puddings with vanilla
   cream 75–6
*Lollipops, creamy lemon 41

Macaroni bake 70
Madeleines 17
Malt loaf 20–1
*Malted sesame sunflower
   spread 112
Mango:
   *lassi 112
   and lime cheesecake 79
   *water-ice with chocolate
      curls 41
Maple:
   cream 51–2

*halvah 62
pecan ice cream 38
sesame scones 14
*soya spread 113
*Marbled lemon cheesecake 84
Marbled summer fool 86
Marmalade:
   and molasses cake 25
   *roll 74
   *sauce 111
*Marrons glacés 97–8
*Marrow jam with ginger 116
Marzipan mice 95
Melba sauce 52
*Melon baskets 91
*Millet flake flapjacks 32
*Mince pies, star 13–14
Mincemeat:
   cake with marzipan cream
      filling 23
   squares 36–7
   *vegetarian 115
Mint carob chip cheesecake 80–1
*Mixed nut brittle 96
Mocha:
   mousse 57
   *popcorn 63
Molasses toffee 97
Mousses:
   *apple pumpkin 57–8
   banana 60
   chestnut crunch maple 59
   lime and mango 56
   Mocha 57
Muffins:
   blueberry buttermilk 9
   carrot 9
   *fruity marmalade 10
   *peanut butter 10

Nectarines:
   and apricot sundae 44
   pancakes 48
*No-bake carob oatmeal bars 37
*No-bake fruit cake 23–4
*No-sugar strawberry jam 116
Nougat 96
Nut:
   cream 109
   and honey slices 120
   -topped caramel cookies 37
Nutty egg custard tarts 13

Oaty lemon meringue pie 106
*Old-fashioned ginger nuts 33
Omelette, soufflé 73
*Orange peel, candied 97
Orange(s):
   *Brazils 95
   cheesecake 81
   and hazelnut slices 16
   and lemon ice cream 39
   and quark pancakes 50

souffléd 54

Pancakes:
  American style, with maple
    cream 51–2
  buckwheat, with kumquat
    sauce 50
  buttermilk 48
  chestnut purée 48
  lemon pie 53
  *lemon spiced, with bananas 47
  nectarine 48
  orange and quark 50
  sunflower honey 49
  see also Crêpes
Papaya:
  flan 100
  ice cream 123
  layer cake 27
Parsnip cup cakes 18
Passion fruit sorbets, in meringue
    shells 42
Pastry 100
Pavlova, kiwi and raspberry 90–1
Peanut butter:
  balls 65
  *cookies 36
  *muffins 10
Peanut sugar puffs 64
Pear(s):
  *and apple sandwich cake 28
  *baked stuffed 93
  *with chestnut chocolate
    sauce 93
  *crumble flan 105
  *'fudge' 66
  *and ginger loaf 21
  and ginger sundae 44
  *and peanut bars 31
  *pie with puff pastry 74
  *strudel bundles 89
Peppermint cream carob truffles 65
Pies:
  *banana custard 103
  *butterscotch and walnut 107
  cinnamon lemon yogurt 105
  honey pecan 104
  lime chiffon 102
  oaty lemon meringue 106
  pumpkin, crunch nut topped 102
  sour cream, with hazelnut
    pastry 101
  *tofu pumpkin 101–2
Pine nut:
  *clusters 98
  *sweets 118
Pineapple:
  and banana fritters 87
  *and ginger crêpes 53
  *jelly cubes 66
  sorbet 41
  *spread 113
  Swiss roll 25

Plum upside-down pudding 73–4
Popcorn:
  honey sesame 63
  *Mocha 63
Praline ice cream 39
Prune:
  and apple fool 85
  *in batter 119
  *whip 59
Puddings:
  *bread, fruit and nut 68
  carrot and almond 72
  *Christmas, traditional 75
  *couscous layer 75
  *exotic rice 67
  lemon suet 70
  little fig, with vanilla cream 75–6
  plum upside-down 73–4
  ricotta 67
  *semolina and date 72
  *steamed chocolate sponge 72–3
  steamed ginger, with cream 69
  *Sussex pond 68–9
  *sweet potato 124
  *winter, with tofu cream 90
Pumpkin:
  *apple mousse 57–8
  creams 71
  crunch nut topped pie 102
  *jam 115
  *tofu pie 101–2

Quick crème brulée with ginger 60
*Quickest ever lemon sauce 111
Quinoa:
  *with pineapple and mint 73
  *rhubarb crumble 91

*Rainbow jellies 59
Raisin:
  *almond ice cream 43
  *and nut carob clusters 95
Raspberry:
  buttermilk ice 43
  soufflettes 56
*Red berry purée 109–10
Red fruit:
  cheesecake 78
  *creams 124
Rhubarb:
  *and fig jam 115
  flan, chilled 103–4
Rice:
  *creamed, with wild apricot
    sauce 68
  *pudding, exotic 67
Ricotta pudding 67
Rock cakes, wholemeal 16
Rosewater:
  and pistachio ice cream 40
  *syrup 120

Scones:

*apple, sliced 14
*date 14
  maple sesame 14
Semolina:
  *and date pudding 72
  *shortbread 36
Sesame:
  crunch 95
  oat bars 31
Simnel cake 28
Sorbets:
  blackberry and apple 41
  cranberry 41–2
  passion fruit, in meringue
    shells 42
  pineapple 41
Soufflé omelette 73
Souffléd oranges 54
Soufflés:
  almond 56
  apricot, chilled 55
  chocolate, with macaroons 56
  coconut vanilla 55–6
  gooseberry and elderflower 55
  lemon, with nut brittle
    topping 55
  raspberry soufflettes 56
Sour cream pie with hazelnut
    pastry 101
*Spiced apple scones 14
*Spiced apple whips with tofu 58
*Spiced banana cakes 16
*Spiced cream sauce 111
*Spiced nut pastry 120
*Spicy granola 62
*Spotted Dick 68
*Star mince pies 13–14
*Steamed chocolate sponge
    pudding 72–3
Steamed ginger puddings with
    cream 69
*Sticky fingers 35
*Stollen 121
Strawberry:
  almond galettes 90
  and 'cream' jellies 58
  *ice cream 44
  *jam, no-sugar 116
  *and kiwi tarts 13
  *tofu cheesecake 83
Stuffed dates 65
Summer fruit gateau with cinnamon
    cream 29
Sunflower:
  honey pancakes 49
  *seed toffee 98
*Sunshine crumble 92
*Sussex pond pudding 68–9
*Sweet peanut spread 112
*Sweet potato pudding 124
Sweet Yorkshire puddings 71
Swiss roll, pineapple 25
Syllabubs:

*dried fruit 57
honey 57

Tahini:
 *cake 22
 *treats 64
Tarts:
 cherry Bakewell 105
 coconut 101
 *lemon cream 13
 Linzer torte 121
 nutty egg custard 13
 *strawberry and kiwi 13
 *wild blackberry 107–8
*Three-fruit marmalade 114
 flan 103
*Three seed flapjacks 32
Tofu:
 *apple slices 34
 *banana cheesecake 84
 *chocolate sauce 110
 coconut dessert 59
 *cream 90

*fresh strawberry cheesecake 83
*with fruit salad ice cream 43
*pumpkin pie 101-2
*spiced apple whips with 58
*Trifle, tropical 92
Tropical fruit:
 *coconut cheesecake 83
 crêpes 51
*Tropical trifle 92
*Tumbled fruit flan 104
*Turkish delight 97

Upside-down yogurt cake 27

Vanilla yogurt ice cream with hot
 blueberry sauce 40
*Vegetarian mincemeat 115

*Walnut bites 64
Water-ices:
 *coffee 117
 *mango with chocolate curls 41
Wheat berry dessert 69

White chocolate brownies 12
Wholemeal:
 hot cross buns 11
 rock cakes 16
*Wild blackberry tart 107–8
*Winter pudding with tofu
 cream 90

Yogurt:
 brulée 61
 cake with rosewater syrup 120-1
 cinnamon ramekins 61
 egg custard 75
 frozen 44
 home-made 61
 and honey eclairs 15
 ring, creamy 57
 vanilla ice cream, with hot
  blueberry sauce 40
Yorkshire puddings, sweet 71

Zabaglione 117-18

365 *plus one* Vegetarian Starters, Snacks & Savouries
JANET HUNT

Looking for a quick meal for one? Needing starters for two? Stuck for party ideas?

Now eating and entertaining the vegetarian way couldn't be easier. Here are mini meals and side dishes for every day of the year – plus an extra one for that leap year occasion.

Janet Hunt's delicious choice of dips and soups, brunches and sweets include inspired ways with pasta and potatoes, wonderful flans and salads, ideas for eating indoors as well as out, all divided into types of meal for easy reference.

All the recipes are vegetarian, many are vegan, and there are plenty of suggestions for variation. Ranging from the simple to the exotic, the inexpensive to the indulgent, from light snacks to substantial fillers, her nutritious nibbles are ideal for lunches, parties, snacks and treats – for everyone – all year round.

The Tofu Cookbook
LEAH LENEMAN

Easy to cook, deliciously versatile and wonderfully healthy, tofu is now readily available in supermarkets and health stores everywhere.

A soya-based bean-curd which has been used for cooking in the Far East for centuries, it absorbs flavours easily and can be used in more interesting and varied ways than any other single food.

Leah Leneman explains how it's made, the different types of tofu, how to store it and how to cook creatively with it – for successful results every time. Her recipes are dairy-free versions of international favourites, including classic dishes such as English shepherd's pie, Mexican tacos, savoury Mediterranean-style risotto as well as soups, salads and desserts from every corner of the world.

High in protein, low in calories and completely cholesterol-free, tofu can be used as a substitute for eggs, dairy products and meat. It is fun to cook and the ideal food for the future.

First Steps in Vegetarian Cooking
KATHY SILK

Whether you are new to cooking, new to vegetarianism or simply want some new ideas *First Steps in Vegetarian Cooking* is an ideal introduction to a delicious, healthy and humane way of life.

Beginning with the basics, Kathy Silk's invaluable book takes you step by step from your first 'V' Day to every day and offers a wealth of useful information about:

- Food: what vegetarians do and don't eat
- The Issues: why a vegetarian diet makes sense
- Nutrition: how easy it is to have a healthy balanced diet
- Ingredients: where to buy them, how to store them and how to cook them
- Recipes: how to provide simple, tasty meals for everyday

and much, much more.

Colin Spencer's Summer Cooking

Recreate the spirit of summer all year round with this inspired collection of recipes from Colin Spencer. His classic and original vegetarian and fish dishes will open a whole new world of enjoyment.

Enjoy al fresco eating in your garden, boat downstream with a moveable feast, transport yourself to a sandy beach with the flavours of the Mediterranean. His fantastic menus for indoors or out will take you on a delicious adventure – and leave your friends and family coming back for more.

Simple to create and sensational to eat, here are meals for two people, menus for six and ideas for 100 more. From picnics to buffets, from hampers to haversacks, whatever the occasion and wherever the location, there is something here to suit your style.

The Vegetarian Vitality Cookbook
JUDY RIDGWAY

To really get the most out of life, a healthy, high-energy diet is a must. Eating well will leave you feeling great – and no longer tempted by fast-food snacks or sweets.

Here are over 150 delicious vegetarian recipes, packed with vital vitamins and minerals, and full of flavour.

- High-energy breakfasts
- Fresh ideas for fruit and vegetables
- Easy packed lunches
- Hot and filling suppers
- Tempting and tasty desserts – that are good for you

High in fibre, low in fat, they are quick and easy to prepare – ideal for a balanced diet – and will leave you full of natural energy.

Eva Batt's Vegan Cooking

Vegans and vegetarians everywhere will welcome this updated edition of Eva Batt's classic cookbook. Filled with creative, nutritious and economical recipes together with a wealth of useful cooking advice, it has something for every occasion:

- Family favourites include Shepherd's Pie, soya burgers, Lotus sausages, cornish pasties and spaghetti bolognese with a delicious range of savoury gravies.
- Fruit and vegetable dishes full of exotic flavours such as peach curry, apple and potato pie, harvest pie, special kebabs and almond rissoles.
- Delicious desserts. If you thought that choosing a dairy free diet meant a farewell to sweet treats, then try banana ice-cream, egg-free pancakes, apple crumble, bread and 'butter' pudding or orange flan as well as the tempting range of cakes, breads and biscuits.
- Festive classics. Proving that there are perfect alternatives for special occasions there are also recipes for mince pies and Christmas cake, shortbread and Christmas pudding.

At a time when more and more people are wanting to follow a compassionate and healthy diet this attractive and timeless collection will be invaluable.

Cecilia Norman's
Vegetarian Microwave Cookbook

Microwave cooking is fast, safe and easy. It's ideal when time is at a premium and good taste is a must.

Cecilia Norman's Vegetarian Microwave Cookbook has been fully revised and includes a new freezer section with extra recipes created to help you to make the most of your microwave.

Here is everything you need to know about preparing, cooking and storing your food, tips on how to choose and use a microwave and how to produce healthy, attractive, delicious food – fast.

Every type of meal is included: from meals for one to family dishes and dinner parties. Here are puddings and pastries, salads and main courses, preserves and sauces and much, much more. Creative, original and delicious, the recipes draw on a wealth of experience and ideas from all over the world. They are ideal for the way we live today.

200+ Vegetarian Pasta Recipes
MARLENA SPIELER

This book is an enthusiastic celebration of the versatility of pasta. Healthy to eat and quick to prepare, pasta can be sweet or savoury, and comes in a variety of shapes and sizes.

Here are pasta sauces, noodle soups, pasta with cheese, hot dishes, cold dishes, stuffed pasta and dumplings.

Everyone loves pasta, and whether or not you are a vegetarian you will enjoy the variety of flavours offered in this sumptuous collection.